Making and Unmaking Disability

EXPLORATIONS IN CONTEMPORARY SOCIAL-POLITICAL PHILOSOPHY (ECSPP)

Series Editors: Naomi Zack (University of Oregon)
and Laurie Shrage (Florida International University)

As our world continues to be buffeted by extreme changes in society and politics, philosophers can help navigate these disruptions. Rowman and Littlefield's ECSPP series books are intended for supplementary classroom use in intermediate to advanced college-level courses to introduce philosophy students and scholars in related fields to the latest research in social-political philosophy. This philosophical series has multidisciplinary applications and the potential to reach a broad audience of students, scholars, and general readers.

1. *Beyond Blood Oil: Philosophy, Policy, and the Future*, by Leif Wenar, Anna Stilz, Michael Blake, Christopher Kutz, Aaron James, and Nazrin Mehdiyeva, 2018
2. *Reviving the Social Compact: Inclusive Citizenship in an Age of Extreme Politics*, by Naomi Zack, 2018
3. *Comparative Just War Theory: Beyond Hegemonic Discourses*, edited by Luís Cordeiro-Rodrigues and Danny Singh
4. *Making and Unmaking Disability: The Three-Body Approach*, by Julie E. Maybee

Making and Unmaking Disability

The Three-Body Approach

Julie E. Maybee
Department of Philosophy
City University of New York

ROWMAN & LITTLEFIELD
Lanham • Boulder • New York • London

Executive Editor: Natalie Mandziuk
Editorial Assistant: Michael Tan

Credits and acknowledgments for material borrowed from other sources, and reproduced
with permission, appear on the appropriate page within the text.

Published by Rowman & Littlefield
An imprint of The Rowman & Littlefield Publishing Group, Inc.
4501 Forbes Boulevard, Suite 200, Lanham, Maryland 20706
www.rowman.com

6 Tinworth Street, London SE11 5AL, United Kingdom

British Library Cataloguing in Publication Information Available

Library of Congress Cataloging-in-Publication Data Available

978-1-5381-2772-8 (cloth)
978-1-5381-2773-5 (paper)
978-1-5381-2774-2 (electronic)

♾™ The paper used in this publication meets the minimum requirements of American
National Standard for Information Sciences—Permanence of Paper for Printed Library
Materials, ANSI/NISO Z39.48-1992.

For Leyna

Contents

Series Editor Foreword

Contemporary Social-Political Philosophy and *Making and Unmaking Disability*

> Now that my ladder's gone,
> I must lie down where all the ladders start
> In the foul rag and bone shop of the heart.

—"The Circus Animals' Desertion," William Butler Yeats

ABOUT THIS SERIES

From Plato through John Rawls, to Jürgen Habermas and Slavoj Žižek, philosophers have developed political philosophy as a stand-alone subfield in their discipline by focusing on political legitimacy, justice, and fundamental political institutions. The work of philosophers who focus on how societal practices and culture are related to politics or government is often subsumed under social philosophy, which has not been a strong, recognizable subfield. Nevertheless, scholars and students who critically examine social practices, traditions, and values, with the goal of improving the conditions of human life, are engaged with political philosophy—especially issues of inequality, oppression, and political power. For instance, philosophers who analyze racial and gender injustice have demonstrated how social norms and political principles can be productively investigated together. Such progressive or liberatory efforts have given rise to a number of questions, such as: How are social values and culture related to political power structures? How do social identities of race, class, gender, ability, religion, and ethnicity affect both individual status and power, as well as quality of life? Can justice be defined without close attention to actual oppression? The result of critical engagement with the questions of both social philosophy and political philosophy has been a new and growing body of method and content that is somewhat informally called social-political philosophy. This hyphenated name signals an intent to address political issues in combination with social and cultural criticism, and/or to conduct social or cultural criticism with the goal of changing political structures.

The aim of this series is to present the best and most interesting work in social-political philosophy at this time, for students, scholars, and general readers—in accessible and clear prose, and by authors who are transparent and self-critical about their methodologies

Social-political philosophy should not be equated with the *application* of theoretical philosophy to social issues. This is because new subjects often call forth and support new ways of theorizing and pursuing knowledge, as we hope will be evident throughout this series. That is, contemporary social-political philosophy, as philosophy that evaluates the social and political conditions of human life, requires reassessing theoretical constructs and methods, as well as addressing practical issues. If the traditional, canonical works and ideas of philosophers could directly be applied to the realities of contemporary human life, then this series would not be needed. As a series of books, Explorations in Contemporary Social-Political Philosophy will share important scholarly work and ideas with a multidisciplinary audience, so that these ideas can be taken up to address some of today's most pressing problems.

—Naomi Zack and Laurie Shrage

ABOUT THIS BOOK

In *Making and Unmaking Disability: The Three-Body Approach*, Julie Maybee focuses a philosopher's eye on disability and disability studies. The core idea is that disabled people are not naturally disabled because something is wrong with their bodies, but that they are made by society *not to be abled*. The result is that although the human body is always something physical, our experience of our bodies and others' experience of them is always "socially constructed." That is, the nature of our physicality is constructed by society, as well as by the socially constructed nature of biology and medicine.

The process of dis-abling those who are disabled results in three distinct socially constructed bodies: the first body is the individual's personal body or body-self; the second body is interpersonal or social; the third body is defined and regulated by social institutions. All three of these bodies interact, and even the first, the personal body, is partly made meaningful to individuals by other people and social structures. Maybee also explains how impairment, or a presumed core of physical dysfunction, is also socially constructed, because what is considered impairment in the contemporary West is not impairment in other geographical and historical contexts. *Making and Unmaking Disability* offers fascinating and engaging concrete examples of disabilities and the experience of disabled people. Maybee also draws on her own family experience.

Maybee's solutions to the oppression caused by the social constructions of disability is to *unmake* the factors that make disability, in attitudes, social practices, workplace expectations, and institutional policies. *Making and Unmaking Disability* is timely, urgent, and engaging. This book will be very interesting to disabled and abled people, including scholars, general readers, and advanced and introductory students.

—Naomi Zack

Preface and Acknowledgments

On November 13, 2002, my daughter, Leyna, had a brain aneurysm at age 12. After Leyna's aneurysm, it did not take me long to realize that, as the mother of a now-disabled child, I would have to fight. I learned that we were largely on our own when it came to caring for our newly disabled child. Leyna was in the rehabilitation hospital only a month (and still in a coma) when the hospital social worker came to talk to me about the fact that her insurance coverage would be running out soon. "What are you going to do?" he asked. "What are *you* going to do?" I thought to myself. Later, I found out that the rehabilitation staff would simply skip Leyna's tilt-table therapy sessions if I was not there to supervise and prevent her from undoing the straps that kept her from falling off the table while being tilted into a nearly upright, standing position. Apparently, no staff was willing or able to supervise her when I was not there.

The nursing staff at a second rehabilitation hospital made little effort to engage with Leyna socially. During afternoons when I was teaching classes and so was not at the hospital, I discovered that staff would bathe Leyna early in the afternoon and leave her mostly alone in her bed with a small personal TV for entertainment for the rest of the day. When I complained that they were not providing her with enough social engagement and stimulation, they began parking her in her wheelchair in one spot near the nurses' station and locking the wheelchair so that she could not move around. Although Leyna was technically in a social space, she was still getting little attention, and whatever social freedom she could have had by slowly scooting herself around in her wheelchair using one arm and one foot was taken away. When Leyna failed to qualify for the hospital's pediatric cognitive rehabilitation program because she needed what they regarded as too much help with activities of daily living (e.g., using the toilet) and the hospital threatened to discharge her home with limited services, I seriously considered moving back to Canada so that Leyna would qualify for rehabilitation services under Canada's nationalized health insurance system. Service providers in Canada were surprised to hear that the American system was apparently ready to give up so quickly on a pediatric client. When the director of the hospital's cognitive rehabilitation unit found out what was happening, however, he worked with us and with the hospital to develop a special schedule for Leyna in their cognitive rehab program. Over time, Leyna was able to join the program full time.

We also soon became familiar with social exclusion, neglect, and ridicule in other places. When we were able to begin taking Leyna out in public, people would stare and/or laugh at her (they still do, sometimes). I learned that we had to scout out places ahead of time to ensure that they were accessible for wheelchair users. While the various predominantly white schools that Leyna had attended in the past had been happy to have her when she was a gifted, black, female student (with a black father and a white mother), we had to fight with the schools for services for our now disabled, black, female child. My husband, who not only is an attorney but also had practiced special education law as one of his areas of expertise, had to threaten to take the director of one school district's disability services office to court to convince the director to instruct Leyna's school to provide the occupational therapy that they had previously denied. "I'll meet you at the administrative law court," my husband told me he said. I wondered how parents who were not lawyers and their disabled children fared in battles with the school district.

During Leyna's journey through various rehabilitation settings (in-patient, day-hospital, cognitive rehabilitation), I was asked to attend meetings with her psychologist to discuss, I was told, Leyna's psychological treatment plan. I found out later during an insurance appeal process, however, that these sessions were billed as "family counseling." It seems that the sessions were about me and not about Leyna after all. Leyna's psychologist told me that I needed to get over my anger and move on to acceptance. But as I came increasingly to recognize that many of the obstacles Leyna faced were socially caused, the psychologist's advice made me even more angry. Was I supposed to stop being angry at and accept the lack of social support and exclusion? Was I supposed to stop being angry at and accept the public ridicule? Wasn't I right to be angry at these things?[1]

I am a philosophy professor who had worked in Africana philosophy and on race, ethnicity, and gender for many years before Leyna's aneurysm, but I had never thought of disability as a socially defined or constructed category of exclusion and discrimination similar to those other categories. To be honest, like many people in Western societies, I suspect, I had not thought of disability as a category much at all. Because Western societies tend to segregate disabled people and exclude them from public spaces, as we will see, people in many Western societies can live large portions of their lives without encountering very many people with disabilities at all. Aside from volunteer work I did in high school with young people with cerebral palsy at a quasi-medical, residential institution in Toronto, Ontario, Canada—encounters that would have reinforced the assumption that disabled people should be segregated in such institutions—I had not spent much time around disabled people myself. When Leyna was—and, by extension, we were—shunned by and excluded from society after her aneurysm, however, I began to recognize the operations of a social, and not medical, category. This book is the result of my attempt to think through how disability and, as I will suggest, impairment operate as socially defined or constructed categories to exclude people we regard and label as disabled, as well as to envision how we might make our world differently in the future.

Portions of this book have been published previously. The idea for the book was born while working with Jesse Prinz and the participants in the 2014–2015 Mid Career Faculty Fellowship Program of the Committee for Interdisciplinary Science Studies at the Graduate Center of the City University of New York—Ken Guest, Andreas Killen, Rachel Kravitz, Tiwi D. Marira, Christina Nadler, Rochelle Rives, and Angelika Seidel. While presenting drafts of the article that was the project for that fellowship, the group members encouraged me to expand the article into a book. This is that book, and it contains passages drawn from the article, titled "Em'body'ment and Disability: On Taking the (Biological) 'Body' out of Em'body'ment," resulting from that project (Maybee 2017). I am grateful to Jesse and to the other participants for inspiring me to write the book, and to Shelley Tremain, the guest editor, and the *Journal of Social Philosophy*, which published the article. Portions of the book have also appeared in two other articles, "African Philosophy, Disability and the Social Conception of the Self" (Maybee 2018) and "Homelessness, Disability and Oppression" (forthcoming in an edited collection published by Brill). I am grateful to the editors of those collections, George Hull and John G. Abbarno, respectively.

I am extremely grateful to Naomi Zack, whose gentle pressure and tireless editing work helped to make this book possible and certainly made it better, though I take full responsibility for any errors and weaknesses. And I am grateful to the many people—students, colleagues, friends—who shared their stories with me, some of which appear anonymously in these pages.

Most of all, I am grateful to Leyna for coming back to me—because, she once said, "they told me you needed me." I certainly did and do. May this book help to make your future in "our" world a little brighter.

Introduction and Theoretical Overview

At the beginning of the short film *The Commute*, directed by Jake Alexander, a man using a manual wheelchair and, as is revealed a little later, carrying a wrapped present in his lap, is refused service by a New York City taxi driver. "I can't pick you up, buddy. I can't do it," the taxi driver says from the driver's seat through the passenger-side window, which has been partially rolled down. "You mean you can't get me in the back?" the man asks. "Nah, I gotta get home," the driver says, as he pulls away in the yellow SUV, leaving the man in the gutter. Afterward, we see the man struggling to get somewhere—thumping down curbs in his wheelchair, dropping his package while navigating poorly maintained streets and sidewalks, rubbing his sore hands. These scenes are interspersed with scenes of children attending a birthday party—a group of young girls hitting each other playfully with balloons, the birthday girl opening her gifts and talking happily with her friends, but also looking around for someone, disappointedly.

The man gets on and off a bus and then rolls through crowded sidewalks to a subway elevator. He goes down the elevator and gets on a train, where other passengers laugh rudely in his direction. He gets off the train, and we see him looking down a long flight of stairs, which he cannot use. He rolls himself up a ramp to get to another subway platform. Meanwhile, the birthday girl, while having fun, occasionally continues to look disappointed.

The man gets on and rides another subway, while, in the party scenes, the birthday girl blows out the candles on her cake. He gets off the subway at what appears to be his destination and rolls down another long ramp. It is dark outside and seems late, as the subway station is quite deserted. We cut away to scenes in which the birthday girl is now asleep in her bed. Once on the street, the man comes to a corner that has no curb-cut or ramp up to the sidewalk, so he backs up his wheelchair and makes a run at the curb, doing a wheelie and launching himself onto the sidewalk. The man rolls along the sidewalk to an apartment building, where, once inside, he approaches an apartment door and uses his key to let himself in. He has obviously missed the party for the birthday girl, who, we now realize, is his daughter. And since she is fast asleep, he will not likely be able to speak with her or give her his gift until the morning. The film, made in 2013, ends with the statement: "There are 468 subway stations in New York City. Only 69 have wheelchair accessibility" (Alexander 2013).

While the film is fiction, it depicts experiences that many wheelchair users have when navigating around towns and cities and using public transportation. After having lived in the Middle East for some years, international journalist and wheelchair user John Hockenberry (2004) noted the "shock" he experienced when he returned to the United States, where, he said, "it routinely took an act of God to hail a taxi" (137). New York cabbies would generally pass him by and pretend not to see him, as he tried not to "look like a panhandler." He often succeeded in hailing a cab, he said, "only to have the driver hand me a dollar" (138). Hockenberry's account suggests that getting a bus is not as easy as the film leads us to believe. While buses in New York City do have wheelchair lifts, Hockenberry tells us that "you have a chance of getting a ride" only "if the driver is carrying a key to operate the lift, if the lift has been serviced recently, if the bus is not too crowded, and if the driver notices you at the stop" (145). Some of my New York City–based students who use wheelchairs have reported that bus drivers routinely pass them by when they are waiting at a stop, even when the bus is not full, because, my students conjecture, the drivers cannot be bothered to take the time to let them get on. Other students have told me about the moans, groans, and rolled eyes that they have observed from passengers on a bus when a driver does stop to pick up a person using a wheelchair.

In a 2017 "Daily 360" video by the *New York Times*, titled "Few Entrances, and Sometimes, No Exit," Google engineer and wheelchair user Sasha Blair-Goldensohn demonstrates the difficulty he has riding the New York City subways. He shows viewers the special entrances he has to use as well as the slots he puts his subway card into so that a mechanism "opens the gate for me, when it's working." He says he was proud of the subway system until his accident, when he found out that "it doesn't work for a whole segment of people." Of the almost 500 stations the system now has, he says in a narrative voice-over, only one-fifth are wheelchair accessible. Meanwhile, in the video, we see him looking at a subway map and rattling off the names of station after station that he cannot use. Even at stations that do have elevators, he says, the elevators are constantly in and out of service, "so you're never assured that when you get on [a subway train], you're going to be able to get off." He talks about the possibility of having to call the police to lift him out of a station, and of the good citizens who once carried him up the stairs. We are with him while he waits on a subway platform for an elevator, unsure whether the elevator will come because the light in the call-button is not working. He points out that, while he himself is willing to risk using the subway with a light-weight manual wheelchair, people who use heavy, electric wheelchairs probably do not bother to take the subway at all, because no one can carry them up the stairs if the elevator is out. Unfortunately, however, he says, when wheelchair users avoid the subway, the Metropolitan Transportation Authority (MTA), which runs the subways in New York City, can get away with its poor service and maintenance record. "At times, it feels like an insult," Blair-Goldensohn says of the inaccessible subway system, "but it's not a malicious one. It's just that you've been forgotten, that you've been left out" (Cott and Mullin 2017).

Yet, there is also a terrific short film by Portuguese director Pedro Amorin called *Midfield*. The film depicts what we are to assume is an ordinary workday in the life of a stevedore, or dockworker. In the film, the stevedore walks around the docks, consults with co-workers, supervises the loading and unloading of containers, and speaks over his walkie-talkie. But on Sunday, when he goes to play soccer with his mates at the gym, he takes his legs off, forgoes arm devices, and plays midfield.[1]

This book is about how today's Western societies might begin to move from the first image and accounts, to the second. In this theoretical overview, I introduce the discipline of disability studies, several models of disability introduced by disability studies scholars, including the distinction between two families of what are called "social models" of disability, and the institutional, social, and phenomenological dimensions of disability and embodiment. These ideas will guide the discussions in the chapters, which are not primarily theoretical, but use biographies, history, experiences of what we call disability and impairment, and comparisons with other cultures to *exemplify* the way in which disability is socially constructed or *made*, as well as how it can be deconstructed or *unmade*.

Outline of this introduction and theoretical overview:

➤ Disability Studies and Social Models of Disability
➤ British/Marxist Social Models vs. American/Minority/Civil Rights Social Models
➤ The Role of the Body
➤ The Three Dimensions of Embodiment or the Three Bodies
➤ Disability Is Socially Defined or *Made* by Societies
➤ Is There a Distinction between Impairment and Disability?
➤ The *Experience* of the Body vs. the Body *Out There*, as an Object
➤ Making Disability
➤ Unmaking Disability

DISABILITY STUDIES AND
SOCIAL MODELS OF DISABILITY

While still angry after my daughter's aneurysm, I tried to convince the director of Leyna's cognitive rehab program that the program was culturally biased because it emphasized cognitive skills that have been privileged in Western societies and cultures, while neglecting cognitive skills that might be more important in other societies and cultures. The director, who knew I am an academic, replied by telling me that there was a then-recent issue of *American Psychologist*, the official journal of the American Psychological Association, that I should read. It turned out that the journal had published a special-topics issue with several articles addressing what the introductory article labeled a "new model" or "new paradigm" of disability, the "social model" of disability (Pledger 2003, 279, 283). Contributors to the issue included psychologists and disability studies scholars Rhoda Olkin and Carol J. Gill. The article by Olkin and co-author Constance Pledger (2003) of the National Institute on Disability and Rehabilitation Research was provocatively titled "Can Disability Studies and Psychology Join Hands?"

Disability studies is a relatively new, interdisciplinary, academic field that focuses, as you might have guessed, on the topic of disability. Unlike scholarship on disability in some other disciplines, however, it is guided by three main principles. First, disability studies is committed to the view that the study of disability should be centered around the perspectives and experiences of people who are regarded as disabled.[2] Second, it aims to challenge prejudice and discrimination directed against disabled people as well as the exclusion of disabled people from our social world.[3] Third, disability studies holds that what we call "disability" is not merely a medical condition or impairment that is located completely in a person's body, but is at least partly socially constructed, much in the same way that scholars today regard gender and race as socially constructed, or as social categories that were invented during a particular historical period in particular societies and then imposed on certain groups of people to justify treating them differently.[4] Disability studies scholars therefore agree that many of the experiences that disabled people have are caused not by their bodies, but by societies' exclusion, prejudice, and discrimination. People we define as disabled are therefore not merely people with disabilities, but people who are actively *dis*-abled—hindered, excluded, or oppressed, that is, *made* to be unable—by society. They are *disabled* (by our society) *people*.

Indeed, disability studies was inspired precisely by the rejection of the medical assumption that disabled people are disabled by their bodies. The "new model" or "new paradigm" of disability described in the 2003 issue of *American Psychologist* also turned out not to be that new. In 1976, a group of disability activists calling themselves the Union of Physically Impaired Against Segregation (UPIAS) proposed a new definition of *disability* that seemed to imply that the physical body has no role to play in defining disability. This "social model" of disability—a term coined by sociologist Michael J. Oliver, who took up and promoted the UPIAS model of disability in academia and the public sphere (Finkelstein 2001b, 2)—rejected the dominant, medical account of disability—as well as the implication that disability is a personal tragedy—by introducing a sharp distinction between *impairment* and *disability*. While *impairment* refers to biological or functional limitations in individuals and hence is a description of the physical body (Oliver 1996, 3–4), *disability* is the social oppression imposed, as they put it, "on top of our impairments, by the way we are unnecessarily isolated and excluded from full participation in society" (UPIAS 1976, 3). Oliver later insists, "Disablement is nothing to do with the body" (4). Instead, as Vic Finkelstein (2001b, 4), one of the original members of UPIAS, claims, a Marxist or materialist approach suggests that the competitive market-based economic structure of capitalism is the primary social structure that disables (and oppresses) people with impairments. What disables people, in this view, is a capitalist economic system that makes it impossible for people with impairments to participate as full members.

BRITISH/MARXIST SOCIAL MODELS VS. AMERICAN/MINORITY/CIVIL RIGHTS SOCIAL MODELS

Marxist-inspired social models have not been the only type of social model endorsed by scholars of disability. As disability studies scholars have often noted (e.g., Shakespeare and Watson 2001, 10; Ellis 2015, 2), there have been two main types of the social model of disability: the original, Marxist-inspired version, which has dominated in Britain, and a second version, the minority or civil rights model of disability, which has been dominant in the United States. The *American Psychologist* articles by Olkin and Pledger (2003, 296–97) as well as by Gill, Donald G. Kewman, and Ruth W. Brannon (2003, 305–6) (which the director of Leyna's cognitive rehab program had recommended to me), endorsed versions of the social model that belong to this second, American family.

Like the Marxist-inspired models, the U.S. version of social models has suggested that disability is located not in people's bodies but in society. As Gill, Kewman, and Brannon (2003) suggested, this social model regards disabled people "as hindered primarily not by their intrinsic differences but by society's response to those differences" (306). However, rather than defining *disability*, as the British social models do, in relation to the economic system of capitalism, the American social models compare the experiences of disabled people to the experiences of members of racial or ethnic minority groups, such as African Americans, and suggest that we should regard disabled people as a minority group similar to those groups (Olkin 1999, chapter 2). According to this model, just as certain sex organs are the physical markers that determine whether someone is a member of the group "women," or certain skin tones, hair textures, and bone structures are the physical markers that determine whether someone is a member of the minority group "black," "impairment" is the physical marker that determines whether someone is a member of the minority group "disabled."[5] *Disability* is, then, the poor treatment that society *imposes* on people so marked. While the Marxist models conceive of society's poor treatment of disabled people in terms of capitalist exclusion or exploitation, the minority models conceive of society's poor treatment of disabled people, as we often do for other minority groups, in terms of discrimination and the violation of civil rights (see also Fine and Asch 1988; Hahn 1996).

Minority models of disability have provided the ideological base for the disability rights movement in the United States. Although there is no single time during which the movement started, a chronology of the movement by Doris Zames Fleischer and Frieda Zames (2001, xxi) dates it to 1817, when the first school for deaf students was founded in Hartford, Connecticut. Deaf and blind people's fight for educational and job opportunities as well as their demand for the recognition and accommodation of sign language and access to Braille have been important parts of the disability rights movement (Fleischer and Zames 2001, 14–32). Beginning in the 1960s and 1970s, people with serious physical impairments fought for the right to be released from long-term care institutions and live independently in the community—a movement that has come to be called the independent living movement (Fleischer and Zames 2001, 33–48). Beginning in the early 1970s, former psychiatric patients started the "psychiatric survivors" movement when they fought for control over their lives and treatment (Fleischer and Zames 2001, 119–21; Braddock and Parish 2001, 49). The disability rights movement has also included the fight for the rights (Braddock and Parish 2001, 46–47), as well as the deinstitutionalization, of people with intellectual and developmental disabilities, approximately 200,000 of whom at the peak in 1967 (Braddock and Parish 2001, 45) were living—often in overcrowded and inhumane conditions (see chapter 2)—in what had become merely custodial institutions offering no treatment or meaningful education or training (Braddock and Parish 2001, 36–37, 41–42).

The disability rights movement also saw the founding of a number of activist groups. In 1935, for instance, the League of the Physically Handicapped was founded by six people who began to conceive of themselves as a minority group when they realized that their files at the Home Relief Agency were being stamped with "PH" (physically handicapped) and they were being denied consideration for government jobs (Fleischer and Zames 2001, 5). Later activist groups include Disabled in Action (DIA), founded in 1970 (Fleischer and Zames 2001, 74), the Disability Rights Education and Defense Fund (DREDF), founded in 1979 (Fleischer and Zames 2001, 77), ADAPT (American Disabled for Accessible Public Transit, and, since 1990, American Disabled for Attendant

Programs Today), founded in 1983 (Fleischer and Zames 2001, 82–84), and Justice for All (JFA), founded in 1995 (Fleischer and Zames 2001, 85–86). ADAPT made the news in recent years when members disrupted U.S. Senate hearings about, and conducted other protests against, bills that would have overturned former President Barack Obama's signature health care law, the Affordable Care Act (ACA) or ObamaCare, as the ACA is often called (Rhodan 2017; Sommer 2017). An article in the *Huffington Post* at the time credited the disabled protestors with having saved the law (Wanshel 2017).

For such activist groups, disability discrimination is similar to discrimination on the basis of race, ethnicity, or gender. DREDF, for example, consciously aligned itself with other civil rights groups and with the civil rights movement more generally (Fleischer and Zames 2001, 79). On this view, disabled people are an oppressed minority group insofar as they are discriminated against and their civil rights are violated when they are systematically denied access to jobs, transportation, education, housing, and other public goods (see chapters 1 and 2). The solution to the problems of disability is therefore not to abolish or reform capitalist systems and structures, as it is for the Marxists, but to fight for civil rights for disabled people as a minority group, through political activism and by working to pass laws intended to prevent discrimination and remove barriers that block access to public goods. In the United States, this approach has been reflected in the creation of laws such as the Education for All Handicapped Children Act (EAHCA), passed in 1975 and renamed the Individuals with Disabilities Education Act (IDEA) in 1997, which guarantees the right of all disabled children to receive a free, public education; and the Americans with Disabilities Act (ADA), passed in 1990 and then amended by the ADA Amendments Act (ADAAA) in 2008, which guarantees the rights of disabled people not to be discriminated against in employment and public services, including transportation, telecommunications, and so on.[6]

Whether these sorts of civil rights laws *can be*, in principle (given how they are designed), or *have been*, in practice (given how they have been implemented and enforced, or not enforced), successful at improving education; increasing employment; increasing access to transportation, housing, health care, and other public goods; or reducing discrimination against disabled people is a hotly contested topic.[7] Scholars and activists who support Marxist social models, such as materialist theorists Marta Russell and Ravi Malhotra (see chapter 1), have been particularly critical of the civil rights approach. On the positive side, Russell and Malhotra (2002) argue that civil rights laws requiring that accommodations be provided to disabled people in employment, as the ADA does, might help challenge capitalism's "expectations of ever increasing productivity rates" (217)—expectations that have played a role in excluding disabled people from jobs (see chapter 1)—and so have the potential to be radically democratic. They note that the independent living movement that was inspired by the disability rights movement, which promotes the rights of disabled people to live independently in homes in the community, has also been helpful (218).

However, because civil rights laws and the independent living movement both presuppose that disabled people will have the resources and purchasing power to challenge discrimination or live independently in a capitalist system in which they are systematically kept in poverty and denied resources (see chapter 1), such a strategy of liberation will be, as they put it, "so impoverished as to be of assistance to only a tiny fraction of the most privileged disabled people" (Russell and Malhotra 2002, 218). This argument is particularly powerful once we acknowledge that the "resources" needed to challenge civil rights violations under the law and live independently would include not only money but also additional skills and social goods, such as education, access to transportation, health care, and so on, that are systematically denied to disabled people as well (see chapter 1). Since disabled people are often socially segregated (see chapter 2), they may even be isolated from people who might have access to such resources and so could provide help.

THE ROLE OF THE BODY

Disability studies scholars have also often disagreed over how much of disability is located in the body and how much of it is socially constructed. As the social model was popularized after 1976, critics complained that it—especially the original, Marxist-inspired, British or UK version of the model (Shakespeare and Watson 2001, 10)—went too far, by ignoring the role that impairment or the body play in shaping the experiences of and defining disability. Because of the social model, sociologists Bill Hughes and Kevin Paterson (1997) argue, "the body has disappeared from disability discourse" (328). The social model, Simon J. Williams (1999) suggests, leads to "the 'writing out' of the body from any discussion, deliberation or debate on the nature of disability itself" (803). Under the social model, sociologists Tom Shakespeare and Nicholas Watson (2001) argue, "impairment is completely bracketed" (14), but since impairment is a salient part of many disabled people's experiences, "it cannot be ignored in our social theory or our political strategy" (15). Shakespeare and Watson endorse what we can think of as a mixed model of disability that combines aspects of the social model with aspects of the medical model in a view that regards disability as multidimensional (20). As Shakespeare (2014) has said more recently, disability is "multi-factorial" (72), such that "people are disabled by society *and* by their bodies" (75).

The criticism that the classic social models of disability neglect the body has resurfaced more recently in the context of the so-called "new materialism" or "new realism" movements (Tremain 2015, 10; Garland-Thomson 2011, 592), particularly in feminist theory. According to disability justice and culture scholar

Rosemarie Garland-Thomson (2011), for instance, although the social model's distinction between *impairment* and *disability* was a politically important move insofar as it recast the "problems" of disability as problems of social justice, more recent disability theory has aimed to address the "embodied aspects of disability such as pain and functional limitation [but] without giving up the claim to disability as a social phenomenon" (592). Garland-Thomson contributes to this goal, she says, by offering "a materialist feminist understanding of disability" through the concept of "misfit" (592). On this view, a disabled person is a "misfit," or is some-*body* who does not fit into a particular environment (Garland-Thomson 2011, 593). These criticisms suggest that one serious problem with the social model of disability is that it ignores impairment, the body, or both. (We investigate these criticisms in chapter 4.)

THE THREE DIMENSIONS OF EMBODIMENT OR THE THREE BODIES

Debates over the role that the body should play in defining disability are complicated, I think, by some confusion about the body. Anthropologists Nancy Scheper-Hughes and Margaret M. Lock (1987) have suggested that three different perspectives can be taken toward the body—what they call the "three bodies" (7). Scheper-Hughes and Lock's distinction provides a good preliminary way of characterizing what we can think of as different levels or dimensions of *embodiment* and will help us to see that human physicality is, or bodies are, always encountered within social contexts and interpretations. In Western societies, we often think of a body simply as an individual person's body. But this is just the *first* body, according to Scheper-Hughes and Lock: the phenomenally and individually experienced "body-self," as they call it (7). I will call this first body or first dimension of embodiment the *personal body*.

The *second* body is what Scheper-Hughes and Locke call the "social body," or collective views of the body. The *social body* refers to how cultures use the body to conceive of social roles, society, or the world (Scheper-Hughes and Lock 1987, 18–23). I will call this second body or second dimension of embodiment the *interpersonal body*. It is the body or embodiment as defined in and by interpersonal social relations, including social roles, such as the roles of being a wife, mother, or soldier, for instance.

The *third* body is what Scheper-Hughes and Locke call the "body politic," and refers to "the regulation, surveillance and control of bodies (individual and collective)" by societies (7). It includes the way foraging societies, for instance, use ostracism to control behavior, as well as the ways in which modern societies regulate both individual and social bodies through racist and sexist systems and structures (Scheper-Hughes and Lock 1987, 8). I will call this third body or third dimension of embodiment the *institutional body*. It captures the ways in which bodies and embodiment are defined by large social institutions or structures. In small-scale, foraging societies, ostracism is a large social institution because a person can be successfully cast out of the society or defined as an "outcast" only if (nearly) everyone in the group (i.e., the whole society) agrees to ostracize or cooperates in ostracizing that person. As Scheper-Hughes and Locke suggest, in many Western European societies, racism and sexism are large social institutions that define a person's body and embodiment. My own body and embodiment are defined in such societies, for instance, by my being a "woman." These social institutions can be formal or informal (or both). Racism, for instance, is formal when it is enshrined in the official policies of social institutions, such as golf clubs whose rules exclude membership by black people, or in law, as when chattel slavery for African and African-descended people was supported by law in the United States. Racism is informal when it is not supported by law or by the official policies of social institutions, but is still practiced widely by individuals in more informal ways. As we will see, ableism is and has been both formal and informal as well.

The following diagram (figure I.1) illustrates the three bodies or three dimensions of embodiment. It depicts the idea that the first body or first dimension of

The Three Bodies

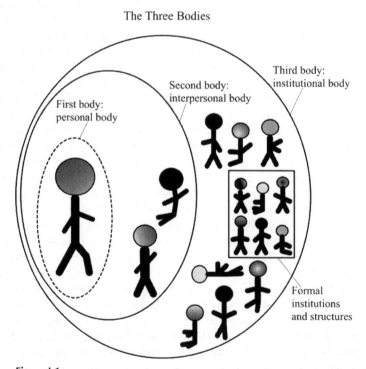

Figure I.1.

embodiment, the personal body, is located in and defined by ever larger social layers of embodiment, namely by the second body or second dimension of embodiment, the interpersonal body, in which people have interpersonal relations and social roles, and by the third body or third dimension of embodiment, the institutional body, in which people are embedded in social institutions and structures. This idea is illustrated by three increasingly large ovals surrounding a stick figure of a personal body, with increasing numbers of (and varied) stick figures representing additional people in the second and third layers. The oval surrounding the stick figure of the personal body has a dashed outline because, as we will see, in some cultures what we think of as the personal body is not regarded as individual or personal, but as social or as already connected to others. For these cultures, there is no solid boundary, so to speak, between someone's personal body and others. The square box with small stick figures in it within the third layer representing the institutional body illustrates the idea that some of the institutions may be formal institutions or official laws and policies.

If we define *embodiment* broadly as what it *is* and *is like* to move about in the world , then we can say that we move around in or negotiate the world as personal bodies (the first body, in Scheper-Hughes and Lock's sense); as interpersonal bodies, insofar as we each have various social roles within the technical, social orders of our societies (the second body, in Scheper-Hughes and Lock's sense); and as institutional bodies, insofar as we are embedded in larger, social/institutional structures and arrangements (the third body, in Scheper-Hughes and Lock's sense).

Noting these different levels or dimensions of embodiment helps to reveal that the classic social models do not ignore the body or embodiment altogether, as critics have charged, but focus attention on the third body, in Scheper-Hughes and Lock's sense, or on the body insofar as it is embedded in large, social/institutional structures and arrangements. The social models' distinction between *impairment* and *disability* and emphasis on *disability*—on socially caused restrictions imposed on people with impairments—focus on the third or institutional body, or on the way in which large institutions and social structures of societies regulate, survey, and control impaired bodies. According to the models, "disability" is not located in the structure or function of people's personal bodies (i.e., in the first body), but in their institutional bodies, or in the ways in which societies' economic, social, and political systems have regulated and controlled the bodies of impaired people. Marxist-inspired theorists, for example (see chapter 1), have suggested that industrial capitalism's separation of home space from work space, its need for standardized, machine-like bodies, and its invention of productivity requirements, for instance, produced not only the class of workers, but also a group of people who were "unfit" and therefore displaced from and "disabled" in relation to the paid workforce (see, e.g., Gleeson 1997, 194–95; Russell and Malhotra 2002, 212–13). Along the third dimension of embodiment, disabled people are cast out of, or are *outcasts* within, the economic system of capitalism (see Charlton 1998, 23–24).

Supporters of the social models are right, in my view, that a full analysis of disability must take account of this third dimension of embodiment or institutional body. My own examination of this dimension is inspired by the British, Marxist, or materialist social models of disability (chapter 1).

DISABILITY IS SOCIALLY DEFINED
OR *MADE* BY SOCIETIES

Notice that this third dimension of embodiment or institutional body is socially defined or *made* by societies. What it *is* and *is like* to negotiate the world as a body in relation to societies' large institutions and structures is defined by those social institutions and structures, that is, by the societies. The second dimension of embodiment or interpersonal body is also socially defined. A society's social roles and, in general, societies' social, technical orders as well as the experiences of those roles and technical orders are defined by societies themselves.

The critics' complaint that the social models leave the body out, however, is really the complaint that the social models fail to account for the first dimension of embodiment, the first or personal body. Because the classical social models make a distinction between *impairment* and *disability*—in which *disability* refers to the socially caused restrictions on activity imposed "on top of" people's impairments—and focus attention on *disability*, the critics are suggesting, the models ignore the role that the personal body plays in defining disability and in shaping the experience of disability. Here, the suggestion is that, while some—possibly even a great deal—of disability is socially caused or shaped by societies, there is something about disability that is pre-social or outside of that social influence, something that is natural or simply given, namely, something about people's individual bodies. There is, on this view, a given, purely objective, pre-social, natural, physical, or biological individual or personal body that the classical social models fail to consider.

Because power can be expressed in intimate and personal ways, the critics are right, I will suggest (chapter 3), that a comprehensive understanding of disability and of our society's ableism must take seriously the first dimension or personal body, as well as the second dimension or interpersonal body, which are *both* neglected by the classical social models' focus on the third dimension or institutional body.

The critics are wrong, however, to say that there is a given, pre-social, purely objective, natural, physical, or biological individual or personal body. Like the other two dimensions, I will suggest, the first dimension of embodiment, or personal body, is also socially defined. There is *no* purely objective, pre-social, natural, physical, or biological body. As cross-cultural comparisons as well as an examination of Western history will show, today's dominant, Western understanding of the personal body and of impairment is just one way of cutting up and defining the world, a way that is socially defined and determined. I do not deny that there is a material reality to the world. I claim only that what that reality *is like*, how it is *defined* or *identified*, is determined by societies. Societies do not make up the world, but they do *define* or *identify* what we perceive and experience as the facts. The claim that there are individual physical, or biological bodies, conditions, or impairments is just one way of forming and organizing the facts that we perceive. Disability is therefore *made*, I will argue, along all three dimensions of embodiment.

IS THERE A DISTINCTION BETWEEN IMPAIRMENT AND DISABILITY?

Because I will suggest that, like the second and third dimensions of embodiment, the first dimension, first or personal body, is socially defined, I am rejecting not only the idea that there is a purely objective, pre-social, natural, physical, or biological body, but also the classical social models' distinction between *impairment*, as a description of a (supposedly) purely objective, pre-social, natural, physical, or biological body, and *disability*, as the social effects imposed "on top of" impairment. This distinction has been endorsed not only by some defenders of the original, Marxist-inspired or materialist, British social models, as we saw, but also by defenders of versions of the American, minority/civil rights model (see, e.g., Morris 2001, 1–2). Criticisms of the distinction therefore apply to many versions of both kinds of social models (Shakespeare and Watson 2001, 10).

Some scholars[8] have criticized the social model's endorsement of the claim that there is a purely objective, pre-social, natural, physical, or biological body or impairment because the claim undermines, they argue, the model's original rejection of the medical model. In an article complaining about the body "disappearing" from social oppression models of disability, for instance, sociologists and disability studies scholars Bill Hughes and Kevin Paterson (1997) criticized the social models for implying that the body is "purely biological," "has no history," and "is an essence, a timeless, ontological foundation" (328–29). Ironically, they suggested, in spite of the fact that the social model was originally intended to undercut the medical model of disability, it ends up agreeing with that model's definition of the body. As Hughes and Paterson put the point, both models "treat it [the body] as a pre-social, inert, physical object, as discrete, palpable and separate from the self" (329). In the end, then, the social model leaves the body to medicine: "The social model—in spite of its critique of the medical model—actually concedes the body to medicine and understands impairment in terms of medical discourse" (Hughes and Paterson 1997, 326).

Defenders of the social model have replied to these kinds of criticisms by suggesting that leaving the body to medicine is an advantage of the model. Oliver (1996), who defends the social model, grants that the original social model developed by the Union of the Physically Impaired Against Segregation (UPIAS) and another group of disability activists with whom they worked, the Disabled Peoples International (DPI), proposes that "impairment is, in fact, nothing less than a description of the physical body" (4). But Oliver argues that the social model's distinction between medical/impairment and political/disability is an advantage of the theory, not a disadvantage. Disability theorists must distinguish those parts of disabled people's lives that need medical intervention from those parts that need policy or political intervention. The failure to make this distinction, he says, has led to "the medicalization of disability and the colonization of disabled peoples [sic] lives by a vast army of professionals when perhaps, political action (i.e., civil rights legislation) would be a more appropriate response" (5).

Oliver is right that we need to distinguish situations in which medical intervention would be appropriate from situations in which it would not, but this point does not require us to adopt the metaphysical apparatus of medicine. There is no pre-social, natural, purely physical, or biological, individual body, as medicine assumes. What we call "embodiment" and "the body," I will suggest, are always experienced and defined in ways that are shaped by the social—by concepts, language, beliefs, and social practices. Indeed, as our exploration of traditional cultures, including traditional European cultures during the Middle Ages, will suggest, the idea that there is a pre-social, purely physical, or biological, individual or personal body is itself just one way of experiencing and defining embodiment and the body. Moreover, continued belief in a mythical, individualized body or experience of a body with supposedly purely objective, biological impairments will only block our research, medicine, and rehabilitation practices from taking seriously the subtle and complex ways in which ableism structures the lives and experiences of disabled people (see chapter 7).

As a result, although I will use the terms *impairment* and *disability* in the two different senses defined by social models of disability, I ultimately reject the distinction. That is, although I will use the term *impairment* to refer to what medicine *presents* as, and people in many Western societies *believe* are, purely objective, pre-social, natural, physical, or biological bodies or conditions, I reject the claim that there really are such things as pre-social, natural, purely physical, or biological bodies or conditions. I am therefore offering what we can think of as a *really social*, social model of disability, according to which *both impairment* and *disability* are socially defined.

I should point out that not all Marxist or materialist theorists of disability adopt the view that the term *impairment* refers to a purely objective, pre-social, natural, physical, or biological body. While B. J. Gleeson (1997), for instance, accepts the distinction between a purely objective and natural body and a socially constructed disability (194),[9] Russell and Malhotra (2002) do not seem to endorse the social model's distinction between *impairment* and *disability* (see chapter 1). Capitalism, they suggest, *created*—and hence defined—the class of people who count as "disabled" (213). And while medical practice helps to establish the boundaries between who counts as able-bodied and who counts as disabled by rating a laborer's body "by the degree of impairment suffered by each of its functioning parts," as they put it, disability is still ultimately defined (in Social Security law, for instance) in terms of whether someone is (medically) able to work (214). For Russell and Malhotra, then, what counts as a medically defined, bodily dysfunction and as "impairment" are ultimately determined by capitalism's demand for workers.[10] Since capitalism has defined and determined the concept of disability as well as who has a medically defined dysfunction or impairment, on their view, both *impairment* and *disability* are socially defined. This view undercuts a distinction between a (supposedly) purely objective or natural body or impairment and a socially constructed disability. I defend a view similar to Russell and Malhotra's (chapter 1).

THE *EXPERIENCE* OF THE BODY VS. THE BODY *OUT THERE*, AS AN OBJECT

Notice that the claim that there *is* a given, purely objective, pre-social, natural, physical, or biological body, which I reject, can actually be interpreted in two ways. First, it can mean that the personal body is *experienced*, from the *inside*, so to speak, in a given way, or that what it *feels* like to have or be a personal body is purely objective and simply a function of a person's natural physical, or biological characteristics. Second, it can mean that what the personal body is, as an object *out there in the world*, is purely objective, that is, that a person's body is a pre-social, natural or physical object in the world. On this view, a person's body, as an object, has given characteristics.

I am arguing against both of those claims. In my view, the personal body is not given or purely objective, but socially defined or defined by societies, both in terms of how it is *experienced* as well as in terms of what it *is*, as an object out there. In other words, *all three* dimensions of embodiment or all three bodies are ultimately identified or defined by societies. Not only are the second dimension or interpersonal body and the third dimension or institutional body socially defined, as I suggested above, but the first dimension or personal body is also socially defined. Table I.1 outlines the argument for this claim:

	The body out there	The body as experienced
Third or institutional body	**Chapter 1:** societies create and define the large, social categories that they recognize as being *out there* in the world. The economic system of capitalism, for instance, defined some people as "disabled," thus creating a new category of "disabled" people out there in the world	**Chapters 1 and 2:** societies define how those categories are *experienced* (e.g., people categorized as disabled experience social exclusion and abuse)
Second or interpersonal body	**Chapter 3:** societies define the social roles that they recognize as being *out there* (e.g., brother/sister, cousin, sexual partner, mother) and which bodies occupy which roles	**Chapter 3:** societies define how those social roles are *experienced* (e.g., disabled mothers in our society experience the role of being a mother as tenuous)
First or personal body	Societies define what a body is, as an object *out there*. **Chapter 4:** society defines what counts as impairment or bodily conditions. **Chapter 5:** the biological body is also socially defined	**Chapter 3:** societies define how one *experiences*, or the *feel* of, one's own body

MAKING DISABILITY

- The Third Dimension of Embodiment or Institutional Body
- Ableism
- The Second Dimension of Embodiment or Interpersonal Body
- The First Dimension of Embodiment or Personal Body
- A Cultural Model of Disability

The analysis of how disability is constructed, socially defined, or *made* begins with the third dimension of embodiment or institutional body. Beginning with the third dimension may seem counterintuitive (why not start with the first dimension or body?), but it is the natural starting point for an analysis of *disability* because it is the dimension that has been emphasized by disability activists and scholars and by the social models of disability, which focus on the ways in which disability is constructed by and embedded in Western societies' institutions and structures. Contrary to popular assumptions, disability activists and scholars have insisted, disability is not a personal characteristic of individuals, but a socially defined grouping that sorts people into categories—the disabled and the non-disabled—that affect how they are treated. From this point of view, the third dimension or body *is* the beginning of the story of disability.

The Third Dimension of Embodiment or Institutional Body

In the case of the third dimension of embodiment or institutional body, the way in which it is socially defined *out there* is closely connected to how it is socially defined in *experience*. Western societies' systems, structures, and institutions, particularly the capitalist economic system and a socially shared structure of public attitudes, not only have invented and defined the *category* of disability—that is, what kind of body and who counts as disabled *out there* according to those systems, structures, and institutions—but also have defined how the category of disability is *experienced* under those systems, structures, and institutions. Chapter 1 explores how the economic system of capitalism came to exclude and disadvantage a category of people that it defined as "*dis*-abled" or as unable to work. Capitalism also produced a corresponding structure of public attitudes that assumes that people will have certain physical and behavioral attributes to participate in community life. This structure of attitudes takes the exclusion of people who do not have the assumed attributes for granted, and helps to ensure that such people are excluded not only from the economic system, but also from other more local, social institutions and structures, such as transportation, education, and health care systems, as well as built environments, such as buildings, cars, or other socially designed, physical structures.

Marxist-inspired or materialist accounts of disability are often criticized for focusing too heavily on the institutional body's economic aspects of disablement, at the expense of its cultural aspects (see chapter 2). In partial agreement with this criticism, chapter 2 explores the development in Western societies, especially during the nineteenth century, of a new structure of public attitudes that increasingly defined disabled people not only as excluded and disadvantaged, but also as a despised group of outsiders. This development is traced through an analysis of the history of the life of Joseph Merrick, who exhibited himself as the "Elephant Man" in freak shows, the invention of the concept of "normalcy," the eugenics movement, the so-called "ugly laws," which expelled people regarded as unsightly from public spaces, an expanded system of segregation for disabled people, and the horrific conditions that disabled people often experienced in segregated institutions. As we will see, however, these cultural aspects of disability were and are intertwined with the workings of capitalism.

Ableism

Because nondisabled people in Western societies use the institutions and structures of the third dimension of embodiment—including structures of attitudes—to define, regulate, and control disabled people, these institutions and structures are *ableist*, or are expressions of nondisabled people's oppressive and discriminatory social power over disabled people. Through these institutions and structures, nondisabled people exclude, disadvantage, and abuse disabled people in ways that they do not do to nondisabled people. But ableism can also be experienced in intimate and personal ways. It affects disabled people, not only along the third dimension of embodiment, in relation to large institutions and structures, but also along the first and second dimensions. Nondisabled people's ableism or oppressive social power affects disabled people's experiences of social capital or value and of social roles (the second dimension or interpersonal body) as well as the very *feel* of their own bodies (the first dimension or personal body, as experienced). Chapter 3 explores ways in which disabled people experience ableism along these other two dimensions. Because negative personal and intimate experiences along the second and first dimensions are defined by societies' ableism; however, they are not merely tragic, personal, or individual problems, but are social and political problems requiring social and political solutions.

The Second Dimension of Embodiment or Interpersonal Body

The second and first dimensions of embodiment are also socially defined—both *out there*, and *in experience*. In the case of the second dimension or interpersonal body, as is the case for the third dimension, how it is socially defined *out there* is closely connected to how it is socially defined in *experience*. How societies use the body to conceive of social roles, society, or the world defines not only which social roles are *out there* and which bodies (including those defined as disabled) have those social roles, but also what the *experiences* of those roles will tend to be like. Chapter 3 explores how ableism, along the second dimensions of embodiment, shapes both the social roles that disabled people have out there as well as how they experience those roles. Disabled people are subjected to a devalued bodily prestige or social capital *out there* that they have to manage, in terms of their *experience*, daily. And while there is a common, *devalued* social role to which they are often assigned *out there*—the "sick" or "handicapped" role—they also tend to be *denied* access to *valuable* social roles, including the social roles of being a sexual partner and parent. These expressions of ableism or of nondisabled people's social power also shape disabled people's *experiences* of these roles. Society's view that disabled women should not be mothers, for instance, leads disabled mothers to experience their motherhood as tenuous. The second dimension of embodiment or interpersonal body is thus socially defined both in terms of its *out-thereness* and in terms of how it is *experienced*.

The First Dimension of Embodiment or Personal Body

Unlike for the third and second dimensions of embodiment, in the case of the *first* dimension or personal body, I separate the analysis of how societies define the personal body in *experience* from the analysis of how they define the personal body as an object *out there*. In fact, my argument for the claim that the personal body is socially defined is divided between three different chapters. Chapter 3 suggests that the *experience* of the personal body, including of personal bodies described as disabled, is socially defined. There is *no experience*, from the inside, of a purely objective, pre-social, natural, physical, or biological body, or the *phenomenologically experienced* personal body is always socially defined. Although we often assume that we experience our own bodies in what seems like an immediate and given way, cross-cultural comparisons as well as an analysis of experiences of disability suggest that the *experience* of this first body or the feel of our own personal bodies is actually socially defined.[11] For disabled people, social contexts, including society's ableism, affect the very *feel* of disabled personal bodies. The experience of vision, for instance, is defined by social context. And society's ableism affects physically disabled people's experiences of fatigue or soreness, cognitively disabled people's experiences of their own intelligence, and the pain experienced by people with sickle-cell anemia.

Chapters 4 and 5 will suggest that, just as there is no *experience* of a purely objective, pre-social, natural, physical, or biological personal body, as chapter 3 proposes, so there is no purely objective, pre-social, natural, physical, or biological body *out there*, as an object. Chapter 4 will suggest that there are no purely objective, pre-social, natural, or physical bodily conditions or *impairments*. As comparisons with the traditional beliefs of some non-Western cultures will suggest, what we call "impairments" and "bodily conditions" are just one way of cutting up and defining the world, a way defined by our languages and learning. Chapter 5 will suggest that there is also no purely objective, pre-social, or natural *biological* body or impairment. Comparisons with the traditional beliefs of Yoruba society in Africa suggest that the discipline of biology and the corresponding practice of medicine are just one of the sets of beliefs that shapes the facts that we perceive, or determines what we regard "as so."

I am not suggesting that individuals can believe whatever they want. Individual beliefs cannot be separated from the socially shared languages in which they are articulated and the worlds those languages presuppose. Given the socially shared meanings of the relevant terms in modern English, for instance, it is just "so" or a fact that so-and-so is your cousin but not your sibling (see chapter 3). For it to be a fact that so-and-so is both (what we would call) your cousin and sibling, the words would have to mean something different from what they do in this socially shared language and in this social world. One would have to be speaking a different language in a different social world altogether. Individuals must reckon with the social, even if they can resist it in various ways. Our worlds will come to reliably have different facts, then, only when we, together, remake our socially shared worlds, including our languages. In chapters 6 and 7 we will explore how such a remaking might begin to be done for disability.

Taken together, then, the arguments of chapters 1–5 will suggest that disability along all three dimensions of embodiment or all three bodies in Scheper-Hughes and Lock's sense is socially defined, both in terms of what there *is* in each dimension, as objects *out there*, and in terms of how each dimension is *experienced*. Disability is *made* along all three dimensions of embodiment, in both of these senses, all the way down to the disabled personal body. Claims about impairment or biological impairment are also socially defined.

A Cultural Model of Disability

I am therefore offering a version of what has been termed the "cultural model" of disability. In a 2005 presentation titled "Generating a Cultural Model of Disability," education, anthropology, and disability studies professor Patrick J. Devlieger (2005) suggested that scholars of disability should continue to develop what he called a "cultural model" of disability that goes beyond the medical or social models (5–6). Anne Waldschmidt (2017), professor of disability studies, sociology, and the politics of rehabilitation, has suggested that, although this approach remains "more like a patchwork quilt" (22), in general, the cultural model of disability uses "a broad conception of culture" to suggest that disability is not "a given entity or a fact" (25) but is socially and culturally defined (cf. Ellis 2015, 2). Under a broad conception of culture, Waldschmidt suggests, *culture* is "the totality of 'things' [whether material or immaterial] created and employed by a particular people or a society," including their (or its) objects, institutions, ideas, symbols, values, meanings, narratives, traditions, customs, social rules, attitudes, identities, and so on (24). My claim is that relatively recent Western cultures—where *culture* includes the societies' complete economic, social, and conceptual systems—have defined or *made* impairment and disability. Western cultures have produced what we organize and perceive as the "facts" of impairment and disability today.

Waldschmidt suggests that cultural models of disability tend to subscribe to three further ideas, which my account also endorses. First, cultural models of disability regard disability not as a feature of an individual's body, but as an "embodied category of differentiation." On this view, what we think of as bodily differences only become relevant "within a given cultural and historical order of knowledge" (Waldschmidt 2017, 25). Bodies are always *embodied*. They are defined and have meaning only insofar as they move about in particular historical, social, and cultural worlds. Although human beings have been different from one another as long as there have been human beings, without access to the relevant cultures, we have no idea how humans from many other cultures and times would have perceived, noted, understood, or classified differences. Second, Waldschmidt says, "disability" and "ability" are produced together and interdependently by particular cultures: there is not "ability" and "disability," but only dis/ability. Just as one ("ability" or "disability") is produced by the sociocultural systems in Western societies, so is the other also produced. Third, Waldschmidt suggests, this approach opens up the possibility of new insights into responses. Instead of continuing only to "stare" at individuals with disabilities, so to speak, Waldschmidt says, "the focus can widen to a look at society and culture in general" (25). Instead of focusing on curing, rehabilitating, or accommodating individuals with disabilities, we can *unmake* disability by changing societies and cultures.

UNMAKING DISABILITY

- Is This Account Like the Human Variation Model of Disability?
- Unmaking Disability along the Third Dimension of Embodiment, the Institutional Body
- Unmaking Disability along the First and Second Dimensions of Embodiment, the Personal and Interpersonal Bodies

Chapters 6 and 7 will explore how we might begin to *unmake* disability and impairment. To say that disability and impairment are *made* or socially defined is to say that societies' institutions and structures—including their structures of public attitudes, concepts, and beliefs—define what counts as disability and impairment as well as how disability and impairment are experienced. As a result, unmaking disability will require changing societies' social institutions and structures. Instead of classifying individual *people* as impaired or disabled and providing individual *accommodations* for people so classified—the predominant way in which disability is currently addressed—we can begin to unmake disability by changing societies' social structures and institutions, including their attitudes, concepts, and beliefs, in ways that increase *access* to social goods for people currently classified as disabled.

Is This Account Like the Human Variation Model of Disability?

Readers who are familiar with disability studies might recognize similarities between this strategy for change and the strategy supported by the view sometimes called the "human variation model" of disability. According to the human variation model, disability is just a kind of human variation. Sociologists Richard K. Scotch and Kay Schriner (1997) suggest, for instance, that we should regard disability "as an extension of the natural physical, social, and cultural variability of the human species" (154–55). Disability has to do with physical and mental variability, which are at bottom just human differences like any other kinds of human differences. However, what we classify as "disability" is a "variability in physical and mental attributes" that goes *beyond* or falls *outside* of what economic, social, cultural, and political institutions routinely respond to (Scotch and Schriner 1997, 155). Human variations in terms of physical or mental characteristics become a "disability" when the differences go beyond what societies' structures and institutions regularly accommodate. Printed books, for instance, can accommodate people who see well along with many people who do not see very well, but cannot accommodate people who do not see at all. Not seeing at all is a "disability," then, because it is a human variation or difference in terms of physical or mental characteristics that falls outside of what printed books, as a currently common social structure, routinely respond to. On this view, as on my view, then, addressing disability requires taking social structures and institutions seriously.

Although my view has affinities with some versions of the human variation model, there are two main differences. First, defenders of the human variation model do not necessarily reject the notion that there is a purely objective, pre-social, natural, physical, or biological body or impairment, as I do. In the quotation above, for instance, Scotch and Schriner include "natural physical . . . variability" among the differences that the model acknowledges, suggesting that there is such a thing, in their view, as a natural, pre-social, physical body—a view I reject. The human variation model is right that what we call disability is a way of defining what we would think of as human differences in the world. But what those human differences *are* is socially and culturally defined. Again, I am not rejecting the idea that there is *something there*, that there are real differences *out there* (to say that they are "human" differences is already to have identified them in a particular way). I am claiming only that what that something *is*, how it is *defined* or *identified*—whether it is "natural," "physical," or a "body," for instance, given the standard, English meanings of those terms—cannot be determined outside of social contexts, outside of language and learning.

Second, the solutions proposed by defenders of the human variation model do not always go beyond providing individual accommodations. In spite of Scotch and Schriner's suggestion that disability is defined in terms of social structures, they go on to propose that unemployment for disabled people, for instance, should be addressed through accommodations that maximize each individual's productivity. As they put it, "Lack of access to employment by persons with disabilities [should] be resolved by cooperatively maximizing each individual's productivity rather than by staking out and defending legal entitlements to employment based on membership in a minority group" (158). Like me (see above and chapter 3), they are skeptical about whether civil rights laws—like the ADA—that are rooted in the minority model of disability can improve the employment participation of disabled people, but their alternative solution mirrors the current, standard approach that addresses disability by providing individual accommodations for individual people. By contrast, I will suggest, since disability is defined by social structures and institutions along all three dimensions of embodiment, unmaking disability will require, not individual accommodations for individual people, but changing social structures and institutions, all the way down to the first dimension of embodiment.

Unmaking Disability along the Third Dimension of Embodiment, the Institutional Body

Chapter 6 explores how disability might be unmade along the third dimension of embodiment or institutional body, including under capitalism. The current shift from a capitalist system dominated by industrial manufacturing to a capitalist system dominated by service industries is reconstructing the category of disability. Unmaking disability will require redefining the structure of work as well as the structures of public attitudes, particularly notions of citizenship, that have been associated with capitalism and with the social system, developed in the nineteenth century in the West, that privileges "normalcy."

Unmaking Disability along the First and Second Dimensions of Embodiment, the Personal and Interpersonal Bodies

Chapter 7 explores what unmaking disability along the first and second dimensions of embodiment, the personal body and the interpersonal body, would be like. Along the second dimension of embodiment or interpersonal body, unmaking disability will require rejecting classifications based on the body and redesigning social structures as well as structures of attitudes in ways that provide disabled people with access to valued social roles, including the roles of being a sexual partner and parent. Along the first dimension of embodiment or personal body, unmaking disability will require reconstructing social contexts and arrangements that define and construct impairment and disability in the first place, including our sciences of medicine and biology themselves. Ultimately, unmaking disability along this first dimension will require remaking our world.

1

Disability and Capitalism

In 1570 in Norwich, England, Elizabeth Mason, an eighty-year-old widow who was lame and had the use of only one hand, worked for her living by spinning and winding yarn. A blind man worked as a baker, and an eighty-year-old blind woman earned a living by knitting. Another blind man earned his living with the help of a fatherless twelve-year-old child, who served as his guide. According to the 1570 population census conducted by Norwich's city authorities, then, historian Irina Metzler reports in her recent book, *A Social History of Disability in the Middle Ages*, neither old age nor disability were necessarily factors that defined a person's ability to engage in productive work and be self-sufficient (Metzler 2015, 76).

As historian Margaret Pelling (2014), who conducted numerous studies on the 1570 Norwich census, suggests, "The sick and disabled were not necessarily excluded from social and economic life" (13; cf. Metzler 2015, 76) and retained, as Metzler (2015) adds, "the possibilities of interactions with others" (76). Although 1570 belongs to the beginning of the early modern period rather than the Middle Ages (which historians typically regard as ending in 1500), Metzler maintains that it helps to reveal what work would have been like for disabled people in Europe during the Middle Ages. After all, she suggests, if people who we would regard as disabled were able to be economically active in 1570, during "the early, modern, post-Reformation period with its Protestant 'work ethic,'" then one would assume all the more economic interaction for [disabled people during] the medieval period" (Metzler 2015, 76).

In her book examining the social history of disability in the Middle Ages, Metzler (2015) also points to other evidence suggesting that medieval people who we would classify as disabled were expected and able to be economically active. The excavation of a mass grave for soldiers killed in battle in 1461 in England found that many of the skeletons had evidence of injuries that had healed, including one individual who had signs of earlier damage to his pelvis that probably caused him to limp. And yet, the fact that he was still fighting as a soldier after his earlier injury had healed meant that he was evidently still regarded, as Metzler puts it, as "fit for action" (39). A contract for work on the York Cathedral in 1368 for the mason Robert de Patrington specified that he would receive a pension even if he could not work because of "blindness or infirmity, as long as he was still able to fulfill an advisory role on-site" (50). There is also an account, from the end of the ninth or early tenth centuries, of a blind man who was raised in a nobleman's court, trained in "all the works of women's art" (56), and worked with women in a textile shop. Is this a case of an emasculated, disabled man, forced to work with women, Metzler asks, or "just an example of finding the 'best' work placement for a disabled man who could not be a warrior, farmer or priest?" (57).

Indeed, according to Metzler (2015), evidence suggests that, during the Middle Ages in Europe, jobs were often tailored "according to individual (dis)abilities" (85). *The Rule of Saint Benedict*, a book of rules written by Saint Benedict of Nursia in the mid-500s to govern the lives of monks in Benedictine religious communities, stated that work for both fit as well as sick or impaired monks should be adjusted to the capabilities of individual monks. The *Rule* even specified that a monk who regarded his tasks as beyond his abilities could appeal to his superior (Metzler 2015, 84–85). Drawing on the work of agrarian historian W. O. Ault, Metzler also notes that, under feudal economic arrangements, when peasants were required to work on the lands that were designated for the lord's use, children and adults who were unable to do heavy harvesting work were allowed to glean the fields, or to do the lighter, but still necessary, work of collecting any remaining heads of grain after the harvest, instead of the professional harvesting work of reaping and binding (78).

Metzler's analysis of work patterns during the Middle Ages suggests that, unlike in today's capitalist, economic system, people were not rendered "dis-abled" or unable to work. Instead, they were expected—and able—to engage in economic activity to the best of their abilities. This participation in economic activities meant, further, that people who we today would regard as disabled were also not excluded from other aspects of social life, or from, as we saw Metzler put it, "the possibilities of interactions with others."

This chapter begins the analysis of the making of disability in terms of the third dimension of embodiment or institutional body. Although beginning with the third dimension may seem counterintuitive, it is the dimension that has been emphasized by disability activists and scholars and by the social models of disability. Disability is not a personal characteristic of individuals, disability activists and scholars have insisted, but a large social category that sorts people into groups: the disabled and the nondisabled (see the introduction). This chapter examines how, beginning in the late Middle Ages, the economic system of capitalism came to define a class of people as "dis-abled" or unable to work. Capitalism defined, regulated, and controlled disabled people by excluding them from the system of paid labor and reducing their social value. It also engendered a structure of public attitudes that justify and reinforce this exclusion by excluding people defined as disabled not only from the capitalist wage market but also from other social structures and institutions, such as the transportation, education, and health care systems and the built environment.

Chapter outline:

➤ Contemporary Exclusion from the Capitalist Wage Market
➤ Capitalism Produces and Defines Disability
➤ Today's Universal Concept of Disability
➤ Other Historical and Contemporary Counterexamples to Disabled Unemployability
➤ Interaction between Exclusion from Capitalist System and Exclusion from Other Systems
➤ A Structure of Public Attitudes
➤ From Paupers to Despised Outsiders
➤ Conclusion

CONTEMPORARY EXCLUSION FROM THE CAPITALIST WAGE MARKET

That disabled people are disproportionately excluded from the wage labor system compared to nondisabled people is undeniable. In January 2018 in the United States, for instance, only 20.4 percent of people with disabilities were employed, compared to 67.8 percent of people without disabilities. Keep in mind that the 20.4 percent employment figure is calculated based only on people with disabilities who would be considered eligible for the workforce. Of the 100 percent of noninstitutionalized disabled people, only 20.4 percent are working. This number is similar to the number obtained in a national, random telephone survey (using both cell and landline numbers) done in 2010 by the Kessler Foundation and National Organization on Disability (NOD) with 1,001 people who self-identified as disabled and 788 nondisabled people. The Kessler Foundation/NOD survey found that only 21 percent of disabled people reported being employed part- or full-time, while 59 percent of nondisabled people were employed—a gap of 38 percent (Harris Interactive 2010a, 22). In January 2018, the unemployment rate among people with disabilities was slightly more than twice the rate of nondisabled people: 8.8 percent vs. 4.3 percent (U.S. Department of Labor 2018).

The economic consequences of being excluded from the labor market are, of course, quite severe. In 2010, the Kessler Foundation/NOD survey found that disabled people in the United States are twice as likely to be living in poverty as nondisabled people—34 percent vs. 15 percent (Harris Interactive 2010a, 12). They were still twice as likely to be living in poverty in 2016. Drawing on the 2016 American Community Survey of the U.S. Census Bureau, W. Erickson, C. Lee, and S. von Schrader (2017) found that the overall poverty rate for disabled people in that year was 26.6 percent (2017). By contrast, the U.S. Census Bureau estimated the overall poverty rate in 2016 to be 12.7 percent (Semega, Fontenot, and Kollar 2017, 12). According to the National Council on Disability's 2017 "Progress Report," although people with disabilities make up only 12 percent of the U.S. working-age population, they live in poverty at twice the rate of nondisabled people (29 percent vs. 12 percent) (National Council on Disability 2017, 21).

CAPITALISM PRODUCES AND DEFINES DISABILITY

- Reevaluating Materialist or Marxist Arguments
- No Universal Concept of Disability in the Middle Ages
- Similar Effects of Capitalism on Punan Bah Society

What explains the disparities in employment rates between disabled and nondisabled people? Researchers influenced by the historical materialist or Marxist perspective have argued that, while the feudal economic system in Europe, or the economic system organized around land owned by a few, feudal lords, allowed people who we today would classify as disabled to engage in productive economic activity and be self-supporting, as capitalism replaced feudalism, people had to find paid work in a system in which labor was now valued based on the workers' productivity. These new productivity requirements excluded people regarded as less able to meet those productivity requirements from getting paid work. Later, under industrial capitalism, according to materialist theorists Marta Russell and Ravi Malhotra (2002), "as production became industrialized people's bodies were increasingly valued for their ability to function like machines" (213).

Capitalists' desire for ever greater productivity also led to the invention of the factory, which contained machines requiring precise movements and standardized bodies, thereby excluding people with nonstandard bodies or abilities from many factory jobs. Capitalism's invention of the factory also separated the home place from the workplace. Whereas most people during the feudal era in Europe would have worked in or near their homes, geographer and urban planner Brendan Gleeson (1997) suggests that industrial capitalism and the invention of the factory introduced a new separation between the workplace and the home place. This separation meant that people who had difficulty traveling to the new workplaces could not access the new spaces of paid work. The structures of capitalism thus excluded many people who we would classify as disabled from the paid labor market—an exclusion Gleeson calls "the sociospatial oppression of disabled people" (195).

The structures of the economic system of capitalism, these theorists argue, thus came to define a class of people as "*dis*-abled" or as unable to work. As Gleeson (1997) points out, Karl Marx (1909) acknowledges in *Capital* that capitalism's "means of production," or the system of facilities used to produce the goods and services that we all need to survive, would create a population of people who, as Marx put it, "are really not capable of working, who are dependent through force of circumstances on the exploitation of the labour of others, or compelled to perform certain kinds of labour which can be dignified with this name only under a miserable mode of production" (Marx 1909, III: "The Process of Capitalist Production as a Whole," 302; cf. Gleeson 1997, 195). Capitalism's production systems and facilities create a class of people who are defined by those very production systems as not capable of working and so are excluded from the wage market. As Marx's quotation suggests, this exclusion forces those people to be dependent on others or to support themselves in ways that are miserable—that demean them or put them in risky positions, for instance—and/or that relegate them to miserable conditions. In other words, the capitalist system dis-ables some people—casts them out of the economic system and confines them to poverty.

Reevaluating Materialist or Marxist Arguments

Metzler (2015) reevaluates the suggestions by Gleeson, Jacques Le Goff, Rob Imrie, and others that disabled people in the Middle Ages were more integrated into the economic system than they later came to be under industrial capitalism (71–83). Metzler, who focuses primarily on the experiences of people with physical and sensory disabilities (8), argues that Gleeson's claim that capitalism's separation between the home place and the workplace excluded and hence "disabled" some people from the system of paid labor is "too simplistic" (74). There were a number of kinds of work in the medieval period that had separate work places, such as mining (57–58) and the building trades, which Metzler suggests not only required workers to go to special work sites but also required workers to be migratory and move from town to town (49, 67). Moreover, Marx's account of people who were defined as "not capable" or "incapable" of working would have applied to any medieval poor person or peasant who was unable to do physical labor, such as widows, elderly people, orphans, sick people, and people who had been injured, since poor people in the Middle Ages were expected (like animals) to work with their bodies (74–75).

However, Metzler (2015) agrees that there were important differences between the economic system of feudalism during most of the medieval period and the later economic system of capitalism—differences that would indeed have affected the lives of people who we would today define as disabled. While an emphasis on the value of work already existed in the Middle Ages, and so predated the so-called Protestant work ethic of the post-Reformation period (44), what *counted* as work or as economic activity during the Middle Ages was different from what counted as economic activity later. The detailed census done in Norwich, England, in 1570 mentioned at the beginning of the chapter reveals that people who we would regard as disabled were engaging in a variety of activities that were considered genuine economic interactions or ways of making a living during the early modern period, such as spinning and winding yarn, knitting, carding and spinning wool, and baking. "In short," Metzler says, "the concept of what was regarded as economic activity in the 1570's and what the industrialized twenty-first century regards as such are not identical" (76). Disabled people would likely have been engaged in even more economic interaction during the Middle Ages, as we saw Metzler suggest, since, by 1570 in the early modern period, the Protestant "work ethic" would already have taken hold. Thus, an expanded definition of what counted as work and how one could earn a living in the Middle Ages (often, but not always, while at home) meant that people who we would regard as disabled were able to engage in economic interactions that would not be possible under capitalism later.

Metzler (2015) explains this difference in terms of what counted as work in the Middle Ages and what counts as work under capitalism by expanding on Le Goff's original distinction between regulated "merchant" time and flexible "peasant" time (71–72) as well as Gleeson's theory (78). In a society that values people according to the length of time they work, rather than the item produced or project completed, those who are slower or regarded as less productive workers are less valued. While the medieval period was dominated by an economic system that valued pieces, products, or projects, rather than time, economic systems in which people worked for wages and were "clocking on/off" and being paid according to the time they worked, were already in existence in the urban centers of the high medieval period. These time-based systems became more common later under the mercantile (trade-based) capitalist economy and under industrial capitalism (Metzler 2015, 73, 77). As we saw Russell and Malhotra (2002) note, industrial capitalism, which began in the late eighteenth century, further increased productivity requirements for workers: as systems of production became industrialized, people were, as they put it, "increasingly valued for their ability to function like machines" (213).

Metzler (2015) therefore recommends distinguishing between, on the one hand, an older, rural system of labor in which medieval people had more flexibility in terms of how they structured their time during the working day, and, on the other hand, urban patterns of work that became more common "with the growth of markets and towns from the high Middle Ages onwards" (77). Under rural conditions of work, a person's physical abilities (or disabilities) in terms of their work "would be relatively negligible" (78). People who could produce products through baking, carding wool, spinning yarn, or knitting could make a living. An emphasis on completing projects also helped. Although feudal, manorial rules allowed children and adults who were unable to do the professional harvesting work to do the lighter, work of gleaning the fields, people "who were caught gleaning when they should have been reaping" were punished (78). The point of such rules, Metzler suggests, was to make sure the reaping and binding were done without undue delays (79), "before valuable resources are allowed to be expended for gleaning" (83). Thus, Metzler concludes, while there is an element of truth to Gleeson's and other theorists' claims that disabled people in Europe were more involved in economic interactions under feudalism than they were later under capitalism, the theory "presents too simplistic a picture of an idealized 'feudal' rural past described through the proverbial rose-tinted lenses" (78).

No Universal Concept of Disability in the Middle Ages

The shift from the economic system of feudalism to the economic system of capitalism also gave rise to another change, namely, to a new, universal concept of "disability." Human development and public health scholars David L. Braddock and Susan L. Parish (2001) suggest that "there was no universal definition or interpretation of disability through this [the Medieval] period" (21), or no definition of disability that would have included all of the people we include under our concept of "disability" today. Metzler (2015) also suggests that there was no single term during the Middle Ages that corresponded to today's concept of "disability" (4). Instead, medieval people offered various interpretations of different disabilities. Braddock and Parish (2001) report that what we would call "intellectual disability, mental illness, deafness and epilepsy" (17) were thought to be caused by demons, for instance, although medical texts from the medieval period also sought natural causes for mental illness (18; cf. Metzler 2015, 148). Metzler (2015) suggests that, because of the common use of mutilations as punishment for crime, a physically disabled body came "to be associated with a criminal body" (29). Moreover, being poor and disabled was regarded as a risk for committing sin (196), and bodily perfection or "physical integrity" was a requirement for joining the priesthood (55, 63–64). People with physical disfigurements were also sometimes required by law to hide their disfigurement (16). However, accidents and disability were also regarded as part of the natural order (46, 102, 113; cf. Braddock and Parish 2001, 21), and physically disabled people who were poor were consistently considered part of "the needy and truly deserving poor" (Metzler 2015, 197).

The fact that there was no universal concept, definition, or interpretation of disability during the Middle Ages helps to explain why people with what we today would call disabilities were integrated into economic activity. The reverse is also true: the fact that such people were integrated into economic activity helps to explain why they were not regarded under a universal concept or definition as "disabled." As we saw at the beginning of the chapter, men and women with what we today would classify as disabilities were able to earn their own living and so were not regarded as unable to work. As the urban system of labor in which people were "clocking on/off" and being paid for the time they worked became more common, however, people who were excluded and hence "dis-abled" under the new system of work not only came to be regarded as a single group, but also came to be increasingly excluded from all aspects of social life. As they lost the ability to be self-supporting and the possibility of interaction with others, to echo Metzler's words quoted at the beginning of the chapter, they lost social value as well.

Similar Effects of Capitalism on Punan Bah Society

Anthropologist Ida Nicolaisen (2008) notes a similar shift in how work is defined—and how people we would regard as disabled fare—among the Punan Bah people of the central region of the island of Borneo in Malaysia. Nicolaisen reports that the Punan Bah have no single concept of disability equivalent to our own, and provide different explanations, which have different implications for the people involved, for various conditions that we would categorize as disabilities (46). People with what we would call mental or physical impairments live in longhouses with other members of the community and family, and so are not segregated; they do their share, to the extent of their ability, of daily household work, depending on their age or sex, which are the only criteria used to organize the division of labor. Women, for instance, look after small children, cook, chase chickens away from rice drying on mats, mend clothes, make sun hats, cut tobacco, and weave baskets and mats for household use or for sale to generate cash. Men craft tools, make chicken cages and fish traps, and mend and make fishing nets (47–48). Nicolaisen reports that she was "taken aback more than once by the capabilities of some of the disabled [people], in particular, those congenitally so" (48).

However, Nicolaisen (2008) continues, since as the Punan Bah began relying more heavily on cash income produced by young men who work for wages for the timber companies or other trades and services beginning the 1980s, "lesser weight is accorded subsistence activities" (54), a shift that disadvantages people we would classify as disabled. As Nicolaisen explains, this shift "diminishes the number as well as the significance of a wide variety of tasks that they were able to carry out, tasks that moreover lent them social value" (54). Thus, as people we would define as disabled became less able to do tasks that contributed to the economic viability of the community, their social standing also diminished. It would be interesting to see if the Punan Bah language adopts a universal concept of disability over time as well.

TODAY'S UNIVERSAL CONCEPT OF DISABILITY

Today in the West, Russell and Malhotra (2002) suggest, we use a universalized and abstract category of disability to divide the "disabled" from the "able-bodied" and to serve "as a 'boundary' category whereby people are allocated to either a work-based or a needs-based system of distribution" (214). This division is aided and abetted by the medicalization of disability, or by the conceptualization of disability as a medical problem. As Russell and Malhotra explain it, "By focusing on curing so-called abnormalities, and segregating those who could not be cured into the administrative category of 'disabled', medicine cooperated in shoving less exploitable workers out of the mainstream workforce" (214). Pushed out of the system of paid labor, people now classified as disabled are forced to obtain assistance from inadequate disability benefits that keep them in poverty (216, 215). Indeed, many of the anti-poverty programs for disabled people in the United States today are designed in ways that discourage them from seeking employment. Eligibility for Medicaid or Medicare, which pay for many of the long-term supports and services for disabled people, is tied to eligibility for Social Security, for instance, and eligibility for disability benefits under Social Security is tied to poverty. Since getting a job and making too much money will make a person ineligible for Social Security and hence for Medicaid or Medicare, disabled people are discouraged from pursuing any job that does not itself come with a quality health insurance program (National Council on Disability 2017, 36–37). The disability benefit system, Russell and Malhotra (2002) argue, thus allows capitalist owners to shift the cost of supporting "non-standard workers" onto the government, "thereby perpetuating their poverty" (215). Today, Russell and Malhotra conclude, "exclusion from exploitation in the wage-labour system, as the 'deserving poor', lies at the core of disabled peoples' oppression in every aspect of modern life" (216).

Russell and Malhotra (2002) argue that the capitalist system shifts the support of nonstandard workers on to the government because it assumes that those workers are more costly or less productive than standard workers—a cost that capitalist owners do not want to shoulder (214). But this assumption is just that—an assumption—that may not accurately describe reality. That is, it is as much an *effect* of our concept of "disability"—a "dis-abled" person is, more or less by definition, "un-able"—as it is a *cause* of our concept of "disability." The concept of "disability" itself implies a leap to the conclusion that the people to whom the term supposedly applies are "un-able," or, in general, cannot do things. The fact that people we would consider disabled were able to engage in economic activity and make a living during the Middle Ages helps to show that those people were in some sense not disabled at all, or that the notion that they should be viewed as "dis-abled" or "un-able" is a function of assumptions and ideology.

OTHER HISTORICAL AND CONTEMPORARY COUNTEREXAMPLES TO DISABLED UNEMPLOYABILITY

There is additional historical evidence that disabled people can work. Colin Barnes and Geof Mercer (2005) report that, during the Second World War, disabled people were pulled into the labor force in Britain—and then pushed out again by labor policies afterward (533).

Further evidence for the productivity of disabled workers can be found in a description offered by disability studies scholar Tomoko Hattori (2016) of three Japanese businesses that employ significant numbers of disabled people: Swan Bakery, Nihon Rikagaku Company, which makes colored chalk and other products, and FP Corporation, which makes and recycles food containers. By breaking down and redesigning tasks, Hattori found, these companies successfully employ people with disabilities—particularly people with intellectual disabilities—and they remain just as productive, or even more productive, as they would be without disabled employees. In terms of redesigning tasks, Nihon Rikagaku Company, for instance, designed special tools that employees who have difficulty reading numbers or characters can use in their work. The company gave one employee color-coded hourglasses (and later color-coded timers that emit sounds) that allow him to measure the precise times for adding different ingredients while mixing a batch of chalk. The company also designed a variety of alternative tools for conducting quality-control tasks. Instead of using electronic weights, employees use color-coded counterweights to test the weight of pieces of chalk coming off the line. Instead of using calipers to measure the dimensions of pieces of chalk, the company designed a mold for employees to use. In terms of productivity, Swan Bakery representatives say that their disabled employees are less likely than nondisabled employees to slack off on their work. Representatives of both Nihon Rikagaku and FP Corporation claim that employing disabled people has increased their productivity. FP Corporation reports that they have an employee retention rate of 99 percent.

As Hattori (2016) notes, these experiences echo the results of a survey conducted in 2010 by the Kessler Foundation and the National Organization on Disability with 411 senior executives and human resource managers at companies that have at least 50 employees. In the survey, 35 percent of the employers said that disabled employees are more dedicated than nondisabled employees, while 62 percent said that disabled employees have the same dedication as nondisabled employees; 33 percent said that disabled employees have less turnover than nondisabled employees, while 58 percent said the turnover was the same (Harris Interactive 2010b, 82, 84). In terms of the costs of hiring employees with disabilities, 62 percent of the employers said that disabled employees cost the same as nondisabled employees, including health care, accommodations, and management, while 33 percent said that they cost more (Harris Interactive 2010b, 89). Thus, the experiences of the Japanese companies as well as evidence from World War II and the Middle Ages suggest that assumptions about the productivity of disabled employees are faulty.

Employers may also find that disabled people are perfectly capable of working under exploitative circumstances. Dan Barry (2014) of the *New York Times* reports that, for more than thirty years, the Texas-based company Henry's Turkey Service paid a group of over twenty men with intellectual disabilities their food and lodging (under unsanitary and abusive conditions), the occasional outing, and a wage of $65 per month to eviscerate turkeys for up to 70 to 80 hours per week at a turkey-processing plant in Iowa. When the men were finally retired by the company, they were asked to train their nondisabled replacements. Henry's Turkey Service never built the men the promised retirement home. After decades of working in the plant, one of the men, Keith, had approximately $80 in his bank account. In 2007, Henry's Turkey Service made $500,000 on the men's contract. In these sorts of cases, even when disabled people are not completely excluded from the capitalist system of paid work, they are still excluded from *benefiting* from that system.

INTERACTION BETWEEN EXCLUSION FROM CAPITALIST SYSTEM AND EXCLUSION FROM OTHER SYSTEMS

The exclusion of disabled people from the capitalist economic system is reinforced by, but also causes, their exclusion from other large social systems and structures. In the 2010 Kessler Foundation/NOD survey of disabled and nondisabled people, 34 percent of disabled people reported that inadequate transportation was a problem, compared with 16 percent of nondisabled people—an 18-point gap (Harris Interactive 2010a, 15). Inadequate transportation affects access to employment as well as other social goods.

In a cross-disability focus-group study with 87 people with disabilities or their family members, Mari-Lynn Drainoni and her colleagues (2006) found that, although many disabled people are able to obtain health insurance through poverty programs such as Medicare or Medicaid (102), other structural barriers still impede their access to health care: a lack of transportation, conflicts with health insurers who lack knowledge about needed services, inaccessible offices and equipment, insufficient time allotted for visits with providers, and poor care coordination (105–8). The 2010 Kessler Foundation/NOD survey found that 19 percent of disabled people (vs. 10 percent of nondisabled people) reported that they had to forgo needed medical care at least once in the previous year (Harris Interactive 2010a, 14).

The survey also found that disabled people are less likely to go to restaurants—perhaps because of the expense, given their higher rate of poverty, or because of inaccessibility or stigma (Harris Interactive 2010a, 121). They are less likely to have graduated from high school, and less likely to use technology to access the internet, though this latter gap was smaller among younger disabled people (Harris Interactive 2010a, 13, 19). There are thus a number of large social structures or systems in our society that regulate and control disabled people by excluding them, which in turn affects their embodiment.

Notice that these systems and institutions exclude disabled people without anyone having to have any bad attitudes in their heads (cf. Maybee 2002, 135–38). No one in the Social Security or Medicaid office, for instance, has to have derogatory beliefs or attitudes about disabled people for the system to discourage disabled people from getting a job. No one at the Metropolitan Transportation Authority in New York City has to have derogatory beliefs about disabled people for the subway system to do its work of excluding disabled people and hence restricting their lives. Google engineer and wheelchair user Sasha Blair-Goldensohn (see the "Introduction and Theoretical Overview") probably had this factor in mind when he said that, although the inaccessible subway system in New York City "feels like an insult," it is "not a malicious one." No one is maliciously intending to exclude disabled people from the subway; disabled people's exclusion is impersonal. They are excluded by the way in which the subway system is designed and maintained. As we saw Blair-Goldensohn explain, "It's just that you've been forgotten, that you've been left out" (Cott and Mullin 2017). At the same time, as we will see next, the fact that disabled people are forgotten or left out when these systems are designed and maintained may be a function of a different kind of structure.

A STRUCTURE OF PUBLIC ATTITUDES

- This Structure of Public Attitudes Reflects the Capitalist System
- This Structure of Public Attitudes Reinforces the Exclusion of Disabled People from Other Structures and Institutions
- "Existential" and "Aesthetic" Anxiety

Social systems such as the economic, transportation, education, and health care systems are not the only kind of social structures that regulate and control—and disadvantage—disabled people. Political scientist and disabilities studies scholar Harlan Hahn (1988) has suggested that we should think of common and widespread assumptions and attitudes in society as a kind of structure—what he called a "structure of attitudes" (42). In our society, there is a structure of attitudes about ability and disability—a structure, as Hahn describes it, of "values, expectations, and assumptions about the physical and behavioral attributes that people ought to possess in order to survive or to participate in community life" (40). These values, expectations, and assumptions, which are reflected in the architectural structures, social institutions, and public policies of our society, require people to have certain functional skills if they are to participate in the social community. As Hahn explains, "Many everyday activities, such as the distance people walk, the steps they climb, the materials they read, and the messages they receive, impose stringent requirements on persons with different levels of functional skills" (40). Before the passage of the Americans with Disabilities Act (ADA) required the main post office in Ithaca, New York, to be modified, for instance, customers could enter the building only by going up a set of stairs. The design of the building thus presupposed that those participating in using the post office would have the functional skill to climb stairs.

Hahn (1988) suggests that the presupposed functional requirements *discriminate* against people who fall outside of the required levels. Disabled people are people who are discriminated against in this way. They are people who do not fit into society's social and architectural environment because they lack the level of functional skills presupposed by the values, expectations, and assumptions of public policies. Hahn also suggested that these presupposed functional requirements are not natural, inevitable, or accidental, but socially defined. As Hahn puts it, "These characteristics of the environment that have a discriminatory effect on disabled citizens cannot be considered simply coincidental. Rather than reflecting immutable aspects of an environment decreed by natural law, they represent the consequences of prior policy decisions" (40). The public policies that assume that people have certain functional skills to survive and participate in community life are *chosen* and *enacted*. Society is *designed* to *disable* certain people, or to *make* people who do not have functional or behavioral abilities presupposed by public policies *unable* to participate.

Nondisabled people, by contrast, are people who fit and so are "abled" by the same values, expectations, and assumptions. As Anita Silvers (1998) has observed, "The main ingredient of being (perceived as) normal lies in being in social situations that suit one—that is, in a social environment arranged for and accustomed to people like oneself" (73–74). For Hahn and Silvers, then, our society can be viewed as a vast affirmative action program for nondisabled people. Our society is *designed* to fit nondisabled people.

This Structure of Public Attitudes Reflects the Capitalist System

The structure of attitudes toward disability that Hahn describes reflects—in attitudes—what the capitalist economic system does in practice. As urban systems of work—in which people were "clocking on/off" and paid for the time they worked—spread toward the end of and after the Middle Ages, the capitalist system began to exclude people regarded as less able to meet certain productivity standards from the wage labor market and defined them as "dis-abled" or as unable to work. Industrial capitalism further raised productivity requirements and came to demand standardized bodies that could function like machines. Capitalism thus excluded people who (were assumed to) fall below certain physical and behavioral standards from paid work. The assumption made by the structure of attitudes that people should meet certain physical and behavioral standards to participate generally in community life reflects, justifies, and reinforces capitalism's exclusive practices.

This Structure of Public Attitudes Reinforces the Exclusion of Disabled People from Other Structures and Institutions

While the structure of public attitudes ensures that the institutions and public policies of society *fit* and so *include* nondisabled people, it takes the *exclusion* and *absence* of disabled people for granted. It therefore reinforces and helps to explain disabled people's exclusion, not only from the capitalist system of wage labor but also from other, more local structures and institutions, such as transportation, education, and health care systems and built environments. It explains why many local structures and institutions seem to have "forgotten" and "left out" disabled people, as Blair-Goldensohn observes about the maintenance practices and design of the subway system in New York City (see the introduction). To the same degree that society's structures and institutions were designed to *fit* non-disabled people, they were designed *not to fit* and so to *exclude* disabled people. Disabled people's absence from the subway system, for instance, is assumed as part of its design and maintenance.

"Existential" and "Aesthetic" Anxiety

Hahn (1988) argues that the structure of attitudes toward disability is ex-pressed in two dominant forms of anxiety that nondisabled people have toward disabled people in our society: "existential" and "aesthetic" anxiety. First, insofar as disabled people deviate from the usual human form or have traits that are regarded as unattractive, they produce in nondisabled people a fear of becoming unattractive, or an aesthetic anxiety. "These fears," Hahn suggests, "are reflected in both the propensity to shun those with unattractive bodily attributes and the extraordinary stress that modem society devotes to its quest for supernormal standards of bodily perfection" (42). Second, insofar as disabled people represent the possibility of a loss of functional abilities, they produce in nondisabled peo-ple a fear of becoming impaired, or an existential anxiety. These fears sometimes rise to people's consciousness when disability leads to thoughts such as "there, but for the grace of God go I," or when people express beliefs that suggest they would rather be dead than live with some kind of disability. "I would rather be dead than live as a paraplegic [or as blind, deaf, or immobilized]," Hahn imagines people thinking to themselves (43).

Marxist or materialist theorists would argue that the phenomena that Hahn calls aesthetic and existential anxiety are products of the capitalist economic system. What people fear is not so much the loss of physical attractiveness or functional ability in themselves, but the social and economic *consequences* of a loss of physical attractiveness or functional ability. Our society classifies people as "disabled" based on both appearance and functional ability. We treat people with facial birthmarks, scars, or disfigurements, for instance, as disabled, even when their functional abilities are not affected (Olkin 1999, 71; Stone and Wright 2013). And, as we have seen, being classified as disabled does have serious economic consequences, including exclusion from the labor market[1] and impoverishment. People therefore fear and try to avoid being classified as disabled—whether based on appearance or functional ability—because they do not want to be subjected to the material disadvantages or poverty that come with being regarded as disabled. As Russell and Malhotra (2002) put this: "Being categorized as 'disabled' . . . and the subsequent impoverishment that so many face when struggling to survive on disability benefits, serves another class function: it generates a very realistic fear among workers of becoming disabled" (215). Or, as Paul Abberley (1987) puts it, the "negative stereotypes and material disadvantages connected to disability" encourage "people, where possible, to normalize suffering and disease so as not to include themselves in a despised and disadvantaged sub-group" (17). The fact that disabled people are a systematically excluded and disadvantaged social group ensures that nondisabled people deny any suffering and disease they may be experiencing as much and as long as possible, to keep functioning in the capitalistic system. Nondisabled people get the message: remain "able," or else.

FROM PAUPERS TO DESPISED OUTSIDERS

So far, we have explored how capitalism and its corresponding structure of attitudes systematically excluded and disadvantaged a group of people who thereby came to be classified as disabled. But we have not yet seen how disabled people became a *despised* group (Abberley 1987, 17).

As we have seen, disabled people have not always been regarded as a *single group*, let alone a *despised* group. They have not even been a despised group throughout European history. The structure of attitudes toward disability in the Middle Ages was mixed. Disfigurement was disvalued and bodily perfection was valued, but accidents and disability were regarded as part of the natural order. Disabled people were also not seen as despised outsiders. They were part of what

Metzler (2015) calls a "multiform category" that included different groups of people who were poor or relied on the support of others: widows, sick people, pilgrims, economically poor, and physically impaired people (157). They were *pauperes*, or paupers, which, she suggests, was a category that applied to people who were either (or both) socially disempowered or economically poor (155). And such paupers were *not* in general, or as part of the structure of attitudes, we could say, treated as outsiders. As Metzler (2015) puts it, a person who required the support of others "did definitely not stand outside or even on the margins of society but instead was an integrated member" (156)—a situation that lasted, she says, until about the twelfth century. Only later in European history, as we will see in the next chapter, did the structure of attitudes in many modern Western societies come to define disabled people not only as an excluded and disadvantaged group but also as a *despised* group.

CONCLUSION

Along the third dimension of embodiment or institutional body (see the introduction), the economic system of capitalism defined, regulated, and controlled disabled people. As the urban system of labor in which people were "clocking on/off" and paid for the time they worked expanded, and with the increase in productivity requirements and the demand for standardized bodies that could function like machines under industrial capitalism, the economic system of capitalism created a category of disabled (or "un-able") people who were excluded from the system of paid labor and economically disadvantaged. This exclusion was then reflected in a new structure of public attitudes, or in a set of values, expectations, and assumptions about the physical and behavioral attributes that people should have if they are to participate in social life. Together, the capitalist system and this structure of attitudes also excluded disabled people from other, more local systems and structures, such as the transportation, health care, and educational systems.

As we saw Abberley point out, however, disabled people came to be defined not only as an excluded and disadvantaged group, but also as a *despised* group. Scholars have often criticized materialist social models for being unable to account for the cultural aspects of disability, or for shared, cultural beliefs and attitudes toward disability. In the next chapter, we will explore how the structure of attitudes or set of cultural beliefs in many Western societies came to define disabled people, not only as an excluded and disadvantaged group but also as despised outsiders.

2

A New Structure of Attitudes

Normalcy, Eugenics, the Ugly Laws, and Segregation

On April 11, 1890, at 3:30 in the afternoon, after four years of living in his private rooms in London Hospital, which came to be called "the elephant house," the now-famous twenty-eight-year-old Joseph Merrick, who had previously worked for five years in the freak-show business as "the Elephant Man," was found lying dead across his bed. In an account of Merrick's life, Dr. Frederick Treves, who had been in charge of Merrick's care at the hospital, implied, but did not explicitly say, that Merrick, who was required to sleep upright to avoid asphyxiation due to his deformities, had committed suicide. Merrick did so, Treves said, because he could not "be like other people." As historian Nadja Durbach (2010) describes it, Treves claimed that Merrick likely committed suicide because Merrick could not "achieve normalcy" (56). However, Tom Norman, one of the best-known show-men of the day who had served as one of four of Merrick's managers when Merrick worked the freak-show circuit (33), challenged Treves's account of Merrick's motivation. Norman maintained, as Durbach summarizes it, that suicide "was Merrick's only way out of being constantly interrogated by the medical gaze." According to Norman, Durbach says, Merrick's suicide was his "last expression of bodily control, an act of manly defiance that was ultimately an explicit refusal to be further objectified and pathologized by medical science" (56).

It is difficult to know what Merrick's own views were, because both Norman and Treves represent themselves in the best light (Durbach 2010, 37). Durbach presents the contrast between Norman's and Treves's accounts of Merrick's life as a conflict between an older view, in which people with physical differences had insisted on their status as "able-bodied" working people while earning a living as entertainers on the freak-show circuit, and a newer view, in which medical practitioners asserted power as experts while depicting people with bodily differences in increasingly dehumanized ways as diseased and pitiful people who, being necessarily unable to work as a result of their deformities, were in need of charity. The competing accounts of Merrick's story are thus a sign of a cultural shift from an older understanding of ability and disability that developed during and after the Middle Ages, to a new understanding of disability that was taking hold in the late nineteenth and twentieth centuries under industrial capitalism.

In the older view, being "able-bodied," as Durbach (2010) suggests, was not associated with deformity of the body but with the ability to labor (18). And, as historian Irina Metzler suggested (see chapter 1), during the Middle Ages and early modern periods, there was also a wider variety of acceptable forms of labor. However, as industrial capitalism's wage labor system and a new structure of upper-, middle-, ruling-class attitudes restricted the range of acceptable forms of labor, bodily differences came to be depicted in increasingly medicalized and dehumanized ways as necessary barriers to employment that should be addressed only through charity and segregation. Merrick himself was segregated from non-disabled people while in residence at the hospital and lived on charity.

The Marxist-inspired or materialist social models of disability (see the introduction), which focus on the *economic* aspects of the third dimension of embodiment or institutional body, are often criticized for failing to take account of the effects that *ideological and cultural aspects* of society, beyond economics, have on the lives of disabled people (e.g., Metzler 2006, 26; Shakespeare 1994). This chapter explores the development of a structure of attitudes, ideology, or set of cultural beliefs that increasingly came to define disabled people, from the point of view of the third dimension or institutional body, not only as an excluded and disadvantaged group (see chapter 1) but also as a *despised* group.

There was a shift in the nineteenth century in Western societies away from a view in which people were regarded as "dis-abled" insofar as they were excluded from or unable to work in the capitalist wage market, as the Marxist analysis suggests (chapter 1), toward a view in which disabled people came to be culturally defined in increasingly medicalized ways as diseased and despised outsiders. This shift is traced through the competing accounts of Merrick's life, the development of the idea of normalcy (and hence also abnormalcy), the eugenics movement, the so-called ugly laws, and the expanding segregation of disabled people, all of which either first appeared or increased in the nineteenth century and continued into the twentieth. These developments solidified and are reflected in today's structures of public attitudes that largely regard disabled people as abnormal and as proper subjects only of medicine, charity, and segregation. Not only were these developments consistent with capitalists' aims, however, but also a full account of them requires paying attention to the workings of the capitalist system.

Chapter outline:

➤ Competing Accounts of the Life and Death of Joseph Merrick and the Development of the Concept of Normalcy
➤ The Eugenics Movement
➤ The "Ugly Laws"
➤ Contemporary Segregation
➤ Conditions in Segregated Institutions
➤ Ending Segregation?
➤ Is the Segregation and Abuse of Disabled People Malicious?
➤ Positive Side Effects of Segregation
➤ Conclusion

COMPETING ACCOUNTS OF THE LIFE AND DEATH OF JOSEPH MERRICK AND THE DEVELOPMENT OF THE CONCEPT OF NORMALCY

• Norman's Account of Merrick as a Defeated, Able-Bodied, Working-Class Man
• Freak Shows and the Invention of Normalcy
• Treves's Account of Merrick as Abnormal, Diseased, and Unemployable
• Treves's Upper- and Middle-Class Account Becomes Dominant

Norman's Account of Merrick as a Defeated, Able-Bodied, Working-Class Man

Born into a working-class household in northern England in 1862, Merrick, who began to develop deformities at an early age, had been employed in unskilled jobs from age 11, including at a cigar factory and as a peddler. He was forced out of his home as a young teenager by family problems. After his mother died and his father remarried, his stepmother rejected him, apparently because she found him grotesque. He was taken in by a kind uncle who worked as a hairdresser, but, not wanting to be a burden, Durbach (2010) reports, Merrick tried to live independently "in cheap lodging houses, before eventually checking himself into the Leicester workhouse where he remained for almost five years" (36).

The showman Norman, the working-class son of a butcher who, like Merrick, had begun working at a young age and left home at age 14 (Durbach 2010, 37), reported that Merrick took the initiative to reach out to a local variety theater from the workhouse "to seek employment as a novelty act," Durbach says. According to Norman, Merrick then "struck a deal with a consortium of showmen, including Norman, who agreed to exhibit him as 'the Elephant Man' in several cities across Britain" (46–47). Durbach suggests that, in Norman's account, Merrick is described "not as a helpless invalid but as a fellow working man who successfully and shrewdly capitalized on an expanding consumer culture by selling the only thing he had left to commodify: his extraordinary body" (37). According to Norman, Merrick's career as a freak-show performer was profitable enough for Merrick to save "a sizeable nest egg for a working-class man" within the first five months (47). Norman maintained that Merrick's ability to earn his own wages was important to Merrick's sense of self, echoing "the discourse of working-class masculine self-reliance" of the day, in line with which the freak show could provide a route for working-class people to "demonstrate that they were independent laborers, and thus to articulate their moral worth" (47, cf. 37). While the freak show was evidently not Merrick's first choice for working and making money—he had tried to obtain other work in the wage market of his day but was pushed out of that market and into the workhouse—it did provide him with a less ideal path for remaining economically independent and self-reliant.

Norman's account of Merrick's attitudes toward his work as a performer is reinforced by Durbach's (2010) arguments that freak-show performers were "heavily invested in their status as 'able-bodied'" working people (19). Durbach writes: "Freaks of all varieties tended to construct themselves as skilled performers whose bodies allowed them to lead normal, if not extraordinary, lives, a fact that was clearly central to their public personae" (20). This account of the attitudes of the freak show performers toward labor is also consistent with Metzler's suggestion that all the social strata of urban society came to adopt the elite's discourse on the intrinsic value of labor, and hence the value of being able to work, beginning in the late thirteenth century and certainly after the spread of the Protestant work ethic in the mid-1600s (Metzler 2006, 43–44). As a result, when Treves confined Merrick to the London Hospital in 1886, he did not rescue Merrick from the "dismal slavery" of the freak show as Treves had claimed, Norman's account suggests, but instead "compromised [Merrick's] identity as an able-bodied, self-governing working-class man" (Durbach 2010, 46). As Durbach writes, "After almost five years in the workhouse, Merrick checked himself out to begin life as a freak. After four years in 'the elephant house' he chose another means of escape" (55).

During Merrick's career as a freak-show performer, Durbach (2010) suggests, although Merrick was marketed as a half-human, half-animal "Elephant Man"—the animal/human hybrid was a common role adopted by freak-show performers (8–9)—he was presented as a *wonder* (45), and not, as he was by the medical profession, a diseased object being made available for the gaze of a healthy observer (46). Merrick's promotional materials insisted that he was not sick or in pain, and was therefore, like the members of his audience, healthy (46)—a common claim by freak-show performers. Indeed, Durbach suggests, "not only did freak acts and their managers resist a medical diagnosis, they took great pains to establish that they were not exhibiting a diseased or unhealthy body" (26). Norman also introduced Merrick by his proper name, "Mr. Joseph Merrick, the Elephant Man," thereby emphasizing Merrick's dignity, humanity, and identity, rather than presenting him as a monster. In fact, Durbach says, Norman maintained "that he encouraged the crowd to see Merrick as 'the most remarkable human being ever to draw the breath of life' rather than as a monstrosity" (46).

Freak Shows and the Invention of Normalcy

Although freak shows were common across Europe in the early modern period beginning in the sixteenth century (Durbach 2010, 2), Durbach suggests that they reached their heyday during the period from 1847 to 1914, at the height of the United Kingdom's status as an imperial power. They also reached their heyday, she says, in the UK in particular (1–2). "It is no coincidence," Durbach says, "that freak shows reached their zenith at the height of Britain's modern and imperial self-fashioning" (1–2). In the freak shows, which also cast racial and cultural difference "as a bodily anomaly analogous to physical deformity" (8), displays of people constructed as "'human oddities' functioned as important spaces for negotiations over the class, gender, racial, ethnic, and sexual meanings of 'normal' and 'abnormal' bodies" (17), and helped to establish the rightness and dominance of the white, European upper and middle classes. As disability studies scholars David L. Braddock and Susan L. Parish (2001) have suggested, in Europe and the United States during the nineteenth century, freak shows displaying disabled people as well as members of racial and ethnic minority groups as abnormal (37–38) helped to construct the concept of "normalcy" as well as of disability as "deviance," and reinforced, in the minds of the white, nondisabled, middle-class population, a belief in their own normality (38).[1]

The concept of normalcy as we understand it today was thus invented around this same time. English and disability studies professor Lennard J. Davis (1995) has argued that the concept of "normal"—meaning common or average—did not come into the English language until 1840, was followed closely by cognate words such as *normalcy, normality, norm,* and *abnormal* (24), and was linked to the invention and spread of the discipline of statistics as well as to the rise of the eugenics movement (28–31). The development of the notion of normalcy was also linked, Davis argues, to the growing dominance of the capitalist middle-class, for whom the "average man," as captured by the new discipline of statistics, became, not merely numbers, but a new ideal. "Middle-class life as a kind of norm" becomes an "ideology," Davis suggests, "the average then becomes paradoxically an ideal, a position devoutly to be wished" (27).

"By the mid-nineteenth century," Durbach (2010) writes,

> the freak show had become a truly international institution. Human oddities from around the world, and increasingly from the colonized areas with which Europeans had the most regular contact, crisscrossed the Atlantic, appearing in both North American and western European cities and towns. Some continued on to Russia or even Constantinople, tracing and retracing what had become an established freak show route. (3)

This is the same time period in Europe and North America, as we will soon see, in which disabled people increasingly came to be segregated, as was Merrick, in what were progressively more medicalized, custodial institutions. And, as we will see later, it is also the same time period in which the discipline of biology was invented (chapter 5).

Treves's Account of Merrick as Abnormal, Diseased, and Unemployable

While Treves's story about Merrick's life has come to dominate popular culture,[2] it was his account, not Norman's, Durbach (2010) argues, that constructed Merrick as abnormal, diseased, and deviant; and it was Treves who confined Merrick and segregated him from the public. Treves had examined Merrick in 1884 when Merrick was performing in a cheap freak show across the street from the London Hospital (35)—until Merrick refused to go back for more examinations (52). It was only when Merrick returned from Belgium destitute after being robbed and abandoned by an unscrupulous showman in 1886 that Treves decided, as Durbach quotes Treves's account, that "Merrick must not again be turned out into the world" and applied to have him become a permanent resident at the Hospital (36).

Treves considered Merrick's segregation in the hospital appropriate because he regarded Merrick as diseased. Durbach (2010) reports that, unlike Norman, Treves described Merrick in "the emotional language of horror and disgust" as a "degraded," "perverted," and "repulsive" "creature" or "thing," and as "'the most disgusting specimen of humanity that I have ever seen'" (38). According to Durbach, Treves and his colleagues also continuously sought "to diagnose [Merrick] as suffering from an identifiable disease that only medical professionals could interpret" (45).

In addition, unlike Norman, Treves undercut Merrick's ability to be self-supporting and self-governing. Although Treves knew of Merrick's career as a performer, Treves claimed that Merrick was unable to find any employment, was physically prevented from learning a trade because of his deformities, and was therefore necessarily a charity case (Durbach 2010, 48–49). For Treves, then, Merrick's deformities were necessarily "dis-abling," or necessarily excluded him from the capitalist wage market. Durbach suggests that Treves's class values led him to regard using one's body for manual labor as acceptable but selling one's body on the freak show circuit as not (49). Treves also could not see Merrick as masculine or as an adult "in any way" (51) and characterized Merrick as childlike, primitive, and feminine (50). "Kept sequestered in his rooms," Durbach reports, Merrick spent most of his time performing tasks such as "building models or weaving baskets" that cast him in a middle-class, domestic, childish, and feminine role (50).[3] It was thus Treves, Durbach suggests, who "undermined Merrick's masculine independence and, in the process, his ability to care for himself and make decisions governing his own body" (52).

Merrick lost control over decisions about his own body, Durbach (2010) argues, because Treves exhibited Merrick for his own purposes in ways that Merrick seemed to find disconcerting. As Durbach describes the situation, although Treves criticized the freak shows, he "staked his own claim to control over the exhibition of Merrick's deformities by placing him under his care at the hospital and thus controlling access to his person" (53). While Treves and the hospital controlled Merrick's access to the outside world, and the outside world's access to him (50, 55), they regularly displayed Merrick in "the elephant house," his private rooms, even for people outside of the medical profession who, as Durbach puts it, "had no professional stake in Merrick's case" (54). According to Norman, Durbach says, Merrick was uncomfortable with the way in which Treves exhibited him. As Durbach explains Norman's report, Merrick was "'keenly conscious of the indignity of having to appear undressed' before this 'never-ending stream' of visitors who did not pay him for his services" (54). Wilfred Grenfell, one of the young doctors primarily responsible for Merrick's care, confirmed Merrick's sensitivity about exhibiting himself at the hospital (54, 51). Treves also exhibited "'the Elephant Man' as a live specimen before the Pathological Society," Durbach reports—a detail Treves "omitted" from his memoirs (40).

"Who, then, 'really exploited poor Joseph?' Norman asked," Durbach (2010) reports. "For, although 'the eminent surgeon' 'received the publicity and the praise' for rescuing Merrick from the freak show," Durbach says, "Norman insisted that Treves was 'also a Showman, but on a rather higher social scale'" (55). Treves had encouraged Merrick "to adopt the trappings of middle-class masculinity" and normalcy by giving Merrick a dressing bag with men's grooming tools and by helping Merrick appear in a three-piece suit in his *carte de visite* or souvenir photograph for guests (52). But by using Merrick's show name, "the Elephant Man," rather than Merrick's proper name, Durbach says, Treves actually undercut "any claim to normalcy" that Merrick might have been making by using the dressing bag and giving out that *carte de visite* to guests. It was really Treves, then, who was the showman who constructed Merrick as irredeemably and inherently abnormal.

Treves's Upper- and Middle-Class Account Becomes Dominant

Treves's story of Merrick's life, and not Norman's, not only came to dominate our understanding of Merrick's particular life, but also reflects what came to be the dominant, public attitude toward disabled people in the West. We will never know for sure whether Merrick took his own life because he could not achieve normalcy, as Treves had implied, or because Merrick's identity as a proud, working-class man was defeated by his confinement to the hospital as a charity case and by the dehumanizing medical gaze, as Norman's account implied. Norman's view was perhaps independently corroborated by D. G. Halsted, one of the other young doctors responsible for Merrick's care at the hospital (Durbach 2010, 13, 19), who, Durbach reports, "regularly had to 'cheer [Merrick] up if he felt depressed'" (56).

But it is Treves's account of Merrick's life, and not Norman's, that dominates Western, popular culture's view of Merrick as what we understand as disabled, with its medicalizing, abnormalizing, and dehumanizing overtones, and its implications of unemployability. Durbach (2010) describes David Lynch's influential 1980 film *The Elephant Man*, which is based largely on Treves's memoir, as a "mawkish and moralizing" story that depicts Merrick in upper- and middle-class terms "as a refined soul trapped in a monstrous body, freed from a life of degradation by Treves, who gave him permanent shelter at the London Hospital" (35). She quotes approvingly historian Raphael Samuel's (1981) claim that "if an 'upper-class evangelical of the 1880s had possessed a cine-camera, this is the film he might have made'" (Durbach 2010, 35; Samuel 1981, 315). Indeed, Samuel (1981) suggests, two of the film's main villains—the invading mob and the evil night porter who "runs a small racket" displaying Merrick for personal profit on the side and "ends up as a small-time torturer"—echo standard upper- and middle-class, mythic depictions of the working class as "cynical, greedy and materialistic" and are not even mentioned in Treves's original account (317).

Still, it is Treves's ruling-class account, which constructed Merrick as necessarily unable to work or "dis-abled" and as a proper subject only of medical diagnosis, charity, and segregation, that has helped to shape our understanding of what we regard as disability and bodily differences today. Treves's depiction is also consistent with capitalists' desires to shift the supposed cost of nonstandard workers onto someone else (chapter 1). Segregating disabled people in medical institutions and making them dependent on charity or state support ensures that employers are not expected to hire people with nonstandard bodies who, employers assume, might be less productive.

THE EUGENICS MOVEMENT

- Forced Sterilization
- Support for Segregation and Restricted Marriage Rights for Disabled People
- Murder

Toward the end of the nineteenth century, around the same time that Merrick went from being a freak-show performer to being confined and displayed in the London Hospital, the eugenics movement arose in Britain, Western Continental Europe, the United States, and Canada. Inspired by the statistician Sir Francis Galton, and the 1883 publication in England of his book, *Inquiries into Human Faculty and Development* (Black 2003b, 16), the eugenics movement aimed to preserve the glorious "Nordic" race by decreasing the population of people considered "unfit" or "defective"—people of color, non-English-speaking immigrants, poor white people who were labeled "feebleminded" (especially women; Kluchin 2011, 17)—a term that, according to investigative journalist Edwin Black (2003b), was never clearly defined (55)—and people with physical, sensory, mental, and intellectual or developmental disabilities.

While, in Britain, Galton struggled to find scientific evidence to support the enactment of policies that would encourage those who were "fit" to reproduce (Black 2003b, 29–30), eugenicists in the United States campaigned to implement policies that would actively *eliminate* members of "unfit," "defective" and hence, in their view, subhuman populations (Black 2003b, 21, 39; cf. Kluchin 2011, 14). Their favored methods of elimination were forced sterilization, segregation, and restrictive marriage laws that aimed to prevent purportedly "unfit" people from being born, as well as murder.

In his book *War against the Weak: Eugenics and America's Campaign to Create a Master Race*, Black (2003b) argues that the eugenics movement in the United States was conceived and promoted "by America's wealthiest, most powerful and most learned men against the nation's most vulnerable and helpless" (7, cf. 57; cf. Kluchin 2011, 14). As Black (2003b) writes, "It didn't matter that the majority of the American people opposed sterilization and the eugenic movement's other draconian measures. It didn't matter that the underlying science was a fiction . . . or that the whole idea was roundly condemned by so many. None of that mattered," Black continues, because the leaders of the eugenics movement in the United States "were not interested in furthering a democracy—they were creating a supremacy." These eugenicists did not fight their battle in public, Black writes. Instead, "they relied upon the powerful, the wealthy and the influential to make their war . . . in the administrative and bureaucratic foxholes of America" (87).

The Marxist historian and activist Herbert Aptheker (1974), writing in the magazine of the U.S. Communist Party, *Political Affairs*, also suggested that the ruling class of American capitalism was behind the eugenics movement's push for sterilization (38). Eliminating disabled people altogether would, of course, be one effective way in which capitalists could reduce the supposed costs of nonstandard workers.

Forced Sterilization

The first state in the United States to pass a law permitting the forced sterilization of institutionalized people was Indiana in 1907 (Kluchin 2011, 15; Black 2003b, 67). By 1942, thirty states in the United States (Kluchin 2011, 16) and two provinces in Canada (Kline 2013) had passed laws permitting forced sterilization. In 1927, the U.S. Supreme Court issued the landmark *Buck v. Bell* decision upholding Virginia's forced sterilization law by a vote of eight to one (Kluchin 2011, 15–16; Buck v. Bell 1927), after which, according to historian Rebecca M. Kluchin (2011), the rate of sterilization increased (16; cf. Black 2003b, 122–23).

In the early twentieth century, supposedly deviant sexual behavior came to be viewed as caused by heredity rather than environment (Kluchin 2011, 13–14). In response, eugenicists increasingly classified poor and working-class white women who violated white, middle-class sexual mores, including prohibitions against interracial attraction (Stubblefield 2007, 177; Roberts 1998, 69; Aptheker 1974, 45), as feebleminded or as "morons" (Kluchin 2011, 14–15; Kline 2005, 16, 27, 29, 32–34; cf. Stubblefield 2007, 176–78). The "moron," a category invented in 1910 by Henry Herbert Goddard, the leading eugenicist in the United States, was a purportedly higher-functioning feebleminded person who could pass as normal (Stubblefield 2007, 172–73).

In the 1930s, poor white teenagers were kidnapped by sheriffs from the mountain regions of Virginia and sent to institutions for the "feebleminded," where they were forcibly sterilized (Black 2003b, 3–4). In the 1960s, eugenicists increasingly targeted poor black women instead of poor white women (Kluchin 2011, 91), and black women were often sterilized using deceit and trickery when they went to hospitals for other surgeries (Kluchin 2011, 73). Civil rights activist Fannie Lou Hamer, who was sterilized without her knowledge or permission when she went to the hospital for minor surgery to remove a uterine tumor in 1961 (Kluchin 2011, 93), called this common practice a "Mississippi appendectomy" (Brown 2017; American Experience/PBS n.d.). By 1961, over 62,000 people, mostly women, had been forcibly sterilized in the United States (Kluchin 2011, 17).

Eugenicists supported forcibly sterilizing not only people who were supposedly "feebleminded," but also deaf and blind people as well as people with intellectual disability, mental distress, physical disabilities, and illnesses such as epilepsy, migraine headaches, and brief fainting spells, even if the spells were caused by exhaustion or heat stroke (Black 2003b, 45, 53, 55–56, 58). Eugenicists' priority targets were people in custodial institutions—hospitals, prisons, and poor houses, for instance—a group numbering, Black (2003b) estimates, up to 1 million (58).

Support for Segregation and Restricted Marriage Rights for Disabled People

Because eugenicists regarded feeblemindedness and many disabilities as hereditary, they also favored segregation and laws restricting the marriage rights of disabled people. In the 1921 edition of *American Government in 1921: A Consideration of the Problems of Democracy*, an enormously popular political science textbook, Professor Frank Abbott Magruder at Oregon Agricultural College claimed, without evidence, that "imbeciles and morons" should be educated apart from other students and are happiest living in institutions with "others of their kind." He reported approvingly that, as of 1921, nine states prohibited marriage between all categories of feebleminded people, including "the morons" (418). He went on to argue that, since "the increased proportion of feeble-minded persons injures our race," and since feebleminded people produce most of society's "criminals, paupers and drunkards, . . . all States should have rigid laws to prevent the marriage of feebleminded persons" (418–19).[4]

According to a "Public Health" note in the *Journal of the American Medical Association* in 1896, a Connecticut law passed in 1895 prohibited marriage between people who were feebleminded, imbecile, or epileptic, if the woman was under 45 years old. The punishment for violating the law was no less than three years' imprisonment ("Public Health" 1896, 1138). As a test case to see if they could convince Americans to pass laws restricting marriages for additional groups of people, eugenicists also tried in the 1920s, unsuccessfully, to pass laws that would restrict the marriage rights of people with purportedly "hereditary" blindness (Black 2003b, 145, 150–51).

Murder

Policies supporting the elimination of "defective" people also led to murder. According to Black (2003a), a mental institution in Lincoln, Illinois, deliberately gave tuberculosis-infected milk to incoming patients, on the assumption that a strong genetic background would make a person immune. The annual death rate of the patients was 30–40 percent. Institutions also murdered residents through deadly neglect (Black 2003b, 255–56). And doctors practiced infanticide, eliminating one infant at a time (Black 2003a; 2003b, 252–54). According to civil libertarian columnist Nat Hentoff (1985)—who was himself the parent of a child with Down syndrome—doctors and parents in the United States, shielded by privacy laws, were still routinely killing disabled infants, one at a time, in the 1980s (54).

Eugenicists in Britain and the United States proposed establishing locally run gas chambers to eliminate feebleminded people (Black 2003a; 2003b, 247–51). In Germany, Adolph Hitler was inspired by the American eugenics movement (Black 2003a; 2003b, 7, 259–60). Beginning in 1939, the Nazis instituted their first euthanasia program, the secretive "T4" program, which murdered an estimated 250,000 children and adults with mental, physical, and intellectual disabilities, primarily through gassing and lethal injection (U.S. Holocaust Memorial Museum n.d.; cf. Black 2003b, 312–13, 317, 369). At the Nuremberg trials after World War II, Karl Brandt, who helped run the Nazi's T4 euthanasia program, cited eugenic ideas and experiences in the United States as part of his defense (Kuhl 2002, 101).

THE "UGLY LAWS"

- The Ugly Laws, Nondisabled People, and Capitalism
- Segregating Disabled People by Expelling Them from Public Spaces and Institutions
- Segregating Disabled People by Shuttling Them into Institutions

Around the same time that the eugenics movement was developing in the United States, disabled people were being rejected and ejected, for supposedly aesthetic reasons, from cities' public spaces—a trend that no doubt helped to generate and reinforce aesthetic anxiety, as we saw political scientist and disabilities studies scholar Harlan Hahn call it (chapter 1), among nondisabled people. Beginning in San Francisco in 1867, cities across America, particularly Midwestern cities linked by railroads, passed what have come to be called "ugly laws": Portland and Chicago (1881), Denver and Lincoln (1887), Omaha (1881–1890), Columbus (1894), Reno (before 1905), New Orleans (1867), the whole state of Pennsylvania (1894 or 1895), and, later, additional cities on the West coast (Schweik 2010, 3). In *The Ugly Laws: Disability in Public*, disability studies scholar and English professor Susan M. Schweik (2010) reports that these laws typically prohibited any person who was "diseased, maimed, mutilated or in any way deformed" from exposing him- or herself to public view (2). Pennsylvania's act and a version that failed to pass in New York City in 1895 (3) also applied to people with cognitive disability, or to "idiots and imbeciles," as New York City's draft law put it (10). There were precursors for these laws in England, Schweik says, but the laws' specific conflation of disability, socioeconomic status, and race, as well as their underlying individualism—which allowed supporters of the laws to cast disability and begging as problems with individual people, rather than as socially caused problems—were uniquely American (4–5). Although no new ugly laws were enacted after World War I, Schweik found that the last attempt to enforce one of the laws was in Omaha, Nebraska, in 1974 (6).

The Ugly Laws, Nondisabled People, and Capitalism

Schweik (2010) shows that, in the patchwork of "unsightly" ordinances or ugly laws, the laws were variously enforced by police, and there were regional and historical distinctions between laws that must be taken into account when assessing their overall impact and meaning (9). Still, she suggests, the laws did affect the lives of both disabled and nondisabled people. For nondisabled people, Schweik argues, the main point of the laws was to condition people to police themselves to ensure that they would not be unsightly or disgusting. In its modern form, nondisabled people are conditioned to "shop at the local drugstore with its aisles of health and beauty products, contemplate the question of cosmetic surgery, respond to the pharmaceutical ads on television" (67), and so on—strategies that, as Schweik hints at, not only ensure that one has a good appearance but also ensure that one feeds the capitalist, personal-care-products-and-services machine. Modern society's devotion to "its quest for supernormal standards of bodily perfection," as we saw Hahn (1988) put it (42; see also chapter 1), supports a significant portion of the capitalist economy. The Personal Care Products Council released a report suggesting that, in 2013, their industry alone—which includes only developers, manufacturers, marketers, and distributors of "soaps, perfume, sunscreen, hair and skin care products, cosmetics, and toothpaste"—made up 1.4 percent of the U.S. gross domestic product (GDP), directly employed over 2 million and indirectly employed another 1.4 million people, and spent over $144 billion on labor (PricewaterhouseCoopers LLP 2015, E1–2).

Schweik (2010) suggests that the ugly laws served capitalist aims in other ways as well. For instance, they eliminated competition from street vendors for local businesses (59) and discouraged chronic pauperism and dissent on the part of nondisabled people who would be regarded as undeserving poor (61). "In this way," Schweik says, "we may come to see the ugly law on a continuum with other means of suppressing labor organizing and social unrest." It follows, she argues, that purely psychological accounts of the laws, or attempts to explain the laws only in terms of people's explicit or implicit attitudes toward disabled people, "are inadequate unless we supplement them with a materialist analysis" linking the laws to the workings of capitalism (56). There is, as we saw before (chapter 1), a symbiosis between the structure of attitudes toward ability and disability and the economic system of capitalism. The ugly laws not only supported the beauty products and services industry, but also, as we will now see, released capitalists from the responsibility of providing jobs for (supposedly) less productive, disabled workers.

Segregating Disabled People by Expelling Them from Public Spaces and Institutions

For people who could not hide their supposed unsightliness, the main point of the laws was to segregate them from the rest of society—and in two primary ways, Schweik (2010) argues. First, expelling disabled people from public view excluded them from many jobs in the capitalist system of paid labor, thereby impoverishing them. Schweik opens her book with the story of a man with clubbed hands and feet who was reported by the "Cleveland Cripple Survey" to have lost his job selling newspapers sometime before 1916 as a result of that city's law. Schweik quotes approvingly Rosemarie Garland-Thomson's suggestion that the impoverishment of disabled people has been "perhaps the most enduring form of segregation" (Schweik 2010, 16; Garland-Thomson 1996, 35). Certainly, the young man interviewed by the Cleveland Crippled Survey was aware of the law's effective economic segregation. The survey reported that, while the young man "'appreciated the meaning'" of the law, he "'considered it ill-advised unless some step went with it for providing other opportunity for work for cripples'" (Schweik 2010, 15).

The widespread attitude expressed by the ugly laws that supposedly unsightly and disturbing disabled people should be hidden from public view led to the expulsion of disabled people not only from the streets of America and from jobs, but also from schools. Education scholars John LaNear and Elise Frattura (2007) discuss an early 1919 court case in the Wisconsin Supreme Court, *Beattie v. Board of Education*, in which Merritt Beattie's parents sued their local school board to overturn the exclusion of their son from the public classroom. Although Merritt was reportedly able to complete his school work and keep up with the other students in the class (92), the court ruled that the school was justified in removing Merritt—who was described in harsh terms as "crippled and defective," with abnormal control of his voice, hands, feet, and body, slurred speech, a "disturbing tone of voice," facial contortions, and drooling—from the public school. The court sided with the school district's argument that Merritt's condition produced "a depressing and nauseating effect upon the teachers and school children," took up too much of the teacher's time, diminishing the attention available to other students, and interfered with school discipline (91–92). But instead of finding ways to help the teacher provide Merritt as well as the other students the attention they all deserved, Merritt's constitutionally guaranteed rights to an education were, as LaNear and Frattura put it, "subjugated to a 'depressing and nauseating effect' on the general sensibilities of the dominant class" (92).

Disabled children were not guaranteed a right to a free, public education until, in 1975, Congress passed the Education for All Handicapped Children Act (EAHCA), which was renamed the Individuals with Disabilities Education Act (IDEA) in 1990. Even today, however, disabled children, particularly students of color, students from urban areas, and students "with specific disability labels (such as autism or intellectual disability)," as the National Council on Disability put it in a 2018 report, are often removed from general education classrooms and educated in segregated spaces (National Council on Disability 2018, 9; see also chapter 7).

Segregating Disabled People by Shuttling Them into Institutions

The second way in which the ugly laws segregated disabled people, Schweik argues, was by shuttling them into institutions—thus shifting responsibility for their support on to charity and the state. San Francisco's early 1867 version of the law specified that those who broke the law should be "committed" to almshouses; the 1880s versions of the laws tended to specify that transgressors could, in lieu of fines, be "cared for" by police until being sent to county poor-farms, thus "diverting some people into institutions" (Schweik 2010, 64). Still later, the laws were amended or written to shuttle disabled people into increasingly medicalized, custodial institutions such as hospitals and "homes." In 1926, the eugenicist Harry Laughlin suggested that state institutions were more effective at permanently segregating disabled people and thus achieving eugenic aims than were the older poor- or almshouses, which tended to have "revolving doors" (Schweik 2010, 66–67). As Schweik concludes, then, "The ugly laws both reinforced and were impelled by a eugenic logic of segregation" (68).

CONTEMPORARY SEGREGATION

- Segregation in Nursing Homes
- Segregation of Individuals with Intellectual and Developmental Disabilities
- Segregation of Wheelchair Users

Attitudes supporting the segregation of disabled people that were developed in the West by the freak shows, the concept of "normalcy," the eugenics movement, and the ugly laws live on, and disabled people continue to experience various forms of segregation. Today, they are shuttled into nursing homes as well as segregated day and work programs, are denied access to many places that are inaccessible to wheelchairs, and are forced to use segregated forms of public services.

Segregation in Nursing Homes

Our society continues to needlessly (ware)house disabled people in institutions, particularly in nursing homes. The U.S. Supreme Court decision in *Olmstead v.*

L.C. (Olmstead v. L. C. [Syllabus] 1999) ruled that helping disabled people live in their communities is required under the Americans with Disabilities Act. But in 2016, the administration of U.S. President Barack Obama sued or threatened to sue several states over policies that needlessly funnel disabled children and adults into nursing homes, instead of helping them live independently in homes in their communities (Apuzzo 2016).

Scholars influenced by materialist or Marxist theory argue that these policies, too, have roots in the capitalist economic system. History professor and disability activist Paul K. Longmore (2005) claims that the policies of states in the United States favor sending people to nursing "homes" because nursing homes are a part of what he calls "the 'Crippling Economy.'" It's not that nursing homes are the only places that can provide care for people with disabilities, or that people with disabilities cannot live successfully and even less expensively in their own homes with help. Instead, Longmore writes, disabled people "are imprisoned in [nursing homes] to profit nursing home operators. Disabled people are the raw materials, the natural resources, of the Crippling Economy. Their bodies are colonized like Third World countries" (40). When increasingly capitalist European countries colonized what are now sometimes called Third World countries, they profited in part by extracting those countries' natural resources or raw materials in ways that harmed those countries. Longmore's quotation suggests that, in a similar way, the capitalist nursing home industry extracts and uses disabled people's bodies—as a kind of raw material—for its own profit, not for the benefit of disabled people themselves, many of whom would prefer to live (less expensively) in homes within their communities. As Russell and Malhotra (2002) argue, "Disabled people are worth more to the Gross Domestic Product when occupying a 'bed' than a home" (215).

Segregation of Individuals with Intellectual and Developmental Disabilities

Today, the majority of individuals with intellectual and developmental disabilities spend their days in segregated contexts. In 2009, 59 percent of people with intellectual and developmental disabilities were attending purely recreational (non-work) day programs, while 20 percent were working in segregated, sheltered workshops. Thus, 79 percent of people with intellectual and developmental disabilities were spending their days in segregated settings (Braddock et al. 2011, 38). In both cases, these settings exclude them from fully participating in the paid wage market. Section 14(c) of the Fair Labor Standards Act permits employers to pay disabled people who work in sheltered workshops subminimum wages (U.S. Department of Labor 2008). As we saw in Henry Turkey's Service's exploitation of a group of more than twenty intellectually disabled men (chapter 1), while the law does not exclude disabled people from participating in the capitalist system of paid labor, it *does* exclude them from fully *benefiting* from that system.

Although sheltered workshops are supposed to be treated as a time-limited placement and bridge to employment in the community (National Council on Disability 2017, 54), repeated studies have shown that they are dead ends. A 2001 study of all programs in the United States by the U.S. Government Accountability Office found that only 5 percent of workers in sheltered workshops leave to take a job in the community (U.S. Government Accountability Office 2001, 4). A study by Robert Evert Cimera (2011) with 9,808 intellectually disabled people who were receiving employment services—half who worked in sheltered workshops and half who did not—found that the participants who were not working in sheltered workshops were just as likely to be employed as the ones who were, earned more than the participants from sheltered workshops, and cost significantly less to serve. A similar study conducted by Cimera and colleagues (2012) with 430 adults with autism spectrum disorder led to the same conclusions for those participants.

Writing for the National Disability Rights Network, Cheryl Bates-Harris (2012) suggests that sheltered workshops provide largely useless work, give workers little choice in what they do, and fail to "promote self direction, self determination [*sic*] or skill development" (47). That is exactly what disability studies scholar Michael Gill (2005), who worked in a sheltered workshop for six years, observed. He called sheltered workshops "a structure that incarcerates disabled people within vocational-like settings" (613).

Segregation of Wheelchair Users

People who use wheelchairs also experience forms of segregation. In a *New York Times* opinion piece titled "If You're in a Wheelchair, Segregation Lives," Luticha Doucette (2017), a black woman who uses a manual wheelchair, criticizes what she describes as the "commonplace and accepted" segregation of public spaces in our society. Many buildings are not accessible to her at all, and, when they are accessible, the ramps or accessible entrances are often in hard-to-find and out-of-the-way places. She notes the irony, as a black woman, of having to access the National Gallery of Art through the back entrance, or having to access restaurants, bars, and other businesses "through back ways, sketchy hallways, side entrances, and kitchens." To get into her favorite bar, she has to go down an alley and then down a ramp that leads to the bowels of the building. "There's no signage, no security cameras," she writes, "and I once saw a bloody towel covering the fire alarm." She points out that the inability to move freely within the community makes it difficult to visit friends and family, producing social isolation.

It also affects employment. The building she works in, Doucette (2017) says, "was built in a time when people with disabilities were almost entirely hidden from society, and architects did not consider how such a person would use the building." Even though the building has been retrofitted for wheelchair users with a sliding door (hidden behind a pillar), she says that the inaccessibility of her work building "eerily mirrors the segregation of blacks in the workplace, where separate doors were not unusual."

Psychologist and disability studies scholar Rhoda Olkin (1999) has gone so far as to suggest that the doctrine of "separate but equal"—originally applied to blacks in the United States and confirmed in the Supreme Court's infamous 1896 *Plessy v. Ferguson* decision, but overturned in *Brown v. Board of Education*—is alive and well for many disabled people. Indeed, Olkin argues, it is not "just tolerated; it is encoded into law and policy" (32). As she explains it, "There are separate entrances (with signs showing that the ramp is around the back), separate drinking fountains, separate buses, and even an entirely separate transit system (usually called paratransit, in a sublime linguistic pun), separate classrooms, separate seating, separate lines, and separate procedures" (32).

CONDITIONS IN SEGREGATED INSTITUTIONS

- Conditions in Mental Institutions
- Conditions in Institutions for People with Physical and/or Intellectual Disabilities
- Why Were Conditions Poor?
- Disability, Race, and an Increased Risk of Abuse

Although some of the later ugly laws couched the shuttling of disabled people to custodial institutions in the language of "care," as Schweik notes (2010, 64, 65, 67), what went on in many of those institutions was not what anyone would call "care." The fact that disabled people came to be regarded in modern Western societies as despised and dispensable outsiders helps to explain the rise and nature of custodial or residential institutions in those societies. During the same time that "freak shows" were popular and disabled people were being defined as a deviant group, Braddock and Parish (2001) suggest, people with disabilities were increasingly segregated into institutions—into schools for deaf and blind children and children with physical disabilities, large mental hospitals for people with mental illness, and residential "schools" for people with intellectual and developmental disabilities (29–39). Although the institutions for people with mental illness and intellectual/developmental disabilities were often established with the stated goal of treating and/or educating residents and returning them to their communities, these goals were quickly abandoned, and the institutions became custodial institutions whose main aim was the preservation of the institutions themselves along with the power of their superintendents (33–37). The optimistic goal that people with intellectual disability could be trained and returned to their communities, Braddock and Parish say, "confronted two difficult realities, [namely] negative attitudes toward persons with mental retardation held by the general public and the lack of supportive social services, family support, and work opportunities in the community" (37). By 1904, twenty-one countries had established 171 institutions for people with intellectual disability; by 1900, there were twenty-five such institutions in the United States alone (37).

Conditions in Mental Institutions

Conditions for residents in institutions for people with mental illness were notoriously abusive and neglectful. Patients were physically abused, kept in rooms with no heat or clothing, chained and restrained, and subjected to forced treatments (Braddock and Parish 2001, 33–34). In the late nineteenth century, some psychiatrists received notoriety for bold and humane care when they simply unchained patients at their institutions (Braddock and Parish 2001, 34). The horrific conditions and abusive practices in mental "hospitals" gave rise, in the twentieth century, to both the deinstitutionalization movement aimed at releasing people from institutions and treating them in the community[5] and the psychiatric systems survivor movement by former "patients" (Chamberlin 1995).

Conditions in Institutions for People with Physical and/or Intellectual Disabilities

Conditions in the residential "schools" were also inhumane. Geraldo Rivera (1972) made his name as a journalist doing an investigative report into conditions at Willowbrook State School on Staten Island in New York City. Watching his exposé today is still heart-breaking. His 1972 report describes children and adults with intellectual disability living in filth with nothing to do and little social interaction, fighting for scraps of paper on the floor to play with. Staff were given only three minutes to help children eat meals, leaving the children undernourished and prey to pneumonia and death—precisely the kind of deadly neglect that Black mentioned in his discussion of the history of the eugenics movement. Twenty-five years later, Rivera was still brought to tears thinking about what he saw at Willowbrook, even though he had been an experienced New York City journalist at the time of the exposé (Fisher 1997, 16:20–16:34).

In the introduction to *Deinstitutionalization and People with Intellectual Disabilities*, Rannveig Traustadottir describes conditions in an institution for people with intellectual disabilities where she had a summer job as a fifteen-year-old in the late 1960s. "The routines and living conditions in the institution were a far cry from what ordinary people would recognize as minimally acceptable," Traustadottir writes. "Over-crowding, lack of privacy, inhumane treatment and abuse were everyday realities. What I remember most vividly when first entering the institution were the smell and the noises. I was horrified" (K. Johnson and

Traustadottir 2005, 15). Rivera (1972), too, had highlighted the haunting sounds and the horrific smell at Willowbrook. Even at age 15, Traustadottir knew there was something wrong. "I was bewildered by the inhumanity of the institution. I was only 15 and could not understand how we, as a society, could treat people this way" (K. Johnson and Traustadottir 2005, 15).

Thomas F. Allen, for instance, became severely physically disabled and difficult to understand after contracting polio at age 2 (Allen, Traustadottir, and Spina 2005, 35). He lived for more than sixty years—beginning in 1928 (Allen et al., 2005, 40)—in "state schools" and a "development center." He describes a life in the first institution with little to do. He had no mobility on his own, and, although staff on the first ward where he lived would place him in a wheelchair during the day, they used one he could not move himself (40). "I could look around, but that was about all I could do all day," Allen reports. "There were no programmes in those days. No school. No work. No physical therapy. No speech therapy. No nothing" (41). His first years at the institution were his most desperate. "I felt like no one understood me nor cared about me. I felt all alone in the world. I was a desperate and angry young man." Instead of trying to understand him, the staff punished him, he says, "for not behaving—sometimes severely. The staff would, for example, put me on the floor in the back of the bathroom door and I had to lay there all day; sometimes without getting anything to eat" (41).

After Allen was punished by being moved to a different ward in an older building, with worse living conditions and more severely disabled individuals, he decided to change and began to help out around the ward. Later, he came to see this change "as a survival strategy." If he had not changed, he says, he would not have survived. He became friends with the staff, who liked him because he helped out. But the work also gave him something to do. "In an institution you have all this time on your hands and many people will do almost anything to have something to occupy them," Allen says. "Having nothing to do makes time go very, very slowly. The work also gave me self-respect and the feeling that I was doing something worthwhile" (Allen et al., 2005, 42). It should be noted that, although Allen was able to take some control over his life and build an identity for himself, the institution itself was not constructed to facilitate this process. Indeed, his ability to build an identity at the institution was made possible by what turned out to be a fortunate accident of being sent to a worse ward with more severely disabled people as punishment, where he was able to help out and become a favored resident among the staff.

Why Were Conditions Poor?

Why did we, as a society, treat people this way? Summarizing the views of the contributors, co-editors Kelley Johnson and Traustadottir (2005) suggest that "the abuse seems to be recognized by the contributors to this book as something that was part of the system" (21). This systemic abuse cannot be explained, however, Johnson and Traustadottir argue, as a natural product of the problems of managing large numbers of people "in difficult circumstances" (25). Instead, the abuse must be explained, they suggest, "within the discourses of intellectual disability itself. Over a period of almost a hundred years, a body of generally accepted knowledge has been developed about people with intellectual disabilities and then put into practice to shape their treatment and their lives" (21). In other words, generally accepted views developed during the nineteenth century and in the eugenics movement in Europe and North America of people with intellectual disabilities as "deviant social menaces" with an "incurable disease," as Braddock and Parish (2001) describe the dominant view at the time (38), conditioned the public to accept warehousing those with intellectual disabilities in large institutions and inhumane circumstances.

Disability, Race, and an Increased Risk of Abuse

Nirmala Erevelles and Andrea Minear (2010) have argued that the risk of institutionalization and abuse is particularly high for people who are poor, disabled, and black. Drawing on the book *Unspeakable: The Story of Junius Wilson*, by Susan Burch and Hannah Joyner, for instance, Erevelles and Minear argue that Wilson's origins in a poor, black family led to his institutionalization and abuse.

When his father abandoned the family, Wilson, who had become deaf as a toddler, was sent to a school for black, deaf children, where students were taught a sign language that was specific to the school. After being sent home from the school for a minor infraction, Wilson's isolation and inability to communicate with others, along with his habit of touching people while stamping his feet and waving his arms, led him to be constructed as dangerous and threatening in the Jim-Crow-law-segregated community in North Carolina where he lived, putting his family, community, and himself at risk. "Perhaps for all these reasons," Erevelles and Minear (2010) speculate, a family friend accused Wilson of trying to rape his wife (134). Wilson was arrested in 1925 and sent to an institution for the criminally insane, where he was castrated and reportedly became submissive seven years later. He worked on the hospital farm until 1970. A civil rights group began litigating to have him released in the 1970s, and in 1994 he was moved to a cottage on the hospital grounds, where he died in 2001. "Hovering precipitously at the boundaries of race, class, gender *and* disability," Erevelles and Minear write, "Wilson had been held in the isolating confines of the institution for more than three quarters of his life" (135).

ENDING SEGREGATION?

In November 2016, the Justice Department of the Obama administration issued a guidance document decrying the segregation of disabled people in the United

States. Michelle Diament (2016), a journalist with the disability news website *Disability Scoop*, reports that the guidance document acknowledged that "'the civil rights of persons with disabilities, including individuals with mental illness, intellectual or developmental disabilities, or physical disabilities, are violated by unnecessary segregation in a wide variety of settings, including in segregated employment, vocational and day programs.'" However, Diament reported in January 2018, this document was rescinded by Attorney General Jeff Sessions under the administration of President Donald Trump, and so has no working link.

IS THE SEGREGATION AND ABUSE OF DISABLED PEOPLE MALICIOUS?

* The Segregation and Abuse Are Not Results of Impairments or Biology

If malicious acts can be performed only by individuals with malicious attitudes in their heads, then, as we saw Blair-Goldensohn suggesting in the discussion of the inaccessibility of the New York City subway system (see the introduction), these institutions are not malicious in that sense. Again (see chapter 1), no one at the Metropolitan Transportation Authority today, which runs the subways, has to have hatred toward disabled people in his or her head for the subway system to do its work of excluding disabled people. The exclusion from the subway system, like the abuse carried out in the residential institutions, as we saw Johnson and Traustadottir suggest, is a result of the system, with its impersonal, institutional policies and organization.

However, we should still regard the segregation and abuse of disabled people as malicious. The exclusion and abuse that has characterized the structures and institutions of Western, European societies, including the economic system of capitalism, have been linked to a structure of attitudes (see also chapter 1), or to a set of values, expectations, and assumptions, in which, during the nineteenth century, people defined as disabled became a despised and dispensable group. If the exclusion of the subway system and the abuse carried out by residential institutions are not produced by individual people's malicious attitudes, they *are* products and expressions of society's *structures* of attitudes. These attitudes qualify as a social "structure" because they are embedded in and expressed by the social institutions and public policies of society. But they are still *attitudes*. While no one in particular may be acting maliciously in these institutions, society as a whole, with its structure of attitudes, is acting maliciously through these institutions. As we saw Hahn suggest (chapter 1), these institutions are designed, by public policies that were chosen and enacted, to do what they do to disabled people. The institutions do not just impersonally forget and leave out disabled people, to use Blair-Goldensohn's description; they *deliberately* segregate disabled people and establish the conditions for abuse.

The Segregation and Abuse Are Not Results of Impairments or Biology

The segregation and abuse of disabled people by structures and institutions can be viewed as *deliberate* because it is not an inevitable consequence of the supposedly natural impairments or biological conditions of the people so targeted. It is not a result of the inability to walk, for instance, or the inability to learn as quickly or to move in certain ways. As we saw Johnson and Traustadottir (2005) suggest, the systemic abuse of people in residential institutions for physically or intellectually disabled people was not a result of the problems of managing large numbers of people "in difficult circumstances" or with difficult impairments (25).

Allen, for instance, who came from a poor family (Allen et al., 2005, 38), lived mostly at home until he was a young teenager. He was sent to live in the institution on a permanent basis, not because of his disabilities, but because of family problems. After his mother died suddenly and his father remarried, his stepmother, who was jealous of her new husband's children and pushed Allen's older siblings away, refused to continue to look after him (39). As Johnson and Traustadottir (2005) write, "It was poverty, abuse and family problems that led many people to leave the community and be placed in institutions. In our view, not enough weight has been given to these issues in considering both people's institutional lives and their subsequent lives in the community" (20). The segregation and abuse is also not a result of natural biology or biological conditions. As we will see (chapter 5), there are no purely natural biological conditions. How societies treat people we regard as disabled is therefore not an inevitable consequence of impairments or biological conditions, but a social *choice* or *decision*.

POSITIVE SIDE EFFECTS OF SEGREGATION

I should point out that, while the deliberate segregation of disabled people establishes the conditions for abuse, it has at times also had beneficial side effects. As disability studies scholars have often pointed out (e.g., Garland-Thomson 1996, 35–36), the segregation of disabled people has sometimes led to the development of positive disability identities and political activism. Disability studies scholar Joseph Shapiro (1993) reports that the physically disabled students who pioneered the independent living movement at the University of California at Berkeley in the 1960s became a politically active group —the group, which included the well-known disability activist Ed Roberts, called themselves the "Rolling Quads"—in part because the students had been forced by the university to live apart from other students in segregated housing at the university's hospital (49).

The segregation of people in schools for blind and deaf students has also led to the development of group identities (Braddock and Parish 2001, 39). Deaf culture and communication scholar Tom Humphries, for instance, who grew up as a deaf person in a hearing culture, characterizes his attendance at Gallaudet University, a university for deaf and hard-of-hearing students, as a cultural shift. As he and his co-author, linguistics and communication scholar Carol Padden (2005), describe his situation, "it was like he had moved to a foreign country where he, alone among them, had no clue how to behave" (146). Later on, however, he came to feel more comfortable at Gallaudet and in Deaf culture (we use a capital *D* when we are referring to Deaf culture) than he had ever felt with his family or in his community of origin. As he and Padden put it, he realized "that he had developed a level of comfort as a signer and that he no longer felt so uncomfortable in his own skin. He felt included in a way that he hadn't felt back home among his hearing family and community" (147). Humphries also began to get involved in political activism (151). For Humphries, then, living in the segregated environment at Gallaudet allowed him to develop a positive as well as a political identity as a deaf person. Thus, while the segregation of disabled people into institutions established the conditions for abuse, in some cases, it also created the conditions for resistance.

CONCLUSION

This chapter has explored the embodiment of disability in terms of the third dimension of embodiment or institutional body, which captures how people are embedded, as social selves, in large, social/institutional structures and arrangements in a society, including structures of public or cultural attitudes. There was a shift, beginning in the nineteenth century, in the structure of attitudes toward people who we today would classify as disabled, in which such people increasingly came to be defined not only as an excluded and disadvantaged social group or as "dis-abled" in relation to the capitalist wage market (see chapter 1), but also as a group of despised, diseased, and abnormal outsiders. We explored the development of this new structure of cultural attitudes through an analysis of competing portrayals of the life of Joseph Merrick, freak shows, the development of the concept of normalcy, the eugenics movement, the ugly laws, the segregation of disabled people, and the conditions in custodial institutions into which disabled people were progressively segregated and confined.

As the Marxist-inspired or materialist social models of disability (see the introduction) would emphasize, this new structure of cultural attitudes not only was consistent with the aims of capitalists but also cannot be fully understood without paying attention to the workings of the capitalist system. Together, capitalism and the structure of attitudes have *made disability* along the third dimension of embodiment or institutional body. To say that the Marxist or materialist social models of disability focus on the third dimension of embodiment, however, is also to say that they leave out other parts of the embodiment of disability, namely, the first dimension or personal body—which captures the phenomenally experienced, individual body—and the second dimension or interpersonal body—which captures how cultures use the body to conceive of social roles, society, or the world.

In the next chapter, we will explore the experience of these dimensions of embodiment. Like the third dimension, as we will see, these dimensions, too, are socially defined or defined by societies (see the introduction).

3

The Experience of the
Socially Defined Body

For twenty years, medical sociologist, disability studies scholar, and polio survivor Irving K. Zola did things the same way that nondisabled people did. He parked his car at the airport like everybody else, for instance, and walked—with the aid of his leg brace—to the terminals and gates. He always arrived at his travel destinations sore, tired, and cramped. Since he had no other airport experiences as points of comparison, however, he said, he never regarded those experiences as problematic. He saw them simply as "part of the cost of traveling and of being Irving Kenneth Zola" (Zola 1991, 4). Only after the independent living movement by disabled people changed his consciousness and he gave himself permission, or was "able," as he put it (4), to use a wheelchair while traveling, did he really *feel* that soreness, fatigue, and cramping, and realize how his travel experiences had been shaped by social practices and expectations. "Only then did I realize," Zola said, "how much of my travel 'experience' inhered not in my disability, but rather in the society in which I lived—socially maintained and socially constructed" (4). In other words, Zola's very experiences of his body while traveling—his experiences of soreness, fatigue, and cramping—were shaped by the social.

In a study conducted in Norway with thirty physically disabled mothers about their experiences of being mothers, sociologists Lars Grue and Kristin Tafjord Lærum (2002) had the following exchange with one participant. "I don't really know how to put it," the mother begins,

> but it's like—when I'm playing with my daughter and she's in her pram while my assistant is pushing it and I'm on the side in my wheelchair saying words like dicky dicky—I've overheard other people saying to each other: "My goodness, poor woman—how she speaks, she doesn't even have a language the poor thing, but look

how happy she is being with the child and what a nice thing to do—that young girl letting her be with them."

How do you feel when you overhear things like that [the interviewer asks?] It's your child, so don't you feel like crying out: "It's really my child!"

Sometimes I do [the mother replies], but then they would probably have thought—how tragic, mental problems as well, she even thinks it's her child. (671)

Grue and Lærum (2002) suggest that the nondisabled strangers were unable to see the disabled mother *as a mother* because of how disability is discussed and understood in society. As they put it, the strangers were "trapped in a discourse of disability that makes it extremely difficult for her to be looked upon and treated as a mother" (672). Society's understanding of disability assumes that disabled women cannot be mothers[1] and led the strangers to see not a disabled mother talking baby-talk to her own child in the presence of an assistant, but a nondisabled mother and child being kind to a disabled woman. The nondisabled strangers' interpretation of the disabled mother's baby-talk as evidence that she was intellectually disabled suggests they were also predisposed to believe that physically disabled people are likely to be intellectually disabled as well—another common assumption among nondisabled people (see, e.g., Sutherland 1984, chapter 6). Indeed, the disabled mother jokes that, even if she had been able to dislodge their assumption that she was intellectually disabled, they would simply have assumed that she must be psychologically disabled instead, which suggests that society's conception of disability inexorably ties physical disability to some kind of mental disability—if not intellectual, then psychological.[2]

The difficulty with seeing disabled women as mothers affects not only how people see (or do not see) disabled mothers, but also how disabled mothers *experience* their own roles as mothers. Clinical psychologist, disability studies scholar, and polio survivor Rhoda Olkin (1999) describes her own reaction to an encounter in which, when she was once struggling with putting groceries in the car while holding her infant son in her arms, a woman who offered help proceeded not to move bags of groceries from the cart into the car, but to grab Olkin's son out of her arms. Olkin says that the woman's decision to rip Olkin's child out of her arms sent Olkin a message. Because we live in a society in which newspaper and scholarly articles often report that disabled people are at risk of losing custody of their children, the woman's decision reinforced Olkin's fear, as Olkin puts it, "that I, as a mother with a disability, could lose my child more easily than a mother without disability" (83). The encounter thus led Olkin to experience her own motherhood as tenuous.

These disabled mothers' stories illustrate how society uses people's bodies to assign (or fail to assign) social roles—in this case, the role of being a mother—and to define the experience of those roles.

Chapters 1 and 2 explore disability in terms of what I call (see the introduction), borrowing from anthropologists Nancy Scheper-Hughes and Margaret M.

Lock (1987), the third dimension of embodiment or institutional body—which captures "the regulation, surveillance and control of bodies (individual and collective)" by institutions or structures in society (7). This is the dimension highlighted by the social models of disability (see also the introduction). The British, materialist, or Marxist family of social models suggests that the economic system of capitalism, as a social institution or structure, defines, regulates, surveys, and controls people it classifies as "disabled." The American, minority/civil rights family of social models focuses on how social structures and institutions—including common public or cultural attitudes—regulate, survey, and control disabled people by oppressing or discriminating against them. Because chapters 1 and 2 examined ways in which Western societies' institutions and structures—including their structures of attitudes—define, regulate, survey, and control disabled people, they offer an analysis of *ableism,* or of the expression of nondisabled people's social power over disabled people.

Because society's ableism can be experienced in personal and intimate ways, as we will see, a full account of the embodiment of disability must explore the experiences of disabled people, not only along the third dimension of embodiment, but also along the first dimension or personal body, and the second dimension or interpersonal body, which refers to how cultures use the body to conceive of social roles, society, or the world (see the introduction). This chapter explores how ableism is experienced along the first and second dimensions of embodiment.

There are two interpretations of what it means to speak of the body or embodiment, however. First, we can speak of the body insofar as it is *experienced,* from the inside. Second, we can speak of the body insofar as it is an object *out there.* To speak of embodiment is thus to speak about both what the body *feels like* (in experience) as well as what it *is* as an object, *out there* (see the introduction). My claim is that societies define or determine the body or embodiment in both of these senses, along all three dimensions of embodiment. (Table I.1 in the introduction outlines how the argument for this claim is organized.) The third dimension or institutional body is socially defined in both these senses. Structures and institutions define not only which categories of bodies there are, *out there,* according to those structures and institutions—in Western societies, the structures and institutions categorize some people as disabled, for instance (see chapter 1)—but also how being a member of the different categories will tend to be *experienced.* In the West, people categorized as disabled tend to experience exclusion and abuse at the hands of societies' structures and institutions (see chapters 1 and 2).

Like the third dimension or institutional body, the second dimension of embodiment or interpersonal body is also socially defined in both of these senses. As we will see, how cultures use the body to conceive of social roles, society, or the world defines not only which social roles are *out there* and which bodies should have which roles, but also what *experiences* of those roles will tend to be like. The transcript of the interview with the disabled mother in Grue and Lærum's study at the beginning of this chapter, for instance, illustrates how societies use disabled bodies to assign (or, in that case, to fail to assign) the social role of being a mother. According to many societies in the West, disabled women should not be mothers; they should not have that role, *out there*. But societies also shape the ways in which those roles will tend to be *experienced*. Olkin's account, for example, illustrates how society's assumptions that disabled women should not be mothers lead disabled woman to experience the role of being a mother as tenuous. In the case of people classified as disabled, then, the assignment of social roles *out there* as well as the *experience* of those role is shaped by ableism, or by nondisabled people's expression of social power.

Although I am arguing that, like the second and third dimensions, the first dimension of embodiment or personal body is also socially defined in both of these senses, unlike the analysis of those other dimensions, which treated both the *experience* and the *out-thereness* together, the analysis of the *experience* of the first or personal body is separated from the analysis of its *out-thereness*. This chapter examines the first or personal body only in terms of how it is *experienced*. The phenomenologically *experienced* personal body or the very *feel* of our own bodies, including bodies categorized as disabled, is defined by society. Zola's account of his airport experiences illustrates how society shaped the very *feel* of his own disabled body. Although we often assume, as Zola did at first, that we experience our personal bodies in a given or natural way, these experiences are shaped by social structures and contexts, including by ableism or nondisabled people's expressions of social power. We will explore what the first or personal body *is*, as an object *out there*, in chapters 4 and 5.

This chapter begins by exploring how, as Zola discovered, experiences of the first dimension or personal body are socially defined by ableism. It also explores how, along the second dimension of embodiment or interpersonal body, bodies classified as normal under capitalism in the West have a positive bodily capital or value, while bodies classified as abnormal or disabled have a devalued bodily capital. In terms of social roles, disabled people have often been assigned the *de*valued "sick role," and they have been denied access to *valued* social roles, particularly the roles of sexual partner and parent. Because some Marxist theorists would criticize my claim that we must analyze disability in relation to the first and second dimensions of embodiment, I end the chapter by addressing these criticisms.

Chapter outline:

➤ The Experience of the Personal Body (First Body) Is Socially Defined
➤ Experiences of the Disabled, Personal Body Are Shaped by Social Structures

THE EXPERIENCE OF THE PERSONAL BODY (FIRST BODY) IS SOCIALLY DEFINED

Let's consider the first dimension of embodiment or personal body and, more particularly, the claim that the phenomenologically *experienced* personal body or the feel of one's own body is socially defined. Scheper-Hughes and Lock (1987) argue that all humans have some form of proprioception and an intuitive self-awareness or sense of being in the world apart from others (7). But, they suggest, that awareness is always shaped by socially shared beliefs. Westerners tend to experience themselves as an "I" or as a mind apart from their bodies—as suggested by the Cartesian model of mind/body dualism that dominates in the West.[3] But certain Buddhists will not experience their subjectivity or interiority as separate from nature or the rest of the cosmos (Scheper-Hughes and Lock 1987, 12–13). The modern conception of an individual self is actually a relatively recent invention, even in the West, they suggest (14).

Some cultures lack a developed, individualized conception of the personal body at all, and, here, people may experience themselves *as social*, rather than as individual. In Gahuku-Gama culture in Papua New Guinea, Scheper-Hughes and Lock (1987) suggest, experiencing oneself as social means that one is most intensely one's self when in physical contact with others. In other such societies, people experience themselves as social by experiencing themselves as a *collection of selves*—as the self that is perceived by the parents, the self that is perceived by other relatives, by enemies, and so on (15).

We can characterize the first dimension of embodiment, personal body or "body-self," to use Scheper-Hughes and Lock's term (see the introduction), then, only *preliminarily* as the experience of an individual body or self, because people in some cultures will not experience themselves as *individual* or as *a self*. To describe the first body as the experience of an individual, personal body, and self is thus already to say too much: the personal body is really only experienced sometimes or in some cultures as *an* (individual) *self*. According to Scheper-Hughes and Lock (1987), the experience of the first or personal body as well as of the second dimension of embodiment or interpersonal body (as we will see later) are both socially defined. As they put it, "the structure of individual and collective sentiments down to the 'feel' of one's body and the naturalness of one's position and role in the technical order is a social construct" (23).

The Suyá Indians of Brazil, who call themselves the Mekin Seji, are an example of a culture in which people seem to experience the first or personal body as social. Scheper-Hughes and her coauthor, anthropologist Mariana Leal Ferreira (2007), recount the story of Dombá, an indigenous Suyá Indian man, who had an inherited kidney disability and received a transplant in 1997 (155–57). What was particularly noteworthy about Dombá's story, the authors suggest, was that Dombá and his community integrated the kidney transplant surgery into their own traditional beliefs (154). Scheper-Hughes has done research on the spread of kidney transplant surgery around the world, particularly in Third World countries. She has found that, in most places, the spread of transplant surgery has largely replaced traditional views with what Scheper-Hughes and Ferreira call a "radical materialism," which they characterize as "a secular, reductionist, commodified view of the body, organs, and tissues, health, disease, and healing" (152) that regards body parts as separate entities that can be sold for money (151–52). This replacement has happened even in cultures where, just twenty years earlier, people would have regarded an amputated foot as (emotionally and spiritually) a continuing part of the person and have held funerary rites for it. Unlike in these other societies, however, Dombá's experience as the recipient of a kidney transplant only strengthened his attachment to his culture's traditional beliefs (161, 179).

Scheper-Hughes and Ferreira (2007) suggest that, in Dombá's case, undergoing a kidney transplant required an adjustment on the part of his whole community because the Suyá define social and kinship relations in terms of a socially shared body. As Scheper-Hughes and Ferreira describe the view, "Suyá social identity and kinship derive from an elaborate corporeal imaginary based on the production and exchange of bodily substances" (171). The Suyá determine kinship not in terms of lineage or heredity but in terms of what Scheper-Hughes and Ferreira call "substance groups" that are defined based on "the sharing of intimate bodily substances, including milk, blood, urine, sweat, feces, vaginal secretions, spit, pus and semen" (171–72). The Suyá believe that substance groups share "body parts (in sex and through birth), bodily secretions, and embodied emotions, feeling, thoughts, and dreams." As a result, Scheper-Hughes and Ferreira report, "what affects one individual in a substance group affects the others" (172). When Dombá received the kidney of a "strange white man" during the transplant, then, "he (and his entire substance group) accepted into their bodies and into their selves a new social and psychological persona." This acceptance was filled both with danger, given the Suyá's often-fraught relationships with whites, as well as with potential power (172), since the successful incorporation of a white man's kidney into their socially shared body would demonstrate increased spiritual power (179). The transplant thus affected all the members of Dombá's entire substance group. "One could say," Scheper-Hughes and Ferreira suggest, "that they are a transplanted community" (179).

The Suyá's commitment to substance groups and to the notion of a socially shared body means that they do not seem to experience their own bodies purely as individual. As Scheper-Hughes and Ferreira (2007) explain, the members of a substance group "are socially, physically, and emotionally bound to each other. One cries; the other weeps. One speaks to parrots; the other befriends parakeets" (172). When Dombá came to believe that eating red peppers "offended his new kidney"—as indicated by painful urination—no one in his substance group was allowed to eat red peppers (172). Indeed, Scheper-Hughes and Ferreira wrote, "to this day [at the time of writing, though Dombá died in 2004], Dombá and his substance group must all follow special dietary and other medical recommendations sent via short-wave radio to Xingu Park [where Dombá resides] by Hospital São Paulo physicians and medical staff" (179).

EXPERIENCES OF THE DISABLED, PERSONAL BODY ARE SHAPED BY SOCIAL STRUCTURES

- Experiences of the Disabled, Personal Body Are Shaped by Ableism

Thinking about disability also helps to show how the experience of the personal body is socially defined. Tanya Titchkosky (2002) has argued, for instance, that blindness itself is contextual. Her partner, Rod, she says, is less blind in some physical and cultural contexts than in others, because some contexts allow him to figure out what he is seeing in the shadows and blurs (106–8). In the vignette about Zola, he offers a personal example that helps to illustrate how the experience of the personal body is socially defined. The example appeared in a speech in which he called for medical sociologists to pay more attention to the body. He told an audience of his fellow medical sociologists that "we" must (to borrow from the title of his article) bring our bodies and ourselves back into the field of medical sociology.[4] The speech was part of his ongoing attempt, he says, "to convey what is at stake in the denial of personal bodily experiences as well as in the difficulty of reclaiming them" (Zola 1991, 2).

One of the difficulties involved in reclaiming personal bodily experiences, Zola (1991) cautions, was that there are "structural limitations" on our abilities to be aware of—and then to write or speak about—our bodies (4). Personal bodily experiences are shaped by social structures that limit our awareness of—and hence our abilities to articulate—these experiences. In Zola's case, his experiences of his body while traveling were shaped by the designs of airports and parking lots, as well as by the social expectation that people should accomplish physical tasks, such as navigating an airport, independently and in as "normal" a fashion as possible. This expectation led him to walk through the airports under his own power, even though walking was tiring for him, rather than using a wheelchair, with (worse) or without (better) help. The feel of his body as sore, tired, and cramped when arriving at his destinations was constructed by these social structures. Social structures also limited the ways in which he felt—and so could explain—his personal bodily experiences. Zola suggests that he did not really even notice the original feel of his body while traveling until after a different social structure—the independent living movement for disabled people—made it possible for him to use a wheelchair and experience his body in another way. And if such "structural limitations" blocked *him*—a sociologist who was trained to spot socially constructed experiences in other contexts[5]—from noticing or articulating his own bodily experiences as a disabled person *for twenty years*, he said, "it must be at least equally difficult for the proverbial man or woman in the street when they try to be aware of and thus to write or speak about their bodies" (4). There is *something* it feels like to be Irving Kenneth Zola, then, but that "something"—the *being* of Irving Kenneth Zola—is structured by the social.

Because social structures shape the very feel of our bodies and act as "structural limitations" that make it difficult for us to notice the ways in which our bodily experiences are shaped by social contexts, Zola (1991) calls for medical sociologists to examine the effects that the practices and assumptions of their own profession have on research results. We need, he says, to "accept at least the metaphor of [Michel] Foucault and turn our gaze on the body ever more inward" (8), by questioning "further some of the most taken-for-granted and cherished assumptions that allowed us to put the word 'scientist' after our name" (8). We will take up Zola's advice in chapter 5.

Experiences of the Disabled, Personal Body Are Shaped by Ableism

Zola's example suggests that experiences of the personal body are shaped not just by social structures or contexts, but by *ableist* social structures and contexts. His experiences of his body were shaped in part by society's expectation that disabled people should do things as much as possible in the same way that nondisabled people do. This expectation is an expression of nondisabled people's social power. The feel of Zola's soreness, fatigue, and cramping while traveling was thus not a personal problem, but a social and political problem. Marxist and other analyses of disability that focus on the third dimension of embodiment will miss the ways in which social expressions of power—in this case, ableism—affect experiences of the first dimension of embodiment, or the very feel of one's own body.

Ableism affects experiences of disabled, personal bodies in other ways as well. Psychotherapist and disability studies scholar Deborah Marks (1999) has suggested, for instance, that the experience of intelligence by cognitively disabled people as well as the experience of pain associated with sickle-cell anemia cannot be separated from the context of ableism. The experience of sickle-cell, she suggests, which primarily affects people of African and Middle-Eastern descent, is also shaped by racism. Cognitively disabled people are aware of the social environment's message that the world would be better if they did not exist and were not a burden, and they often misdirect or internalize appropriate rage about this message against themselves (Marks 1999, 618–19). The external and resulting internal message that it would be better if they were dead, Marks says, creates anxiety that reduces their capacity to think. She quotes clinician Valerie Sinason: "Faced with an internal and external death-wish the handicapped child or adult can cut off his or her intelligence further so as not to see, hear or understand what is going on in a hostile world. Only when we take that on board can we understand the stupid smiling behavior" (619; quoting Sinason 1992, 38).

In the case of sickle-cell, racism and ableism combine to lead medical staff to be suspicious about the periodic attacks of pain associated with the condition, and hence to undertreat it, which causes more pain (Marks 1999, 620–22). This oppression also creates anxiety, which further increases the pain. As Marks puts it, "Social, cultural and emotional oppression contributes to spiraling feelings of desperation, panic and helplessness. As the attack worsens, patients feel increasingly abandoned. Anxiety makes the pain worse" (622). Domba's and his substance group's experiences of their socially collective body during Domba's kidney transplant were also shaped by whites' racism. As we saw, the feeling of having the kidney of a strange white man in their collective body was shaped by the racism and ethnic conflict that the Suyá experienced at the hands of whites. In these cases, then, ableism and racism affect the very feel of one's own personal body or collective body.

The *experience* of the first dimension of embodiment or personal body, or the feel of one's own body (though, as we saw, in some cultures the body may not be experienced as a personal, individual self at all), including of the disabled body, is thus socially defined. Although we often assume, as Zola at first did, that we experience our own bodies in a given or natural way, there is *no experience* of a given, natural, or pre-social personal body. (We will examine how the personal is socially defined as an object *out there* in chapters 4 and 5.)

THE SECOND DIMENSION OF EMBODIMENT, SECOND BODY OR SOCIAL BODY, IS SOCIALLY DEFINED

> • Some Cultures May Not Use the Body to Define Social Roles

The second dimension of embodiment or interpersonal body is also socially defined. It is socially defined both in terms of how it is *experienced* and in terms of what it is *out there*. Let us first begin by looking more closely at what the interpersonal body is. The interpersonal body is illustrated when cultures draw connections between the body and the social world. The Akan of Ghana, for instance, who have a matrilineal culture (Scheper-Hughes and Lock 1987, 19), believe that mothers pass on a blood principle that determines a child's kinship group (lineage and clan) (Wiredu 2003b, 290; 1992). Fathers pass on what African philosopher Kwasi Wiredu (2003b) calls a "charisma principle" (290; 1992), which determines a child's membership in another (largely ceremonial) social group. Thus, the Akan use the body to define a person's social roles: one's social role and hence experience as a member of a certain lineage or clan, for instance, is determined by one's blood. We must be careful, however, not to think of the Akan body as a pre-social, purely natural or biological body in the Western sense. As Scheper-Hughes and Lock (1987) note, many cultures do not employ the body/mind(spirit) or natural/supernatural distinction (9–11). African philosophers often maintain that traditional African metaphysics tends not to subscribe to Western dualisms, including the natural/supernatural and matter versus mind/soul/spirit distinctions (Teffo and Roux 2003, 165). As Wiredu (2003b) says of the Akan blood and charisma principles, "Suffice it to warn that the physical/spiritual dichotomy is unlikely to be a source of light in this connection" (198–90; 1992).

Domba's and the Suyá's commitment to the concept of substance groups that we saw a moment ago in the discussion of the first dimension of embodiment or personal body can also be used to illustrate this second dimension of embodiment or interpersonal body. Their use of substance groups as a principle of social organization involves using the body—in particular, shared intimate bodily substances—to define the social roles of kinship relations.

Some Cultures May Not Use the Body to Define Social Roles

However, we should avoid assuming that all cultures use the body to define social roles. Feminist scholar and sociologist Oyèrónkẹ́ Oyěwùmí (1997) has argued that Yoruba society, a society located today largely in Nigeria and Benin, "is not focused on the body" (14), and she criticizes feminists for assuming that the body is central to social organization and that gender is a universal phenomenon. Since gender is socially constructed, there may be some cultures in which it was not constructed at all (9–11). Oyěwùmí argues that traditional Yoruba culture had no concept of gender, but instead was organized around a seniority system defined according to when one joined the household or lineage, either by birth or marriage (13, 35, 39).[6] Concern for biology was limited strictly to procreation and pregnancy (36) and carried no social weight (9). In traditional Yoruba society, the social world was based purely on social relations, and not on the body at all (36). In such a society, individuals (and their bodies) would be defined by relative seniority (depending on who was present in any situation), and no-*body* is a woman. We will examine Oyěwùmí's arguments for these views in chapter 5.

BODILY CAPITAL

- Bodily Capital, Normalcy, Ableism, and "Damaged Goods"
- Managing Devalued Bodily Capital

We can begin to assess how the interpersonal body is socially defined in many Western societies by thinking about what disability studies scholars and policy analysts Patricia McKeever and Karen-Lee Miller (2004) call, borrowing a term from sociologist and social anthropologist Loïc J.D. Wacquant (1995), "bodily capital." Wacquant uses the term to refer to a kind of capital that he argued boxers possess—though, as Wacquant notes, their managers often possess the rights to turn that capital into value (90 n. 5). If *capital* is defined, as Pierre Bourdieu defined it, Wacquant says, as a materialized form of accumulated labor (e.g., a business, investments, or money) that has been privately appropriated by an agent or group and that enables the appropriator to wield social energy, then trained boxers have what we should think of as *bodily* capital (66). Their bodies become the privately held capital that they work on or appropriate and then convert into value—in the boxers' cases, into value in the form of, as Wacquant puts it, "recognition, titles and income streams" (67). Bodily capital thus provides access to valued social roles as well as material rewards.

Bodily Capital, Normalcy, Ableism, and "Damaged Goods"

As we saw in the discussion of the capitalist economic system (chapter 1), the invention of normalcy, the eugenics movement, the ugly laws, segregation, and conditions in custodial institutions (chapter 2), in many Western societies, having what came to be defined as both a functionally and aesthetically normal body increasingly determined whether one was included in the economic system and could avoid unpleasant and harmful living conditions. Functioning and appearing as what is defined as normal has become a form of bodily capital.

Like boxers, people work on their own bodies to be normal, as we saw Harlan Hahn (chapter 1) and Susan M. Schweik (chapter 2) suggesting, and those bodies become a privately held form of capital that has value. In such societies, people who are regarded as visibly or functionally disabled therefore have a *devalued* bodily capital. Their bodies are used by our society to assign them devalued social capital and roles, less recognition, and less income. English professor and disability studies scholar Marilynn J. Phillips (1990) observes, for instance, that disabled people in the United States report that they tend to be regarded as "damaged goods"—a term that echoes the capitalist implications of the notion of bodily capital. "Although the phrase more often refers to products than to people," Phillips writes, "it can be metaphorically transferred from product to person in a society which idealizes commodity and functional predictability. . . . Those failing to meet such standards are reclassified as irregulars, seconds, damaged goods" (850). Like the social expectations that shaped Zola's airport experiences, the assignment of devalued bodily capital to disabled people or their classification as damaged goods is an expression of ableism, or of nondisabled people's social power.

Managing Devalued Bodily Capital

Individuals who are visibly or functionally disabled have to manage their devalued bodily capital on a daily basis. McKeever and Miller (2004) report that mothers often compensate for their disabled children's devalued bodily capital, or lack of bodily prestige in society, for instance, by ensuring that their children are meticulously dressed and groomed. As they put it, "Mothers spontaneously reported that they invested enormous cost and effort to ensure their children were dressed well and fashionably regardless of each family's class position, ethnocultural background, or extent of disability" (1187). In a similar way, in their examination of how the caregivers of severely disabled people construct their disabled loved ones as human, sociologists Robert Bogdan and Steven J. Taylor (1989) argue that the caregivers engaged in "managing [the] appearances" of their disabled loved ones—through dress, hairstyle, and so on—to "downplay visible differences and accentuate individuality. They [the caregivers] sought to present the person to outsiders and to themselves as normal" (143).

Disabled people themselves may also use dress to manage their devalued bodily capital. A former student with visible disabilities who took one of my classes admitted that she played up her traditionally feminine good looks—by wearing make-up and nice skirts or dresses—in part to compensate for her disability. A black professor I know who has visible disabilities told me he has a conscious policy of making sure he is the best-dressed guy in the room. Whenever he left the house, he was, as he used to say in the lingo of the day, "stickin." In these cases, people with disabilities or their caretakers use dress to compensate for the ways in which nondisabled people use their bodies to assign them devalued social roles.

They attempt to improve their own or their children's experiences as a particular personal body (the first dimension of embodiment or first body) by using dress to enhance their status as an interpersonal body in the social technical order (the second dimension or body). We could also include here the smiling behavior of intellectually disabled people, which attempts not only to shut out, but also to appease, the negative responses of nondisabled people.[7]

People with nonvisible disabilities manage bodily capital differently. Ellen Samuels (2003) describes the "coming out" process of people with nonvisible disabilities as a process of "coming out *to*" others, rather than as a process of coming to terms with one's own identity, which is how the "coming out" process is often described by gays and lesbians. Nonvisibly disabled people face what Samuels describes as "the daily challenge of negotiating assumptions about bodily appearance and function" (239). In this case, the challenge as an interpersonal body (the second dimension or body) is to convince others that one's personal body (first dimension or body) is *not* nondisabled.

A DEVALUED SOCIAL ROLE:
THE "SICK ROLE" OR "HANDICAPPED ROLE"

One social role that modern Western societies have often assigned to disabled people is the "sick role" or, an extension of this role, the "handicapped role" (Fine and Asch 1988, 12). As psychologist and education scholar Michelle Fine and bioethicist and disability studies scholar Adrienne Asch explained it, the handicapped role is defined by "helplessness, dependence and passivity." Disabled people are expected to act out the social role of being helpless, dependent, and passive, and, in turn, society assumes that they are helpless, dependent, and incompetent. Fine and Asch note that the connection between the handicapped role and the sick role betrays the influence of the medical model of disability (12), which regards disability as a medical problem and so conflates disability and sickness (see the introduction). As Veterans Administration research scientists Jeanne Hayes and Elizabeth "Lisa" M. Hannold (2007) observe, "The medicalization of disability has often relegated people with disabilities into a 'sick-role' in which they are exempt from social role obligations and expectations of productivity, and instead, are viewed only as passive recipients of health care resources" (362–63). Because the handicapped or sick role assumes that disabled people will not contribute socially or be productive, it is a devalued social role.

Fine and Asch (1988) describe how the medical model of disability leads nondisabled people to assign the "sick" or "handicapped role" to disabled people. As they explain the thinking, "The nonhandicapped person equates having a disability with a *bad and eternal* flu, toothache or broken leg" (12), which are sicknesses that would ordinarily lead nondisabled people to be unsteady and out of sorts and would exempt them from their usual social responsibilities. Non-disabled people then impose this experience on to disabled people by assuming that disabled people are unsteady and out of sorts and should be exempted from age-appropriate social roles. Because nondisabled people are imposing their own experiences on to disabled people, or are interpreting the experiences of disabled people in terms of their own experiences, it is a form of ableism, or a reflection and expression of nondisabled people's social power.

Being assigned the devalued social role of being "sick" or "handicapped" leads to its own forms of discrimination. Asch, who was blind (Asch 2001, 3, 16; 2004, 11–12, 28), describes, for instance, how strangers often assumed that the only way to interact with her was to offer help. "Sitting beside a stranger waiting for a lecture to begin at an academic conference, the stranger whispers loudly not 'Hello, my name is Carol,' but 'Let me know how I can help you,'" Asch wrote. "What help do I need while waiting for the speaker to begin? Why not introduce herself, rather than assume that the only sociability I could possibly want is her help?" (2001, 3; 2004, 11). In fact, Asch suggests, denying disabled people opportunities to play age-appropriate social roles is itself a form of discrimination:

> Much of the daily discrimination faced by people with disabilities is not the overt hostility of being shot at or lynched, although the institutionalization, involuntary sterilization, and school exclusion . . . [faced by disabled people] are blatant enough; rather, it is the experience of being denied the opportunity to play the social roles expected of one's nondisabled age-peers. Many commentators note that people with disabilities are expected to play no adult social role whatsoever. (2001, 2; 2004, 10–11)

The expectation that disabled people should play no adult social roles has also led to other forms of discrimination. As we saw, many Western societies actively tried to prevent disabled people from playing adult social roles through forced sterilization and institutionalization (see chapter 2). Two adult social roles that have routinely been denied to disabled people include the roles of being a sexual partner and parent.

THE DENIAL OF ACCESS TO THE SOCIAL ROLES OF SEXUAL PARTNER AND PARENT

- The Denial of the Sexuality and Reproduction of Intellectually and Developmentally Disabled People
- The Denial Is Fueled by Worries Reminiscent of the Eugenics Movement and by Assumptions of Incompetence
- The Ableist Denial of These Roles Affects Experiences of the Roles

In most Western societies, disabled people's roles as sexual partners and as parents have been devalued and curtailed. In the case of disabled women, as disability studies scholar and disability rights activist Corbett Joan O'Toole (2002) puts it, "'hot sexy mama' are three words that disabled mothers will never hear strung together except perhaps from their lovers. Both the literal and figurative components of that phrase are culturally precluded from mothers with disabilities" ("Introduction," para. 1).[8] O'Toole, whose article focuses on the sexual experiences of physically disabled mothers, tells the story of how her own sexuality was treated when she was growing up. "Growing up with cerebral palsy," she writes, "my sexuality was rarely acknowledged or, if it was, it was often invalidated. I learned not to asked [*sic*] questions about sex or talk about boys I liked because I would get teased by adults or older children [and told that] my questions or comments about sex were 'silly' and my 'crushes' were 'cute.'" O'Toole continues, "Just like my disability, I got the message that sexuality[,] particularly my own[,] was not a topic for discussion. Needless to say, it was enormously damaging to my self esteem [*sic*]" ("Myths and Assumptions," para 13).

Raymond J. Aguilera (2000), a disabled writer who works on queer and disability issues, has noted that, although there are nondisabled people—they call themselves "devotees"—who are sexually attracted specifically to physically disabled people, particularly amputees, they have tended to be regarded by scholars either as diseased/disordered or as predators. That is how the psychologist Richard Bruno, for instance, Aguilera suggests, treated devotees in a 1997 study. While the issue of devotees is controversial,[9] Aguilera points out that both of those views assume that disabled people could not possibly be the objects of genuine sexual attraction (Aguilera 2000, 258–59; Bruno 1997). As literature and art professor and disability studies scholar Tobin Siebers (2012) has remarked, "One of the chief stereotypes oppressing disabled people is the myth that they do not experience sexual feelings or that they do not have or want to have sex" (39).

Western societies have avoided assigning disabled people not only the social role of being a sexual partner but also the social role of being a parent. The stories about physically disabled mothers at the beginning of the chapter illustrate how our society tends not to regard disabled women as appropriate or competent mothers. According to O'Toole (2002), a disabled woman's "training against motherhood begins when a woman is diagnosed as disabled and continues throughout her childbearing years" ("Introduction," para. 12). This training, O'Toole suggests, takes the form of denying disabled women access to sex education, training them for celibacy, teaching nondisabled people that disabled women are unfit partners, denying disabled women access to information about sex and sexual health, training women to avoid abuse but not to have positive sexual lives, sterilizing and institutionalizing disabled women who then do not have sexual lives, divorcing women who become disabled after marriage, and preventing women who become pregnant or mothers from becoming or remaining mothers, through abortion or through public policies that facilitate the removal of children from disabled mothers' homes ("Introduction," para. 12).

The Denial of the Sexuality and Reproduction of Intellectually and Developmentally Disabled People

Intellectually disabled people's sexuality and reproduction has also been denied and curtailed in many Western societies. As educators and advocates Winifred Kempton and Emily Kahn (1991) note in a historical analysis of the sexuality of people with intellectual disabilities, "Their sexual needs were ignored; their sexual behavior was punished; they were randomly sterilized; they were closeted in their homes or isolated in large institutions, segregated by sex to prevent them from reproducing" (93–94). As Siebers (2012) reports, even today, "group homes and long-term care facilities purposefully destroy opportunities for disabled people to find sexual partners or to express their sexuality" (45). Staff members prevent residents from being "alone in their rooms with anyone of sexual interest," residents are "subjected to intense surveillance," and people are not even permitted "to sit together alone in the same room" (45). Siebers says that when these facts are combined with the fact that "many people with disabilities are involuntarily confined in institutions, with no hope of escape . . . the enormity of their oppression becomes palpable" (45). A number of students who have taken my master's of disability studies classes and worked for agencies that run group homes for intellectually and developmentally disabled people reported that many such homes regularly give women birth control pills and men the same drugs that prisons use to chemically castrate sexual offenders, generally without the residents' knowledge or understanding, but sometimes with parents' permission.

The Denial Is Fueled by Worries Reminiscent of the Eugenics Movement and by Assumptions of Incompetence

Issues of sexuality and reproduction are linked, of course. As Kempton and Kahn (1991) note, fears about reproduction have reinforced societies' efforts to control and restrict the sexualities of intellectually disabled people (93–94). Ora Prilleltensky (2003), who works in counseling and human development, has suggested that disabled women are discouraged from having children not only because of the myth that they are asexual and unable to attract partners, but also for reasons reminiscent of the eugenics movement (see chapter 2). Our society's "pursuit of perfect babies suggests that people living with disabilities are really a tragic mistake of nature," Prilleltensky suggests (23). As a result, even though many disabilities are not hereditary, since disabled women "are perceived as being at risk for producing children with disabilities," they are discouraged from having children because of "concerns that they will give birth to 'defective' babies'" (23).

They are also discouraged from becoming mothers because of assumptions—assumptions that are embedded in the "sick" or "handicapped" role as well—about their dependence and incompetence, or, as Prilleltensky (2003) puts it, because of "prejudicial assumptions about their capacity to care for children" (22). Asch, who was born blind (2001, 16; 2004, 28), tells the story of how people who had known her for years and considered themselves close friends of hers "would," as she put it, "prefer that a high-school-age stranger take care of their six-year-old son for an evening than have me do it, even though I have known their son and their home ever since his birth" (2001, 3; 2004, 12). Asch's friends' preference for the strange, high-school babysitter betrayed an assumption that disabled women are not capable of looking after children. Disability studies scholar Alison Sheldon (1999) has pointed out that these preconceptions have meant that, unlike for nondisabled women, for whom reproductive rights have typically been associated with the right *not* to have children—the right to access birth control and abortion—for disabled women, reproductive freedom has meant the right *to* have children (651).

The Ableist Denial of These Roles Affects Experiences of the Roles

Society's attempts to deny disabled people the social roles of being a sexual partner and parent not only shape the ability of disabled bodies to have those roles *out there*, but also affect how disabled people *experience* those roles, when they do. These experiences are functions of ableism, or of nondisabled people's assertion of their social power to restrict disabled people's access to social roles.

In an article that—echoing Zola—urges disabled people to pay attention to their bodies, including their sexuality, poet, essayist, and activist Eli Clare (2001, 361–62), who describes himself as disabled, transgender, and queer (in various senses of the word), notes the shame that he had about his body because of society's message that his body was wrong. "I stored the taunting, the gawking, the shame in my bones," he says, "they became the marrow" (361). This shame affected his experience of being a sexual partner. "I think of my lover cradling my right hand," Clare writes, "saying, 'Your tremors feel so good'; saying, 'I can't get enough of your shaky touch'; saying, 'I love your CP [cerebral palsy].' Shame and disbelief overwhelm me until I stop and really listen to the words" (364).

Artist and professor Riva Lehrer (2012), who identifies herself as "crip" (240)—a self-defining term derived from the word *cripple* sometimes used by physically disabled activists—describes how society's message that she is not an appropriate object of sexual interest affected her sexual encounters with her first boyfriend. "I hid from him even while we were tangled up together," she explains (244). She notes the panic she experienced as another lover put hands on, in, and under her clothing. "A Panic Inventory," she writes: "There. Is. Not. One. Inch. Of. Me. That. Is. Normal" (248).

As we saw in Olkin's account at the beginning of the chapter, society's reluctance to assign disabled women the social role of being a mother also affects disabled women's *experiences* of that social role. As in Olkin's story, Grue and Lærum (2002) found in their study with thirty physically disabled mothers in Norway that, because other people often failed to recognize their roles as mothers and because the disabled mothers felt pressure to prove that they were good mothers, the mothers experienced their motherhood as "fragile" (676). As a result, they often performed their roles in ways that were designed to convince others of their competence and suitability as mothers—a strategy intended, Grue and Lærum suggest, "to legitimate their motherhood" (677). Grue and Lærum found that the women also "carefully monitor their own performance in their role as mother and accordingly as woman" (678). In a similar way, Prilleltensky (2003), who is herself a mother with disabilities (25), found in her study with thirteen physically disabled mothers that they often felt under surveillance and intruded upon by personnel who were gatekeepers for needed services (31).

PROBLEMS OF DISABILITY ALONG THE SECOND DIMENSION OF EMBODIMENT OR INTERPERSONAL BODY ARE NOT PERSONAL PROBLEMS, BUT SOCIAL AND POLITICAL PROBLEMS

- Some Societies Do Not Deny People We Would Classify as Disabled the Roles of Being a Sexual Partner or Parent

Scholars and activists who support exploring the sexual and reproductive experiences of disabled people sometimes explicitly regard this work as a *corrective* to what they suggest is the social model of disability's emphasis (some might say overemphasis; cf. Liddiard 2017, 1) on the political aspects of disability (see the introduction). Zola, who called for medical sociologists to bring the body back into their research, quotes approvingly a passage by Barbara Waxman and Anne Finger (1989) that criticizes the disability rights movement for ignoring issues of sexuality: "Many disabled people find sexuality to be the area of greatest oppression. We are more concerned with being loved and finding sexual fulfillment than getting on a bus" (2; quoted in Zola 1993, 22). As one disabled man interviewed by sociologist and disability studies scholar Russell P. Shuttleworth (2002) put the point, "'I don't give a flying fuck about the ADA because that's not gonna get me laid!'" (113).

Finger (1992) suggests that exploring sexuality has perhaps been hampered by a discomfort with the subject matter. As she puts it in an often-quoted passage,

"It's easier for us to talk about—and formulate strategies for changing—discrimination in employment, education, and housing," she wrote, "than to talk about our exclusion from sexuality and reproduction" (9).

Because the social models focus on the third dimension of embodiment or institutional body (see the introduction), these scholars and activists are right that the models neglect important aspects of the embodiment of disability, namely, the first and second dimensions, or the personal and interpersonal bodies. Analyses of these dimensions are therefore important correctives. However, since sexuality and the social roles of being a sexual partner or parent (in the case of the interpersonal body) are socially defined and have been systematically denied to disabled people in many Western societies because of ableism or nondisabled people's expression of social power, explorations of experiences of these roles is a social and political analysis. While acknowledging the importance of the way in which the disability rights movement shifted attention from supposedly problematic disabled bodies to social injustice, Clare worries about the tendency of activists to ignore their bodies. "Sometimes we who are activists and thinkers forget about our bodies, ignore our bodies," Clare (2001, 359) writes. But experiences of disabled bodies, including of their sexuality, cannot be untangled from oppression, which is political. Oppression lives, for instance, Clare says, in his shame over his tremors when lying with his lover (361, 364).

Shuttleworth (2002) argues that the self-claiming of sexuality (a phrase introduced by anthropologist Anne Guldin [2000]) against cultural assumptions that desexualize disabled people is itself a political act. As Shuttleworth puts it, "The claiming of sexuality by disabled people . . . against the cultural assumption of their asexuality is . . . a bid for full subjectivity," which is "one reason why the issue of disabled people's sexuality has assumed such political importance" (122).

The experiences of disabled women who choose to have children are also political. As Grue and Lærum (2002) suggest, while disabled women are made social objects by society, those who choose "to have children are resisting preconceptions of what social roles they may fulfill" and hence are *remaking* themselves as social objects (673). Thus, problems experienced along the second dimension of embodiment or interpersonal body are not personal, but social and political.

Some Societies Do Not Deny People We Would Classify as Disabled the Roles of Being a Sexual Partner or Parent

Indeed, not all societies regard people who we would consider disabled to be asexual or unfit parents. According to anthropologist Ida Nicolaisen (2008), the Punan Bah people of Malaysia, for instance, who have no single concept of disability equivalent to our own (see chapter 1) suscribe to a notion of a person that is closely tied to the continuation of their society and to a sense of their own mortality. Full personhood is therefore defined by "taking part in subsistence activities to satisfy physical needs, by the begetting of children, and by the carrying out of elaborate funerary and secondary funerary rites to safeguard the rebirth of the deceased" (53). Although, beginning in the 1980s, the ability of disabled people in Punan Bah society to take part in subsistence activities is being altered by the incursion of capitalism and the increasing reliance on wages (Nicolaisen 2008, 54; see also chapter 1), Nicolaisen suggests that many people who we would classify as mentally or physically impaired have been part of the social entity of full persons. Like others, they are regarded as "living incarnations of ancestors" (53) and they are expected to marry and have children to become full persons. Nicolaisen reports that there have been people who we would classify as intellectually disabled who have married and had children of their own (52).[10]

While it is true that the Punan Bah regard characteristics such as severe mental or physical impairments as reducing a person's marriageability, so can other factors, such as infertility, ugliness, being overweight or too skinny, having a hot temper, laziness, or selfishness. Nicolaisen (2008) also suggests that "the Punan Bah deal with this issue of achieving full personhood as a social and moral problem, not of the individual, but of the family" (52). Rather than seeing a failure to achieve full personhood as a social or moral problem inherent in an *individual* and trying to fix or change the individual, in Punan Bah society, full personhood is achieved through a moral system in which sisters and brothers—a familial relationship that includes people we define as first cousins—are morally expected to give a childless sibling one of their own children as a gift. "Due to this custom, few Punan Bah are left without a child of their own" (52). Dreams can also create parent-child relationships. "The net result," Nicolaisen concludes, "is that to my knowledge no one ends up being denied full personhood in this society; no one is structurally disabled" on account of what we would define as impairment or disability (52).

Thus, the second dimension of embodiment or interpersonal body is socially defined both *out there* and in terms of how it is *experienced*. What social capital people have, which social roles *there are* in a society—whether there are substance-group members or first cousins (rather than just sisters and brothers)—as well as who is regarded as appropriate for which social roles, how someone comes to have a social role, and how roles are *experienced* (or, in some cases, are prevented from being experienced) are all socially defined.

MARXIST OBJECTIONS TO MINORITY/CIVIL RIGHTS STRATEGIES AND TO EXPLORING PERSONAL EXPERIENCES OF IMPAIRMENT AND DISABILITY

- Minority/Civil Rights Strategies of Liberation Are Flawed Because They Leave the Capitalist System Intact
- Does Analyzing the First and Second Dimensions of Embodiment Return Us to the Rejected Tragedy Model of Disability?

Recall from the introduction that scholars of disability have offered two main families of social models of disability: the British, materialist, or Marxist-inspired models, which we explored in chapter 1, and the American, minority/civil rights models. The Marxist models conceive of society's poor treatment or oppression of disabled people in terms of exclusion and disadvantage under the economic system of capitalism. For them, liberating disabled people requires addressing capitalism. Minority models conceive of society's poor treatment or oppression of disabled people, as we do for other minority groups, in terms of discrimination and the violation of civil rights. For them, liberating disabled people requires passing and enforcing civil rights laws that prevent discrimination against disabled people.

Marxist theorists have offered criticisms of the minority/civil rights strategy of liberating disabled people that might lead someone to reject my claim that a full account of disability should include an analysis, not just of the third dimension of embodiment or institutional body and capitalism, but also of the first and second dimensions, the personal and interpersonal bodies. Vic Finkelstein, for instance, a member of the activist group in Britain that originally proposed the social model of disability (see the introduction), offered a metaphor that summarizes well the thrust of some of the main Marxist arguments against civil rights approaches to disability liberation. "Our society is built on a competitive market foundation and it is this social system that disables us," he once wrote (Finkelstein 2001b, 4).

> From this point of view disabled people are forced to live in a social prison. While no one can object to campaigning for "rights" so that the prison in which we live is made more humane[,] it is only a political buffoon who believes that exploring prisoner experiences can lead to emancipation! Nothing less than dismantling the prison and replacing it with a non-competitive form of society can break-down the doors which bar our emancipation. (Finkelstein 2001b, 4)

Minority/Civil Rights Strategies of Liberation Are Flawed Because They Leave the Capitalist System Intact

In this quotation, Finkelstein is offering two criticisms against the idea that we can liberate disabled people by passing laws protecting their civil rights. First, he suggests, a legalistic, civil rights strategy leaves the capitalist economic system intact, thereby leaving in place the main mechanism, according to Marxists, that disables certain people.[11] In Finkelstein's metaphor, *capitalism creates* the social prison that excludes and confines disabled people, and while passing civil rights laws might make living in the prison more humane, the laws never dismantle the prison or system of capitalism itself.

Minority/civil rights models of disability are plausible. Scholars such as Hahn and Olkin are right that disabled people in Western societies are targeted in many ways as a kind of minority group (cf. Hahn 1985, 1988; Olkin 1999, chapter 2). As sociologist Richard Scotch and social work researcher Kay Schriner (1997), who are critical of the model, acknowledge, disabled people "are subjected to prejudiced attitudes, discriminatory behavior and institutional and legal constraints that parallel those experienced by African Americans and other disadvantaged and excluded groups" (149), which the minority model helps to explain (151) and civil rights laws can help to address. However, as Finkelstein's metaphor suggests, because capitalism and its associated structures of attitudes toward ability and disability play a crucial role in defining people as disabled and in shaping the embodiment and experiences of disabled people (see chapters 1 and 2), a civil rights approach toward liberation that does not challenge the ways in which capitalism disables people will have only a limited effect (see also the introduction).

Does Analyzing the First and Second Dimensions of Embodiment Return Us to the Rejected Tragedy Model of Disability?

There is a second criticism of civil rights approaches in the quotation. Finkelstein (2001b) is rejecting any approach that involves, as he puts it, "exploring prisoner experiences," or that involves describing personal experiences of impairment and disability. He worried that sharing bad personal experiences of impairment or disability in a way that is not connected to an analysis of capitalism would return us to a model in which disability is merely a personal tragedy—a view that many scholars of disability and disability activists have rejected—rather than a form of social oppression (2). He might therefore be reluctant to go beyond the Marxist analysis to explore the first and second dimensions of embodiment or the personal and interpersonal bodies.

Since ableism is experienced in intimate and personal ways, however, as we saw, a comprehensive understanding of disability and of our society's ableism should take seriously the experiences of embodiment all the way down to the first dimension or personal body. Also, because experiences of the first and second dimensions are always socially defined, as we have seen, the analysis of these dimensions is a social and political analysis, and not only an exploration of personal experiences. Finkelstein is right that we should avoid analyses that treat disability merely as bad personal experiences, but bad experiences of disability along the first and second dimensions of embodiment or personal and interpersonal bodies are social and political problems, and not personal tragedies.

CONCLUSION

A full understanding of the experience of embodiment will require an analysis, not only of the third dimension of embodiment or institutional body (chapters 1 and 2) but also of the first and second dimensions of embodiment, the personal body and the interpersonal body. Because social power can be experienced in intimate and personal ways, and because the British, materialist, or Marxist social models and theories as well as the American, minority/civil rights social models focus attention on the third dimension of embodiment or institutional body, critics are right to suggest that something is left out of these models and theories: an examination of ways in which social context and ableism shape experiences of disability in relation to the interpersonal body (the second dimension) and the personal body (the first dimension).

However, like the third dimension or institutional body, the first and second dimensions of embodiment are also socially defined. In the case of the second dimension or interpersonal body, societies define both what social roles there are *out there* as well as how those roles are *experienced*. In the case of the first dimension or personal body, so far I have argued only that the phenomenologically *experienced* personal body or feel of one's own body is socially defined. There is no *experience* of a given, pre-social, natural, biological, or physical personal body. Because experiences of the first and second dimensions are socially defined, an analysis of these dimensions is a social and political analysis, and so does not, as some Marxist theorists worried, reinvoke a model of disability according to which disability is merely a personal tragedy.

In chapter 4, I develop the claim that the first dimension or personal body is socially defined, not only in terms of how it is *experienced*, as we saw in this chapter, but also in terms of what it *is*, as an object *out there*. We will need a social and political analysis of how Western societies have defined what the body *is*, *out there*, as an object.

4

The Socially Defined Body in Society

On July 12, 1794, thirty-six-year-old Post Captain Horatio Nelson of the British Navy was wounded and lost sight in his right eye while commanding His (or Her) Majesty's Ship (HMS) Agamemnon in an attack on the fort of Calvi, Corsica. In 1796, Nelson was promoted to commodore, and in early 1797, he was promoted again, to rear admiral of the blue, after being instrumental in the British victory against the Spanish in the Battle of Cape St. Vincent. On July 24, 1797, while leading a losing assault on the Spanish island of Tenerife, Nelson's right arm was fractured and an artery severed just above the elbow by a musket ball. He was taken to HMS Theseus, where his arm was amputated. The next day, the ship's surgeon, James Farquhar, wrote in his journal that Nelson was issuing orders to his men within thirty minutes of the surgery.

After the amputation, Nelson sailed home to recover from complications. But he was called on once again to command a squadron of ships by the spring of 1798 because of another crisis in the war against Spain. He was promoted to rear admiral of the red in 1799, and to vice admiral in 1801. During the Battle of Copenhagen that year, Nelson, who had a history of defying orders to win battles, put his telescope over his sightless right eye and claimed he could not see the signal from his superior to cease action. The sea battle continued until Nelson proposed a truce and negotiated peace with Danish officials. The British regarded the battle as a great victory, and Nelson as its hero.

At the end of 1803, after Britain declared war on France, Nelson was made Mediterranean commander-in-chief. On October 21, 1805, while commanding the fleet in the Battle of Trafalgar from the flagship, HMS Victory, Nelson was shot through his shoulder and into his chest by a sniper on the enemy's ship. Approximately three hours and fifteen minutes later, he died.[1] However, he was credited with having won the battle, and there is a statue of him standing proudly, missing part of his right arm, in Trafalgar Square in London. While Nelson continued to serve in the British Royal Navy after losing sight in his eye and having part of his arm amputated, today, by contrast, he would have been discharged from military service because of his impairments.

This biography suggests that, in the 1790s and early 1800s in England, Nelson did not have "impairment" in the way that we understand the term today. The Royal Navy did provide small pensions to sailors for various wounds, and, indeed, Nelson himself petitioned the Navy for such a pension while home recovering from his amputation in 1797 (a pension he would likely have lost once returning to duty). Since the damage to his right eye was not apparent, he had difficulty convincing the Navy that it had been wounded and was required to provide, as evidence, "formal certificates from the doctors who had treated him," as Colin White, the editor of a collection of Nelson's letters puts it (Nelson 2005, 190). Still, although the practice of medicine was advancing in the West by Nelson's time, he lived before its dominance (in the mid-nineteenth century) and before the dominance of the medical model of impairment and disability. As a result, while he was regarded as having battle injuries—one of which temporarily required him to return home to heal—his wounds were never regarded, as they would be today, as diseases, defects, or impairments that required discharge from military service. Once he recovered from his arm injury, he was once again fit for duty.

As David M. Turner (2012) has argued in his book on the history of disability and impairment in eighteenth-century Europe, what we call impairment has not been defined in the same way across different historical time periods, or, as he puts it, "Impairment is . . . not trans-historical" (12). Nelson's life thus helps to suggest that not only is *disability* socially defined, as social models of disability have suggested (see the introduction), but also *impairment*, too, is socially defined. There is *no* such thing *out there* as a purely objective, pre-social, natural, or physical body. Understandings and identities of bodies and of what bodies are like *out there*—including whether they have impairment—I will suggest, are all socially defined.

Recall that my claim that there is *no* purely objective, pre-social, natural, physical, or biological body can be interpreted in two ways. First, it can be interpreted to mean that there is no purely objective body *out there*, as an object, and, second, it can be interpreted to mean that there is no purely objective *experience* of the body (see the introduction). For the second and third dimensions of embodiment, the interpersonal and institutional bodies, there is no purely objective body in *both* of those senses. In terms of the second dimension or interpersonal body, which refers to how societies use the body to conceive of social roles, society, or the world (see the introduction), what social roles are available *out there*—which roles are offered by a society—are defined by societies, and so can change from culture to culture as well as over time. How those roles are *experienced* is also socially defined (see chapter 3). In terms of the third dimension or institutional body, which captures how institutions and structures in societies regulate, survey, and control people (see the introduction), social institutions and structures define not only what identities or categories of people there are *out there*, such as whether there are people categorized as disabled, but also how those categories are *experienced* under the institutions and structures (see chapters 1 and 2).

In the case of the first dimension of embodiment or personal body, however, so far, chapter 3 argued *only* for the second interpretation, that is, for the claim that there is no purely objective, pre-social, natural, physical, or biological *experience* of the individual, personal body. The phenomenologically experienced personal body or the very *feel* of our own bodies is always socially defined (see chapter 3). But, as Nelson's biography suggests, societies also define what a body is like as an object *out there*, including whether it is *impaired*. My claim is that there is *no* purely objective, pre-social, natural, physical, or biological personal body *out there*, as an object, along this first dimension of embodiment, or that what bodies are like *out there* is always defined by society. This chapter will suggest that *impairment*, facts of impairment, bodily features, and conditions—which are ways of describing personal bodies out there—are all socially defined; chapter 5 will add that the discipline of *biology* as well as the notions of *biological bodies* or *biological impairment* are also socially defined.

The chapter begins by reviewing some confusions that have obscured discussions of impairment by scholars of disability. It then uses explorations in anthropology, Africana philosophy, and philosophy of science to suggest that not only is the concept of impairment socially defined, but also smaller categories of impairment—such as autism or mental illness—as well as claims about bodily features or conditions, are also socially defined. For, in general, what we perceive as the facts—and hence as people's identities as objects out there—is determined by our society's languages and learning.

Chapter outline:

➤ Confronting Some Confusions about Impairment
➤ The Concept of Impairment Is Socially Defined
➤ Are People's Identities (as Objects Out There) Completely Socially Defined?
➤ Smaller Categories of Impairment and Bodily Conditions or Features Are Also Socially Defined
➤ Conclusion

CONFRONTING SOME
CONFUSIONS ABOUT IMPAIRMENT

- Confusion Caused by Shifting from the Experienced Body to the Body *Out There*
- Confusing the Material with Physical Objects: Another Shift from a Socially Constructed Body to a Given, Physical Body
- A False Distinction between Denotation and Connotation

Confusion Caused by Shifting from the Experienced Body to the Body *Out There*

Scholars of disability do not always clearly distinguish between the *experience* of the body and the body as an object *out there*. This confusion sometimes clouds their discussions of the first dimension of embodiment or personal body and, particularly, their discussion of impairment. Sociologists and disability studies scholars Tom Shakespeare and Nicholas Watson (2001), for instance, complained that the British, Marxist-inspired social model's distinction between *impairment* and *disability* (see the introduction) completely brackets or sets aside impairment (14). Because the social models focus on disability, or on the social consequences of having an impaired body, they suggest, the models end up ignoring impairment altogether. But this is a mistake. "Experientially," they write, "impairment is salient to many," or affects the experiences of many disabled people, so "it cannot be ignored in our social theory or our political strategy" (15). The social model also brackets or fails to address impairment, they suggest, in the sense of reduced functioning or genetic conditions (15–16). A theory of disability should be able to explain when it is appropriate to take "action on impairment—and even [on] various forms of impairment prevention" (Shakespeare and Watson 2001, 17). This discussion does not clearly distinguish the *experience* of impairment from impairment as an object *out there*. While the *salience* of impairment is about the *feel* or *experience* of the body, functions and genetic conditions are characteristics that we ascribe to bodies as objects *out there*.

Because Shakespeare and Watson's description of *how* the models bracket impairment here does not clearly distinguish between the *experience* of the body and what the body is, as an object *out there*, they end up offering a somewhat incoherent account of impairment. While the discussion of the *experience* of impairment leads them to argue for the claim that impairment or the body is socially constructed, in their account of what disability is as an object *out there*, they fall back into a biological account of impairment, which not only is the dominant account of impairment in the West today, but also takes impairment and the body to be given in the world, rather than socially constructed (see chapter 5). These two views are therefore not compatible with one another.

Let's begin with Shakespeare and Watson's (2001) discussion of the *experience* of impairment. According to the social models, like the term *sex*, the term *impairment* is supposed to refer to purely objective physical or biological features, and, like the term *gender*, the term *disability* is supposed to refer to socially created restrictions or oppression (10). However, Shakespeare and Watson argue, this distinction that the social models make between "impairment (bodily difference)" and "disability (social creation)" is "unsustainable"— a point that becomes clear, they say, when we ask, "Where does impairment end and disability start?" (17). Pain (an *experience* of impairment), they suggest, can be affected by sociocultural factors (i.e., by disability)—a point we explored earlier (chapter 3). And while impairment may trigger disability (*experiences* of the social consequences of impairment), disability can "create or exacerbate impairment." (Shakespeare and Watson do not offer any argument or examples for this claim.) Impairment and disability thus bleed into one another (Shakespeare and Watson 2001, 18). As a result, just as many feminists have argued that sex—and not just gender—is socially constructed (Shakespeare and Watson 2001, 17), so we must say that impairment—and not just disability—is socially constructed. "There is no pure or natural body, existing outside of discourse," they conclude (18).[2]

As they shift from talking about *experience* to offering a definition of what disability is as an object *out there*, however, talk of biology and a biological body sneaks back into their account. Impairment and disability are not "dichotomous," they suggest, "but describe different places on a continuum, or different aspects of a single experience," and we cannot tell "where impairment ends and disability starts" (22). As a result, they say, "Disability is a complex dialectic of biological, psychological, cultural and socio-political factors, which cannot be extricated except with imprecision" (22).

The suggestion that disability is determined in part by biology implies that impairment is biological. But the claim that impairment is biological is inconsistent with their claim that impairment is socially constructed, because the discipline of biology assumes that biological features are not socially constructed or defined, but purely objective, pre-social, natural, or physical (see chapter 5). While Shakespeare and Watson explicitly endorse the view that impairment is socially constructed, then, they end up with a definition of disability in which disability is determined (in part) by a purely objective, pre-social, natural, or physical biology or impairment. As sociologist Bill Hughes (2007) has said of their view here, "These claims about disability and the body to which I am (mostly) most sympathetic tend to give way to a body that is overendowed with nature and over-determined by its natural limitations. They also give way to an ontology for disability studies that must privilege impairment and the biological at the expense of disability and the political" (677).

Carefully distinguishing the *experience* of the first dimension of embodiment or personal body from what the personal body is as an object *out there* helps us to keep in mind that the claim that impairment is socially constructed or defined is inconsistent with a purely physical or biological definition of impairment according to which impairment is given, pre-social, or natural. If the personal body and hence impairment, which is a description of such personal bodies, are socially defined, as I claim, then they are socially defined both in terms of how they are *experienced* (chapter 3) and in terms of what they are *out there* (this chapter and chapter 5).

Confusing the Material with Physical Objects: Another Shift from a Socially Constructed Body to a Given, Physical Body

There is a similar problem with disability justice and culture scholar Rosemarie Garland-Thomson's (2011) suggestion that we should use the concept of "misfit" to theorize or understand disability. The concept of misfit is supposed to combine the feminist insight, first suggested by philosopher and gender theorist Judith Butler, for instance, that bodies are discursively constructed (595)[3]—or constructed and defined by our concepts and practices—with more recent feminist materialist attempts to move away from thinking of things as merely linguistic constructions toward thinking of things as material (Garland-Thomson 2011, 592). To be disabled is to "misfit," Garland-Thomson suggests, where *misfit* refers both to a person who does not fit in a certain environment, as well as to "the act of not fitting" (593). Because environments help to construct what counts as a "misfit," misfits and misfitting are socially constructed, but their construction is material, rather than discursive. "Misfits are inherently unstable rather than fixed," Garland-Thomson writes, "yet they are very real because they are material rather than linguistic constructions" (593).

When Garland-Thomson outlines the details of the concept, however, as in Shakespeare and Watson's account, we seem to end up talking about given, physical bodies and functions once again. Garland-Thomson distinguishes the way in which disabled people are misfits from the way in which people of color are misfits. While people of color might be misfits in a perceptual and social sense, she suggests (596), disabled people are literal and material misfits. "People with disabilities become misfits not just in terms of social attitudes—as in unfit for service or parenthood—but also in material ways. Their outcast status is literal when the shape and function of their bodies comes in conflict with the shape and stuff of the built world" (594). Misfitting, Garland-Thomson says, is about "the discrepancy between body and world" (593). Garland-Thomson illustrates a lack of fit between the body and built environment by using the example of a wheelchair user who encounters a flight of stairs. In this case, Garland-Thomson suggests, the woman's body, together with the "built-ness or thing-ness of the space" determines whether she can enter (595). In spite of Garland-Thomson's attempt to acknowledge the feminist insight that bodies themselves are (and the category of sex, in particular, is) socially constructed, then, we end up once again talking about what seems like a physical or biological body, with (purely objective) bodily shapes and functions that literally—and not just socially—cast disabled people out.[4]

The problem with Garland-Thomson's account is that it confuses the material—the out-thereness of the world, so to speak—with physical objects and overlooks the ways in which the imaginary wheelchair user's inability to get into the building—that materiality—is shaped, not by her body and the stairs, but by social contexts and expectations. Garland-Thomson fleshes out the materiality of the wheelchair user's misfitting in purely physical terms as an interaction between what seems to be a given, physical body and a socially constructed, but still physical, environment (the stairs).

But the wheelchair user's inability to get into the building is shaped by the same Western cultural values that shaped medical sociologist, disability studies scholar, and polio survivor Irving K. Zola's experiences of navigating the airport like everyone else and arriving at his destinations sore, tired, and cramped (see chapter 3). Zola's experiences were shaped by the values of individual, physical independence and "normalcy," or by the assumption that it is important to accomplish physical tasks—such as getting up the stairs or navigating the airport— by oneself and in as "normal" a fashion as possible. Zola walked around airports with the help of his leg brace, instead of using a wheelchair, and arrived at his destinations sore, tired, and cramped because he internalized this assumption and so strove to accomplish the physical task of navigating the airport on his own and in as "normal" a fashion as possible. According to this assumption, it is better to walk with a brace than to use a wheelchair (worse still to have someone else push the wheelchair), and better to have a ramp so that—if one does use a wheelchair—one can get into the building or accomplish that physical task by oneself.

International journalist and wheelchair user John Hockenberry (2004) has remarked jokingly, however, that, in Arab countries, people will insist on carrying you "up a flight of stairs whether you wanted to go or not" (149). In such a society, stairs would not pose the same problem that they pose in individualistic, Western cultures focused on physical independence and normalcy, and ramps might hardly seem to be necessary. In a society with different social arrangements and expectations, then, the woman Garland-Thomson imagines might well be able to get to where she wishes to go, without a ramp.[5] Thus, the materiality in question—the wheelchair user's inability to get into the building—is a result not of a physicality (a given, physical body in combination with a socially constructed but still physical environment, namely the stairs), but of social context or social values, assumptions, and expectations.[6]

If the wheelchair user's misfitting is constructed by social contexts, however, then, contrary to Garland-Thomson's claim, there is no distinction in terms of materiality between the kind of misfitting that occurs to (nondisabled) people of color and the misfitting of disabled people. Garland-Thomson's distinction between racial misfitting and disability misfitting seems to be grounded in the idea that there is a materiality—which she fleshes out in terms of physicality or physical objects—to the wheelchair user's misfitting that is not present for a non-disabled person of color. Unlike in a case of race alone, where the misfitting is caused purely by social context, Garland-Thomson is suggesting, for the disabled person, the wheelchair user's body, as a physical object, along with the socially constructed physicality of the stairs, constitute the materiality of the misfitting. However, once we give up the idea that the out-thereness or materiality of the wheelchair user's misfitting is defined in terms of *physical objects* (seemingly given, physical bodies plus socially constructed but still physical stairs), then there is no difference between the misfitting of nondisabled people of color, which is defined by social context, and, as I have suggested, the equally, socially defined misfitting of disabled people. Being the only one who is frisked by security at the airport or being the only canvasser singled out by police because one is the only person of color in the group is as much a real and material form of misfitting as is being unable to get up the stairs in a particular society while using a wheelchair.[7]

If bodies are socially defined, as Garland-Thomson suggests, then we must say that the wheelchair user's body and bodily conditions are not purely objective, but are also socially defined. There are no purely given or objective, physical bodies. What we would call human differences are real, but what those differences *are*, how they are *defined* and *understood*, I will argue, is socially determined. Indeed, as we saw in the discussion of Domba's kidney transplant and the Suyá belief in substance groups and in a socially shared body (chapter 3), even to regard someone as an *individual* body is already to have cut up the world in a particular way.

A False Distinction between Denotation and Connotation

Confusion about the nature and status of the concept of impairment is compounded by a false distinction between what is called connotation and denotation. Scholars are sometimes willing to grant that the meanings *associated* with impairment—the *connotations* of impairment, let's say—have changed over time and so are socially constructed, while holding on to the idea that impairment refers to (or *denotes*) a pre-social, biological body.

Vic Finkelstein (2001a)—one of the founders of the original social model and its distinction between *impairment* and *disability* (see the introduction)—for instance, noted the large statue in Trafalgar Square of Admiral Horatio Nelson "flouting his impairments" (9). Indeed, as Finkelstein points out, not only was

Nelson missing part of his right arm, as the statue depicts, but he was also blinded in one eye, as we saw earlier. And yet, Nelson was promoted four times by the Royal Navy—twice after part of his right arm was amputated in 1797—and continued to command ships and fight in battles until being fatally wounded in 1805 (National Museum of the Royal Navy 2004). In the late 1790s in Britain, then, it was possible to be blinded in one eye and missing part of an arm and still be a highly respected member of the military. Nelson was impaired, Finkelstein suggests, but the connotations were different at that time. In particular, having an impairment did not mean being *dis*-abled (not able) or *in*-valid (not valid). As Finkelstein (2001a) puts it, "Admiral Nelson was not a disabled person" (9).

By the time Franklin Delano Roosevelt ran for president of the United States in the 1930s, however, Finkelstein relates, having an impairment automatically meant that one was *dis*-abled—a status regarded as inappropriate for a president. As a result, F. D. R. hid his inability to walk from the public (Finkelstein 2001a, 9). In fact, the American public was still debating whether his statue should depict him sitting in a wheelchair in 1997 (Stout 1997). Thus, Finkelstein (2001a) suggests, sometime between the 1790s and the 1930s (and until 1997), the connotations or social meanings associated with impairment changed. Today in Britain, as he notes, it would not be possible for Nelson to remain in active, military service (9).

Finkelstein's distinction between what the concept of impairment refers to or denotes and its social meanings or connotations, however, is a false one. To say that the meaning of impairment is historical and can change over time is to say that the concept of impairment itself—its denotation—is socially defined or constructed. As philosopher and scholar of disability Shelley Tremain (2015) has argued—and as I will argue—impairment is not a natural characteristic for which only its "signification or significance" (31) or connotation changes over time or from culture to culture. Rather, the very idea that impairment refers to a natural, bodily characteristic is part of the meaning (denotation) of our concept or category of impairment itself. In the 1790s and early 1800s, under a definition in which being able-bodied was linked to the ability to labor and before bodily differences came to be defined in medicalized and biological terms (see chapters 2 and 5), Admiral Nelson did not have impairment. By the 1930s, impairment was a biomedical defect or dysfunction that would have automatically disqualified F. D. R. for the job of president. Thus, Nelson and F. D. R. did not have the same kind of characteristic—impairment—that had a signification or connotation that changed over time; they did not have the same characteristic at all. As soon as we grant that impairment as we understand it is socially constructed, as feminist scholar and sociologist Oyèrónké Oyěwùmí might remind us (see chapter 3), we must also grant that there may be some societies in which it was not constructed at all.

THE CONCEPT OF IMPAIRMENT IS SOCIALLY DEFINED

- All Concepts Are Metaphors: They Combine Different Things Together as the Same, and Forget the Differences
- Small-Scale Societies Are Unlikely to Develop an Abstract Concept of Impairment at All

All Concepts Are Metaphors: They Combine Different Things Together as the Same, and Forget the Differences

We can begin to see how impairment is socially defined by thinking about the nineteenth-century German philosopher Friedrich Nietzsche. As Nietzsche (1976) argues, all concepts are metaphors. "Every concept is produced through the equation of the not-equal," Nietzsche writes. "As, certainly, no leaf is entirely equal to another, so, certainly, is the concept of leaf formed by dropping any of these individual differences, by a forgetting of the discriminating" (46 [§1]; alternate translation). Today's concept of impairment is extremely abstract. It equates quite a lot of things that are not equal—not only various physical (paralysis, lameness, palsies, deformities) and sensory (blindness, deafness) impairments, but also intellectual, mental (e.g., epilepsy), and psychological impairments.

In the Middle Ages in Europe, according to historian Irina Metzler, there was no single abstract term that put together or included all and only the conditions we think of as physical impairment today. Medieval people recognized that some conditions might make someone unable to work. The rules of one parish guild founded in 1357 in what is now Yorkshire, England, for instance, which served as a model for other guilds, listed a range of situations that would make someone eligible to receive social benefits from the guild's coffers. A member of the guild would be entitled to support upon becoming "infirm, bowed, blind, dumb, deaf, maimed, or sick," whether permanently or temporarily, in old age or in youth, or if "borne down by any other mishap that he has not the means of living" (Metzler 2015, 70). Metzler describes the list of conditions in the rule as "the more or less complete range of physical impairments recognized in the Middle Ages" (70). However, the abstract terms that were used to refer to what we would think of as physical conditions or impairment also included other conditions that we would not think of as impairment. People might speak of the "infirm," "debilitated," "weak," or "impotent," for instance, Metzler suggests, which were terms that referred to people who were powerless because of a lack of physical ability and encompassed what we would call orthopedic impairments or paralysis as well as the effects of old age. But these terms also included people who were, as Metzler puts it, "suffering from poverty," or were powerless because of a lack of *economic* ability (4–5).

As anthropologists Benedicte Ingstad and Susan Reynolds Whyte (1995) point out, the concepts of disability and handicap were invented under particular historical circumstances in Europe. "In many cultures one cannot be 'disabled' for the simple reason that 'disability' as a recognized category does not exist," they write. "There are blind people and lame people and 'slow' people, but 'the disabled' as a general term does not translate into many languages" (7). The Maasai term that is translated into English as "disabled," for instance, they say, "actually refers to a lizard that walks in an awkward way" (7), and so is a description of physical movement. It therefore does not include what we would think of as intellectual or psychological impairments.

Small-Scale Societies Are Unlikely to Develop an Abstract Concept of Impairment at All

It is not clear how much weight some smaller-scale societies would give to what we would regard as impairments—blindness or walking in an awkward way, for instance—in defining a person's identity. Anthropologists Jessica Scheer and Nora Groce (1988) have argued that—unlike in modern, Western societies, where the practice of institutionalization has meant that many able-bodied people have no contact at all with disabled people—in small-scale, traditional societies, close contact with people with what we call impairments would be common (33). At the same time, there may only be one or a few individuals at once with what we would identify as impairments in any such society (26). Because people have regular face-to-face contact with each other and are embedded in complex, social relationships, however, what we call an impairment is typically regarded in such societies as merely a single, personal characteristic that does not define one's identity (31). As Scheer and Groce remark, "An individual who is disabled may well be viewed as a fellow villager or clan member, age-mate, skilled artisan and so forth, rather than solely as someone who is unable to see, hear or walk" (30). Thus, in small-scale, traditional societies, identities are defined by social relationships and roles. What we would classify as a specific impairment only comes to have meaning and be associated with social roles if there is a high number of persons with the characteristic, at which time cultural traditions "will often emerge to explain why such events occur and to support the participation of the disabled persons in whatever roles that society deems appropriate" (30).

Because there may only be a few individuals with what we call impairments in small-scale, traditional societies, and because these societies will tend to regard such features as uniquely personal characteristics unassociated with social identity, those societies would be unlikely to develop a concept of impairment that abstracts across the wide range of conditions that our concept of impairment does. Someone in such a society might be blind or lose a leg,[8] but there is no reason to think that members of the society would come to regard those two characteristics as the same, one kind of abstract thing (i.e., "impairment").[9] Indeed, it is not clear what use our level of abstraction has outside of the stigmatizing and exclusive social and economic practices (see chapters 1 and 2) that were invented in the West sometime between the time of Admiral Nelson and that of F. D. R. Given the wide range of conditions that can count as an "impairment," to say that someone is impaired does not give us any precise information at all about what the person or his or her life is like—it says only that the person is *dis*-abled, less able to work, and *in*-valid. The modern, Western, highly abstract concept of impairment is thus socially defined.

ARE PEOPLE'S IDENTITIES (AS OBJECTS OUT THERE) COMPLETELY SOCIALLY DEFINED?

- Communalism in Africana Philosophy and the View That People's Identities Are Essentially Social
- An Objection to Communalism: People Have Individual Features or Attributes That Are Not Socially Defined
- Are There Smaller Categories of Impairment That Are Not Socially Defined?

Communalism in Africana Philosophy and the View That People's Identities Are Essentially Social

Drawing on views regarded as having deep roots in a number of traditional, African cultures, some philosophers and scholars who work in Africana philosophy (philosophy rooted in beliefs and traditions found in African cultures and the African diaspora) have suggested that people's identities (out there) are always socially defined. These scholars have defended a version of communalism, according to which people are *essentially* social in the sense that their identities are always determined by their social communities. Indeed, in the "Introduction" to their anthology, *I Am Because We Are: Readings in Black Philosophy*, Africana studies scholars Fred Lee Hord (Mzee Lasana Okpara) and Jonathan Scott Lee (1995) argue that the social conception of identity, according to which a person cannot be defined or have an identity outside of a social community, is one of two themes that constitutes the "black philosophical tradition." As they put it, "The first generative theme constitutive of the black philosophical tradition highlighted therein [in the anthology] is the idea that the identity of the individual is never separable from the sociocultural environment" (7). According to this view, Hord (Okpara) and Lee explain, "a person's identity is constructed in and at least partially by a set of shared beliefs, patterns of behavior and expectations" (7–8).

African poet and scholar Okot p'Bitek (1998), for instance, defends a social conception of the person while poking fun at what he takes to be the overly individualistic Western conception of freedom, according to which freedom is merely individual freedom from constraint. From that Western point of view, he says, "'Son,' 'Mother,' 'Daughter,' 'Father,' 'Uncle,' 'Husband,' 'Grandfather,' 'Wife,' 'Clansman,' 'Mother-in-law,' . . . 'Chief,' 'Medicineman,' and many other such terms are the stamps of man's unfreedom" (74). Since social roles constrain what we can and cannot do, if freedom is the mere absence of external constraint, then those social roles make us unfree. But in fact, p'Bitek continues, "it is by such complex titles that a person is defined and identified. . . . The central question 'Who am I?' cannot be answered in any meaningful way unless the relationship in question is known. Because 'I' is not only one relationship, but numerous relationships" (74). Our freedom to do and be something and hence our identities are determined by our communities, particularly by our social roles and relationships.

Our communities also define us, in this view, insofar as they determine *how* we should live out our socially defined identities. As p'Bitek notes, the social titles he lists "order and determine human behavior in society" (74). We can use the work of the nineteenth-century German philosopher G. W. F. Hegel to flesh out p'Bitek's claim. Hegel argued that concepts are not only descriptive but also *prescriptive*. The concept of hammer, for instance, describes a hammer and also tells us something about what a *good* hammer is like. A hammer is only *truly* a hammer if it is a good hammer; a hammer that is broken into pieces is not only no longer a good hammer, it is also not really a hammer at all. Similarly, concepts of social roles are also prescriptive.[10] To truly *be* a teacher, I have to live up to that role, at least to a minimal degree, in a way that could be recognized by others in the community as living up to that role. As sociologist and disability studies scholar Sharon N. Barnartt (2010)—whose work focuses on analyzing disability in terms of social roles—has observed, "Although people may have some choice about the degree to which they will follow the role prescriptions, they must follow some of them or they will not be seen as performing that role adequately" (8; cf. 2001, 56). I cannot claim to be a teacher and then behave in ways that no one would recognize as "being a teacher."[11] Thus, people's identities out there are always socially defined, not only in terms of what identities get ascribed to people, as objects out there, but also in terms of how people carry out or live up to the ascribed identities.

An Objection to Communalism: People Have Individual Features or Attributes That Are Not Socially Defined

However, African philosopher Kwame Gyekye (2003) has criticized what he views as an overly extreme form of African communalism, according to which a person's identity is regarded as *completely* social. "[A] person is by nature a social (communal) being, yes," Gyekye writes, "but he/she is by nature other things as well (i.e. a person possesses other essential attributes). Failure to recognize this may result in pushing the significance and implications of a person's communal nature beyond their limits" (301). Gyekye argues that the ability to be rational, to be morally virtuous, and to make moral judgments belongs to people *as individuals*, not in virtue of their social communities: "It is not the community that creates these attributes; it discovers and nurtures them" (305). Although the features that Gyekye highlights are not what we would think of as bodily conditions, in a similar way, someone could argue that, although persons are defined by their social roles, they are also determined—as individuals—by other attributes, including specific attributes that define them as disabled. In the West today, these attributes would typically be described in terms of specific categories of physical or biological (bodily or mental) functioning—as smaller categories of impairments.

Are There Smaller Categories of Impairment That Are Not Socially Defined?

Following the same kind of reasoning offered by Gyekye, someone might argue that, while the abstract concept of impairment as a whole may be culturally specific and hence socially defined, as we have seen, there are still smaller categories of impairment, more specific kinds of conditions, that are pre-social, purely objective, and purely physical, and that define people's identities out there. In his criticism of the American, minority/civil rights version of the social model of disability (see the introduction), bioethicist and disability studies scholar David Wasserman (1994), for instance, grants that "there is reason to be skeptical about the impairment classification," because "the impact of conditions classified as impairments varies widely across environments and goals, the scientific basis of that classification is obscure, its elasticity makes it highly susceptible to abuse, and its application to particular conditions, from homosexuality to congenital deafness, has been plausibly challenged." Nevertheless, Wasserman suggests, "there is an objective category of impairments, even if it is narrower and less significant than commonly supposed" (183).

According to the minority group model of disability, disabled people are a socially defined minority group—much like women or people of color—who are oppressed or disadvantaged by the larger society's individual and social attitudes and practices. But this model incorrectly ignores the fact that people are also disadvantaged by their biological or physical conditions, Wasserman says. "[A] person whose major life activities were limited *only* by other people's attitudes or practices would be 'disabled' only in a derivative sense," Wasserman writes. "The disadvantages experienced by people with disabilities arise from the interaction of their physical conditions and their social environment; those disadvantages can rarely be attributed to biology or social practice alone" (9). There is, then, Wasserman says, a "fact of biological impairment" (10),[12] even if those facts must be captured by categories that are more narrow than the category of "impairment."

One problem with trying to reinterpret the concept of "impairment" in terms of smaller facts of biological impairment is that—even if we assume for a moment that the concept of biology is not itself problematic (a view I will question in chapter 5)—it is not clear that some of the things classified as impairments are biological. Autism, for example, is typically diagnosed by using a list of largely social characteristics, such as lack of eye contact, hand flapping, or weak pragmatic language skills. As Kristin Bumiller (2008) notes, the medical definition of autism is highly indeterminate, and there are no blood, brain, or other medical tests that can be used to confirm a diagnosis (969). A student in one of my disability studies classes reported that she spent the first year her son was in preschool fighting with the school district over whether her son should be diagnosed as autistic. She grew up in an African culture in which young people were taught that making eye contact and speaking with elders when not directly spoken to or questioned was rude and disrespectful—social customs that she passed on to her own children. The New York City school district staff believed that, because her son refused to make eye contact and was socially shy and awkward, he must be autistic. Thus, autism is not defined in terms of biological features or characteristics, but is constructed out of social—and hence socially defined—characteristics. (We will return to an examination of claims about biology in chapter 5.)

SMALLER CATEGORIES OF IMPAIRMENT AND BODILY CONDITIONS OR FEATURES ARE ALSO SOCIALLY DEFINED

- The Social Construction of "Mental Illness"
- Facts and Hence Identities (Out There) Are Socially Defined
- Languages Determine the Facts That We Perceive
- Facts Are Theory-Laden, or Presuppose Socially Learned Commitments about What the World Is Like
- Bodily Features or Conditions Are Socially Defined

As my student's experience points toward, then, Wasserman's suggestion has a bigger problem: not only is the concept of impairment as a whole socially defined, as we have seen and as he grants, but smaller categories of impairment—such as autism—are also socially defined.

The Social Construction of "Mental Illness"

Take the category of "mental illness," for instance. Psychiatric systems survivors and university professors Anne Wilson (a pseudonym) and Peter Beresford (2002) have argued that the medicalized and supposedly scientific concept of "mental illness," which treats mental distress as parallel to physical disorders, is flawed (144–47). The concept of "mental illness" is not a scientific concept that captures something that is simply given in the world, but a socially constructed concept, they argue. Supposed mental illness is diagnosed using lists of symptoms created by committees of psychiatrists who do not always agree with one another. After that, individual psychiatrists will disagree about how those lists should be applied to individual patients, so that individual diagnoses are based largely on the subjective judgments of psychiatrists. And, although the psychiatric profession has searched for underlying biological or genetic causes for many conditions, there is, as they put it, "still no definitive 'laboratory test' for any specific mental illness" (Wilson and Beresford 2002, 147).[13] Wilson and Beresford do not deny that people experience "very real mental and emotional distress" (144), but maintain that such distress is experienced by all people and can vary as well as ebb and flow over the course of a lifetime in response to different situations.

The notion of mental illness, however, presupposes that mental illness is an individual defect within a specific person and is permanent, so that people can be neatly divided into the categories of "normal" and "mentally ill" (Wilson and Beresford 2002, 144). Wilson and Beresford go on to criticize the standard social models of disability (see the introduction) for assuming that impairment is a biological characteristic at all. Instead, they support the view that impairment itself is socially constructed (155).

This argument suggests that Wasserman's attempt to get around the suspicious and socially defined nature of the concept of impairment by appealing to smaller facts or categories of impairment will not work, because smaller categories of impairment are also socially defined. Just as the concept of "impairment" captures a particular socially defined way of characterizing bodies, so the concept of "mental illness" captures a particular socially defined way of characterizing some of their distress.

Facts and Hence Identities (Out There) Are Socially Defined

Wasserman's attempt to appeal to smaller facts of impairment as a way of avoiding the socially defined nature of the concept of "impairment" also fails because *facts* themselves are socially defined. African philosopher Ifeanyi A. Menkiti (1984) has argued that facts are socially constructed because they are constituted by the languages in which they are expressed. In his classic defense of African communalism and the view that a person's identity is essentially social or communally defined, Menkiti emphasizes the role that languages—which, as he notes, "belong to this or that social group" (172)—play in constructing a person's identity. The individual comes to identify himself "as a durable, more or less permanent fact of this world" (7), Menkiti says, by reference "to the language which he speaks . . . which is no small factor in the constitution of his mental dispositions and attitudes." As a result, Menkiti says, "the sense of self-identity which the individual comes to possess cannot be made sense of except by reference to these collective facts" (172).[14]

Although Menkiti talks about a person's self-identity, because the identities he has in mind are "facts," as he puts it, they are the kinds of identities that define someone *out there* as an object, and so could be used by an individual him- or herself or by others to define the individual. Thus, Menkiti is arguing, people's identities (out there) are determined as facts in the world, but since languages—which are social—shape the facts that we perceive, identities themselves are shaped by the social. It would follow from Menkiti's argument that accounts of people's identities that appeal to smaller facts of impairment are also socially defined.

Menkiti does not really explain how language shapes the facts that we perceive—either about our own identities, as he suggests, or others' identities, as I would add. He goes on instead to defend the "processual," as he puts it (172), or normative conception of the self that is embedded in some traditional African cultures, according to which personhood is an honorific status that has to be earned over time in a community—a concept of "person" similar to the definition of personhood offered by the Punan Bah people of Malaysia (see chapter 3). This notion of personhood takes the concept of "person" to be both descriptive and prescriptive—as Hegel suggested concepts are generally. It both describes what a person *is like*, and *prescribes* what a person *should* be like, or what a *good* instance of a person would be like. In this view, being a genuine person is a *process* (hence the term *processual*), because a person is not just someone who meets a certain description, but someone who also lives up to the community's standards of what a good or accomplished version that description (i.e., of a person) should be like (we will return to this topic in chapter 7).

Languages Determine the Facts That We Perceive

Although Menkiti does not really explain his claim that language determines the facts—and hence the identities—that we perceive, the work of the philosopher of science Norwood Russell Hanson (1969) supports Menkiti's claim. Hanson argues that facts themselves are socially constructed because they are always shaped by the languages in which they are expressed. As he puts it, "The character of what we call 'the facts' is affected fundamentally by the logical-grammatical peculiarities of the language in which those facts are expressed. Those peculiarities provide a 'set,' as it were, a context in which the world looks one way as opposed to another way, or in terms of which the facts are construed in one way rather than in another" (183). He did not claim that language *produces* what we see or think about, but rather that it *forms* or *organizes* what we perceive as the facts. As he puts it, "the (logico-grammatical) form of language exercises some formative control over our thinking and over our perceiving, and over what we are inclined to state as the facts (and indeed *how* we state those facts)" (184). Our languages, he suggests, "screen the world into two conceptual hemispheres, the noticed and the unnoticed" (184).

Hanson speculates, for instance, that people who did not have a number system in their language—who counted only "one, two, three, few, many," for instance—would perceive different facts about the world (181). Philosopher of science Jesse Prinz (2014), who argues for the view that language imposes a structure on our perceptions of reality, cites a study conducted with the Pirahã people, who do not have words for numbers. The study suggests that members of the Pirahã people were able to keep track of quantities up to two or three items, but had difficulty tracking the number of items after four (186). For them, as Hanson (1969) speculated might happen, the fact that, to use Hanson's examples, John's Chapel has four spires or a gallon has eight pints would be inexpressible (181). Prinz (2014) goes on to discuss other studies that suggest that color words in various languages as well as the grammatical gender of words in certain languages, such as German and Spanish, can affect how people perceive the world. As Prinz concludes, "The way we divide categories and experience the world is not fixed by what's out there or by what is innately specified within. Learning, including linguistic mastery, can impose a structure on reality that is not biologically inevitable" (190).

Facts Are Theory-Laden, or Presuppose Socially Learned Commitments about What the World Is Like

Hanson (1969) argues that facts are theory-laden in the sense that they presuppose commitments about what the world is like—commitments that are provided by what we learn when we learn languages. These commitments can be captured in sets of *that* clauses (193). We can see Hanson's point by returning to Wilson and Beresford's criticism of the concept of "mental illness" for a moment. Wilson and Beresford do not deny that people experience very real distress. What they deny is that this distress is best captured by the concept of "mental illness," or that there is a "fact" of mental illness, given the theoretical commitments associated with that fact. We can capture the theoretical commitments of the concept or fact of mental illness in a series of *that* clauses based on Wilson and Beresford's analysis: *that* the distress is mental or emotional, *that* it is a defect within the individual, *that* it is like a physical disorder, *that* it is permanent and fixed, *that* it is one side of a dichotomous pair according to which someone is either "normal" or (permanently) "mentally ill," and so on. Such *that* clauses are examples of the sorts of theoretical commitments that are embedded in the concept of "mental illness." These embedded beliefs, to use Hanson's (1969) words, "provide the logical matrices through which we *see* the world" (196), and that we learn when we learn the concept of "mental illness." The *distress*—as part of an account of what it is like for someone to move about in the world—is real, but what the distress is like—where it is located, what its sources or causes are, what kind of thing it is, its relationship to other ways in which people move about in the world, what one should do in response to it—is determined by the associated *that* clauses we use to perceive the world and that are provided by our societies when we learn languages.

As author and journalist Andrew Solomon—who has researched what we would call depression around the world—suggested in an interview for *The Guardian*, "Depression exists universally, but the ways that it's understood, conceptualized or even experienced can vary a great deal from culture to culture" (Leach 2015). He notes that Western-trained mental health workers who traveled around the world to provide psychological assistance after crises were sometimes sent away by local people who thought the Westerners did more harm than good. A Rwandan man who ran an organization that worked with women raising children born of rape as a result of genocide complained to Solomon that the Westerners' approach was intrusive and re-traumatizing. "Their practice did not involve being outside in the sun where you begin to feel better. There was no music or drumming to get your blood flowing again. There was no sense that everyone had taken the day off so that the entire community could come together to try to lift you up and bring you back to joy," the Rwandan man said, according to Solomon. "Instead they would take people one at a time into these dingy little rooms and have them sit around for an hour or so and talk about bad things that had happened to them. We had to ask them to leave" (Leach 2015). As journalist Ethan Watters, whose book, *Crazy Like Us: The Globalization of the American Psyche*, criticizes the Western steamrolling of indigenous understandings of mental health and madness around the world, told *The Guardian*'s Anna Leach (2015),

> In the west a soldier coming home might be troubled by their battlefield trauma. They think of the PTSD [post-traumatic stress disorder] as a sickness in their mind and they take time away from responsibilities to heal. That makes sense to us and it's neither wrong nor right but conforms to our beliefs about PTSD. For a Sri Lankan, to take time away from their social group makes no sense because it is through their place in that group that they find their deepest sense of themselves.

Notice that Watters's description of what the soldier thinks he or she should do in response to the distress echoes the "sick role" often ascribed to disabled people, especially the assumption that people should give up their usual social responsibilities (see chapter 3).

Bodily Features or Conditions Are Socially Defined

Hanson's argument against regarding facts as independent of the social will apply generally to any account of disability that appeals to objective bodily features. The philosopher Elizabeth Barnes (2016), for instance, rejects naturalistic accounts of disability (13–21) as well as the distinction between *impairment* and *disability* (21) in favor of what she calls "a moderate social constructionism," according to which "disability is socially constructed" based on "objective features of bodies" (38). According to her account, which is intended to define only physical disability (2), someone is disabled if he or she is in some bodily state that—and here is the social constructivism—the disability rights movement classifies, as least in some contexts, as the sort of physical condition for which the movement is seeking to promote justice (46). Not every person in the same type of state will necessarily be disabled—some people with asthma, for instance, may be disabled (in severe cases) while some may not be (in mild cases). And some people with one condition may be disabled given their context while others in the same condition may, in a different context, not be disabled (Barnes 2016, 47–48).

Still, Barnes suggests, whether or not someone is really disabled is determined by what his or her body is like. As Barnes (2016) writes, "The question of whether someone is disabled ought to be a question of what their body is (really) like. . . . It's a matter of whether they in fact have particular bodily features" (38). It is true, she says, that our society determines whether some particular bodily features are *important* to us and hence are used to classify people, or, put another way, it is true that which bodily features are used to classify people "is due to the way we think about bodies" (38). Still, she says, while societies determine which bodily features are important, they do not determine which bodily features *there are*. Whether someone has particular objective bodily features determines, in part, whether someone is disabled. As she writes, "Whether you are disabled is in part determined by what your body is (objectively) like" (38).

As Hanson's argument suggests, however, our languages and societies do not merely determine which bodily features or states are important to us; they determine which objective features or states—which smaller facts of impairment or bodily conditions—there are at all. What someone's body is objectively like, or what facts there are about someone's features, are all socially defined.

CONCLUSION

The concept of impairment as a purely objective condition is socially defined. It was invented by European cultures during a particular time period, did not exist in the way we understand it today in the Middle Ages or even up until the 1790s in Europe, as Admiral Horatio Nelson's biography suggests, and did/does not exist in many traditional cultures at all. Wasserman's attempt to get around the socially defined and hence suspicious nature of the concept of "impairment" by appealing to smaller categories or "facts" of impairment as well as Barnes's appeal to supposedly objective bodily states also fail, because the facts (or states) that we perceive are already shaped by what we learn as members of our societies, particularly when we learn languages. As Hanson (1969) remarks, "Given the thesis that changes in our language (and, *ipso facto*, changes in our conceptual framework) can change our appreciation of the nature of the world, the notion of *fact* is no antithesis, antidote, or corrective to this thesis" (198). Insisting that there are smaller categories or facts of impairment or objective bodily features or conditions is no antithesis, antidote, or corrective to the thesis that languages shape the facts that we perceive. As Oyěwùmí (1997) writes, "Language carries with it the world-sense of a people" (28). *We* describe people in other times or other cultures as blind or missing parts of arms or as having *spina bifida*[15] because that is how we speak and cut up the world, but our descriptions tell us little about how the people in those other times or cultures would have cut up the world or spoken, what facts they would have perceived.

Moreover, as disability activists would remind us—and as I will return to later (in chapter 5)—our own descriptions or "diagnoses" tell us little about what a person's life can be like, or what the person can do. Our "facts" are a restricted or perhaps even distorted range of facts. Insisting that there are simply *facts* about people's bodies or physical conditions does not overcome the socially defined nature of those facts. As we will see next, appeals to biology will not support the notion of a purely objective body either, because biology itself is just one of the concepts and sets of beliefs that shape the facts that we perceive.

5

The Socially Constructed Body in Biology

In the United States or Canada today and in many Western countries, the first question often asked about a new baby is "is it a boy or girl?" In many hospitals, volunteers knit little pink and blue hats, and babies born at the hospital are given a hat that matches their biological sex. In traditional Yoruba society in Africa, however, that question would never be asked and such color-coded items would not be given, because, according to feminist scholar and sociologist Oyèrónké Oyěwùmí (1997), the traditional Yoruba did not regard babies as having a sex at all.

Traditional Yoruba recognized, of course, that people had different roles in the process of human reproduction, and they had words to distinguish those roles: *obinrin* (the ones who have babies) and *okùnrin* (the ones who do not have babies). But because children have no role in reproduction, these words applied only to adults, and never to children (Oyěwùmí 1997, 33–34). The Yoruba word for *offspring, oyo*, was also sex- and gender-neutral (40–41), as were most other nouns and pronouns, and even proper names (40–42). Indeed, Samuel Johnson, an early twentieth-century cultural anthropologist, reported in 1921 that, when Yoruba translators tried to use the Yoruba language to express the idea of sex, they ended up having to invent words that made no sense to ordinary Yoruba people at the time (Oyěwùmí 1997, 41; Johnson and Johnson 2010, xxxvii).

The difference between the traditional Yoruba view and the Western view is that Westerners now conceive of people according to the discipline of biology. They perceive human beings in terms of development and functioning, with only two, opposed, biological sexes. Together, these beliefs lead us to regard babies as either (immature) women or (immature) men, even though babies do not play any role in human reproduction. From the point of view of biology, then, there is a fact about whether a baby is a girl or boy. For traditional Yoruba, by contrast, because children have no role in human reproduction, the fact is that no child can be an *obinrin* (one who has babies) or *okùnrin* (one who does not have babies). This example illustrates how the discipline of biology shapes the facts that we perceive. It also suggests that, given different socially shared beliefs, one could cut up the world differently and perceive different facts. Because biology, as a set of socially shared beliefs, shapes the facts that we perceive, including about the body, there is no such thing *out there* as a purely objective, pre-social, natural, *biological* body.

This claim continues the argument, begun in chapters 3 and 4, for the thesis that, in terms of the first dimension of embodiment, personal body or "body-self," to use anthropologists Nancy Scheper-Hughes and Margaret M. Lock's phrase (see the introduction), there is *no* purely objective, pre-social, natural, physical, or biological personal body. That is, not only is there no purely objective personal body *in experience* (see chapter 3), but there is also no purely objective personal body *out there*, as an object (see the introduction for more on the distinction between the *experience* of the body and the body *out there*, as an object). According to our accounts and reasoning in chapter 4, our societies' languages form and organize the facts that we perceive, including about people's identities as objects out there. Whether people have impairment, smaller *facts* of impairment or certain bodily conditions are all socially constructed. This chapter builds on that insight to show how there is also no purely objective, pre-social, natural, *biological* personal body out there, and hence no *biological* impairments, because biology itself is socially created.

There have been interesting genealogical critiques, inspired by the work of the French philosopher and social theorist Michel Foucault, of the Western concept of biological impairment and of biology in general. Genealogical arguments trace the history or origin (i.e., the genealogy) of concepts or beliefs as well as the social, economic, and political conditions that made the development of the concepts or beliefs possible. By revealing the social, economic, and political conditions that gave rise to a concept or set of beliefs, these arguments cast doubt on the idea that the concept or beliefs capture a purely objective reality, or a reality that is not already shaped and defined by societies and cultures. Since the concepts or beliefs were invented by particular groups of people to serve particular social, economic, or political interests, they are inseparable from the social interests that gave rise to them, are tainted by those interests, and so are socially defined. Genealogical arguments have been offered to show that the Western concept of biological impairment and the discipline of biology are rooted in and hence tainted by particular social, economic, and political conditions. According to these arguments, there is *no* purely objective, natural, pre-social *biological* impairment or body, because the biological body and impairment are socially defined.

Philosophy of science as well as African philosophy and scholarship also suggest that the discipline of biology is part of the language and learning that shapes the facts that we perceive. From these perspectives, there is no purely objective, natural, pre-social *biological* body or impairment, because the concept or discipline of "biology" itself is a socially shared set of beliefs that shapes the facts that we perceive. Indeed, as disability studies scholars have suggested, the emphasis in Western culture on biology and on (supposed) facts of biological impairment leads us to focus only on a restricted and distorted range of facts.

Chapter outline:

➤ A Genealogical Argument against Biological Impairment
➤ A Genealogical Argument against Biology
➤ Biology Is Tainted by Social and Political Interests
➤ Arguing against and Pointing beyond Biology
➤ Confronting Some Objections
➤ Conclusion

A GENEALOGICAL ARGUMENT AGAINST BIOLOGICAL IMPAIRMENT

- Medicine, Biology, and the Expression of Bio-Power
- Bio-Power Defines the Concept of Biological Impairment
- Aligning Tremain's Account with the Accounts of Earlier Chapters
- Another Really Social, Social Model of Disability
- Government Surveys and Questionnaires Do Not Find Impairment; They Define It
- Do People Deny Being Impaired Only to Avoid a Stigmatized Status, or Are They Employing a Different Definition of *Impairment*?

Beginning in the 1960s, Foucault suggested that, if we trace the genealogy or evolution of various scientific concepts, or the ways in which those concepts developed in the context of social institutions in Western societies, we will come to see not only that the concepts were socially constructed but also that they were constructed by political elites to maintain control over people and over societies as a whole. For instance, he suggested that if we look at the evolution of the concept of "mental illness" in relation to the growth of madhouses and other institutions in Europe in the nineteenth century, we will see not only that the concept of "mental illness" was constructed at a particular point and in particular places in history, but also that it was constructed to control those who might challenge values and beliefs that allowed the capitalist elites of the day to maintain power.[1]

Medicine, Biology, and the Expression of Bio-Power

Philosopher and scholar of disability Shelley Tremain (2001) uses Foucault's genealogical strategy to suggest that the concept of biological impairment as well as the concept's assumption that there is a pre-social, *biological* body, are both socially defined. She suggests that the growth of the medical profession and its clinical discourse about the human body beginning in the late eighteenth century created both that body as well as the belief that there is a socially independent reality of that body (618–19). Medicine and biology were "technologies of normalization" that developed to create, identify, classify, divide (into groups) and control "social anomalies," including people who came to be defined as impaired (619). "Bio-medicine" (620), the practice of medicine rooted in the discipline of biology, is thus an expression of what Foucault had called "bio-power" (618), which is an assertion of social and political power that is rooted in and justified by claims about biology.

The discipline of biology was used to convince people to categorize themselves and others based on their bodies—to classify bodies in certain ways—and to believe that the categories were natural, inevitable, and inescapable. This belief led people to be more likely to do, and to encourage others to do—on their own and without coercion—what the dominant group in society said people who belong to that category are supposed to do. As Veterans Administration research scientists Jeanne Hayes and Elizabeth "Lisa" M. Hannold (2007) put the point in an article examining the social control that doctors assert over disabled people, Foucault's work shows that "institutional standards in and of themselves do not exert power over the lives of people. The power of institutional standards originates when people interpret their world in accordance to these standards and elect to abide by them" (357). Bio-power's definition of the body under the discipline of biology thus allowed and made it easier for dominant social and political groups to discipline, control, and constrain people. It produced, as Tremain (2001) puts it, "a 'docile' body, that is, one that can be subjected, used, transformed and improved" (622).

Bio-Power Defines the Concept of Biological Impairment

As part of the assertion of bio-power, bio-medicine invented and defined the notion of biological impairment as well as the belief that impairment is a socially independent, "real" entity (Tremain 2001, 623). Bio-medicine's definition of disabled people as permanently diseased (see chapter 2) and its consignment of them to the "sick" or "handicapped" role (see chapter 3) is a form of social control. As psychologist and education scholar Michelle Fine and bioethicist and disability studies scholar Adrienne Asch (1988) suggest, the sick or handicapped role "compels the occupant to suspend other activities until recovered, to concentrate on getting expert therapy, to follow instructions, to get well, and only then to resume normal life" (12).

Bio-medicine's exertion of control over disabled people is starkly illustrated by the life of Joseph Merrick, who had exhibited himself in freak shows as "the Elephant Man" in the late 1880s. As we saw (in chapter 2), it was Dr. Frederick Treves and his colleagues at the London Hospital who sought to diagnose Merrick "as suffering from an identifiable disease that only medical professionals could interpret" (Durbach 2010, 45) and confined Merrick to the hospital. After living in segregated and isolated conditions in private hospital rooms for four years, Merrick committed suicide in 1890. Defining "impairment" as a real, biological, given, natural, and fixed identity from which people cannot escape thus made people easier to control and constrain (Tremain 2001, 622–23).

Contrary to that belief, however, Tremain (2001) suggests, biological impairment is not a socially independent, real entity, but an expression of bio-power—a concept that was socially created and defined by a particular class of people for particular social and political purposes, about which we should be suspicious. As Tremain puts it, impairment is "an historical artifact of this regime of knowledge/power" (623).

Aligning Tremain's Account with the Accounts of Earlier Chapters

Does Tremain's historical account of the invention of the concept of biological impairment as we define it today align with the accounts I offered in earlier chapters, which took the economic system of capitalism to be centrally important to the development of the concept of disability? In earlier chapters I suggested that, beginning in the late Middle Ages, the spread of capitalism and particularly of the urban system of work in which people were "clocking on/off" and being paid for the time they worked, together with a narrowing of what counted as work or as genuine economic activity under capitalism, increasingly excluded people who were regarded as less productive and hence more expensive workers. Such people were defined as "*dis*-abled" or as unable to work, which reduced their social power. Under these conditions, "able-bodiedness" came to be understood in terms of the ability to labor in the capitalist wage market.

Admiral Horatio Nelson (see chapter 4), who was active in the British Navy in the 1790s and early 1800s and continued to be viewed as suited for his job after his injuries, was able-bodied in this sense. Still, even by Nelson's time, medical doctors were already influential as (supposed) experts on bodies and bodily conditions and as official gatekeepers for services. Nelson was required by the British Navy to submit certificates from doctors substantiating his claim that his right eye was sightless when he applied to receive a pension while home recuperating from his amputation. But he was pressed back into duty once his injury had healed. Thus, although the discipline of biology and practice of medicine were already gaining ground in England by this time, they and the biomedical definition of impairment that they invented, according to Tremain's account, did not yet define Nelson as impaired and as necessarily "dis-abled" or unable to work.

Beginning in the mid- to late eighteenth century, industrial capitalism increased productivity requirements as well as a demand for workers with standardized bodies that could function like machines, thereby progressively excluding people with nonstandard bodies from the capitalist wage market (see chapter 1). This exclusion was reinforced, in the nineteenth century, by the invention of the concept of normalcy within the disciplines of statistics, medicine (chapter 2), and as we can now add, biology. (The term *biology* first appeared in 1802, as we will see below. English and disability studies professor Lennard J. Davis has suggested that the term *normal* was first used in English to mean "common" or "average" in 1840 [see chapter 2].)

Unlike Nelson, who was active almost a hundred years earlier (1790s to early 1800s), Merrick, who had been excluded from the wage market and spent five years living in a workhouse before joining the freak show circuit, was active (in the late 1880s) after the discipline of biology and the concept of normalcy had been developed and the practice of medicine gained further prominence. Still, there were those who rejected the newer view even during Merrick's life, and accounts of his life illustrate the *shift* to new definitions of impairment dominated by the concept of normalcy and bio-medicine (see chapter 2). This is the shift and time period that Tremain's account highlights. So far, then, Tremain's account and the account offered in earlier chapters align.

Philosophically, Tremain's and my accounts can be aligned by noticing the intertwining of class issues with the development of biology and the concept of normalcy. As the discussion of Merrick's history suggested, the class of people who came to assert power through the claims of bio-medicine, which Tremain's account highlights, were the same upper- and middle-class people who, as we saw (chapter 2), benefitted from capitalism and the invention of normalcy. It was not the working-class-bred showman Tom Norman, but Treves, with his ruling-class values and expectations, who regarded Merrick as abnormal (Treves used terms such as *degraded* and *perverted*) and diseased and as "dis-abled" or necessarily unable to work, and defined Merrick as an object only of charity, segregating him in and confining him to the medical institution. It was thus Treves's biomedicalized definition of impairment that helped capitalists avoid having to employ those regarded as less productive employees. Treves's definition also provided work and fame for doctors like Treves and his associates and for medical institutions like the London Hospital (chapter 2).

Socioeconomic class may also have played a role earlier in Nelson's life. Not only the time during which he was active—in the early days of the dominance of medicine and the invention of biology and the concept of normalcy—but also his relatively high social status, based on his background in a moderately well-off family and occupational status as an officer in the navy, probably helped to ensure that he was defined under the older account linking able-bodiedness to the ability to labor. Historian Irina Metzler suggests that there was a tendency in the Middle Ages to regard people of higher status as suited for intellectual work and people of lower status as suited for mechanical and physically demanding work (Metzler 2015, 85). The fact that Nelson's particular injuries did not prevent him from engaging in the predominantly intellectual labor of commanding ships and devising battle strategies (though there were some tasks of his job for which he received help) together with those older, medieval values (to the degree that they still had sway) might help to explain why he continued to be seen as suited for his job.

Another Really Social, Social Model of Disability

Like my approach (see the introduction),[2] Tremain's (2001) approach does not deny that there is a materiality to the body, but suggests, as she puts it, "that the materiality of 'the body' cannot be dissociated from the historically contingent practices that bring it into being, that is, bring it into being as that sort of thing" (621). The disciplines of medicine and biology, which developed during a particular time and in a particular place for particular social and political purposes, are historically contingent: something else could have developed (or they could have been different), and, indeed, other views developed in other times and places, as we will see further below. Instead, the modern, Western disciplines of medicine and biology invented and defined both the concept of the "body," as we understand it today, as well as a set of beliefs about what kind of thing the body is, or about what the body is like.

For Tremain (2001), then, the problem with the classic social models of disability (see the introduction) is that they mistakenly treat impairment and the biological body as given, or suggest that impairment and biology can be identified outside of historically contingent social practices. *Impairment* and *disability* are *both* socially defined, she suggests, or, as she puts it, "impairment has been disability all along" (632). Like me (see the introduction), Tremain offers a *really* social, social model of disability, which regards not only disability but also impairment, as socially defined.

Government Surveys and Questionnaires Do Not Find Impairment; They Define It

Tremain illustrates her view that impairment is socially defined by using the example of a questionnaire that was distributed in the United Kingdom to determine eligibility for government services. Drawing on the work of Margrit Shildrick and

Janet Price (1996, 100–104), Tremain (2001) suggests that the questionnaire distributed to applicants under the UK's Disability Living Allowance welfare policy did not discover supposedly "pre-existing and stable" impairments in people, but asked deeply personal and individual questions (about, e.g., menstrual cycles, fatigue, and difficulty using household appliances) that *constructed* how the abstract concept of impairment should be defined (633).

In the twenty-eight-page questionnaire, Shildrick and Price (1996, 102) report, respondents were required to construct an exhaustive picture of their failed bodies. "What is demanded of her [a respondent]," they write, "is that she should police her own body, and report in intricate detail its failure to meet standards of normalcy" (100). The form's detailed questions, they suggest, meant that "no area of bodily functioning escapes the requirement of total visibility" (102). Because the respondent is required by the form to specify "the minutiae of functional capacity," the form implies that impairment "is a fixed and unchanging state which pre-exists its observation," Shildrick and Price suggest (102).

But the questionnaire did not discover fixed, unchanging, preexisting states that constitute "impairment," Tremain (2001) points out; it *determined* or *defined* both what states there are out there as well as the idea that those states are the states that constitute impairment. Tremain concludes that "through a performance of textual confession ('the more you can tell us, the easier it is for us to get a clear picture of what you need'), the potential recipient [of the allowance] is made a subject of impairment (in addition to being made a subject of the state), and is rendered 'docile,' that is, one to be used, enabled, subjugated and improved" (633). The questionnaire constructed the applicants as impaired subjects who were then expected to passively follow out the roles assigned by the state to those so constructed, such as seeking treatment so that they could be improved.[3]

Tremain's argument that such surveys *construct* and *define* the concept of impairment is reinforced by disability studies scholar and sociologist Irving K. Zola's criticism of the way disability statistics have been collected and used. Zola tells the story of serving on a committee that was charged with increasing the participation of women, minorities, and people with disabilities in the sciences and engineering. The agency sponsoring the committee had been sending out annual surveys asking respondents the question: "Are you physically handicapped?" Only 1–2 percent of respondents had answered "yes" to that question on the survey each year. As Zola (1993) recounts, during a meeting of the subgroup of scientists with disabilities, although "scarcely anyone, including myself," he says, "did not use some obvious assistive device from guide dogs to wheelchairs to canes, braces and hearing aides" (20), the members of the subgroup discovered that not one of them had ever answered "yes" to the question on the survey about whether they were "physically handicapped." Two years later, however, Zola says, when a revised version of the survey asked more specific questions about "the presence of chronic conditions, activity limitations, and the use of assistive devices," the percentage of scientists and engineers indicating that they were disabled on the survey "jumped nearly 10-fold" (20–21). One possible explanation for this jump is that, as Tremain might say, by specifying what counts as "impairment," the new survey *constructed* more of the respondents as impaired and hence as disabled according to the survey itself. There is another possible explanation, however.

Do People Deny Being Impaired Only to Avoid a Stigmatized Status, or Are They Employing a Different Definition of *Impairment*?

Zola (1993) suggests that the low number of respondents willing to answer "yes" to the original question about whether they were "physically handicapped" can probably be explained by the fact that disability is disvalued and being disabled is a stigmatized status in our society (20). He goes on to warn that attempts to measure the presence of disability are often affected by such "unarticulated value assumptions" (21). According to this explanation, people did not answer "yes" on the original survey because they wanted to avoid applying the disvalued and stigmatized category of disability to themselves. But when the survey asked questions about chronic conditions, activity limitations, and the use of assistive devices, Zola is suggesting, the respondents truthfully reported that they were disabled.

In a similar way, the philosopher Elizabeth Barnes (2016) has argued that claims such as "I've never thought of myself as disabled" are not claims that we should grant as true, but are best understood as attempts to avoid the stigmatized status of disability, which regards disability as "nothing more than a loss or lack" (34–35). On this view, Zola and his colleagues were truly "handicapped" all along, but failed to answer "yes" on the original iteration of the survey only because they were resisting the stigmatized status of impairment, handicap, and disability.

People may well work to avoid ascribing a stigmatized status to themselves, and such avoidances may help to explain the low number of respondents willing to answer "yes" to the question about whether they were handicapped. However, inspired by Tremain's argument, it would not follow that Zola and his colleagues answered "no" on the survey *only* to avoid a stigmatized status.

A professor I know who would appear, to outside observers, to have some physical activity limitations once told me that he never considered himself disabled because he has always been able do any activities that he regarded as important to him and to his identity, particularly his scholarly activities. From his point of view, he has no "impairments." Perhaps the scientists on the subcommittee who, like Zola, had answered "no" on the original surveys, did not consider themselves handicapped for the same reason. After all, they were successful scientists or engineers, and so were perhaps, like the professor, not prevented from doing anything of value to them. Perhaps, given their own understanding of what constituted impairment or "handicap," they did not regard themselves as "handicapped." From this point of view, the second iteration of the survey—which asked specific questions about chronic conditions, activity limitations, and assistive devices and led to higher numbers of respondents indicating that they were disabled—did not "discover" impairments that had always been there, but constructed and imposed on the respondents a definition of *impairment* that led more respondents to consider themselves "impaired"—and so as "disabled"—under that definition.

Indeed, Barnes (2016) suggests that "we are, all of us, limited by our bodies" (186). As she explains the view, "Whatever way your body is, there will be bad effects of having a body that's like that" (186). There is always something that individual bodies cannot do, or cannot do easily. "But the disabled body," Barnes continues, "is a pathologized body" (186). The disabled body is a body whose particular disadvantages or bad effects are pathologized or treated as an illness or disease. If every body has some bad effects or limitations, then to insist that the particular limitations of Zola or his colleagues were "impairments" that defined them as handicapped or disabled is precisely to impose a special label on the particular limitations of the scientists and engineers, and hence, again, to impose a concept or definition of *impairment* on them, and not simply to recognize the presence of some supposedly real, preexisting impairments.

As Michael, an urban, working-class, black student remarked,

> "Everyone is born with something, so it's not like a disability. People say, you have dyslexia da-da-da, but to me it really didn't do anything. I just had to work harder [at school]. . . . You're normal just like everyone else. Coz in life, people with learning disabilities *don't* have to work harder. It doesn't take a genius to work at McDonald's." (Connor 2006, 155, ll. 11–15)

Michael is well aware of the stigmatizing effects of being labeled as having a learning disability and being shuttled off to special education classes ("you hear all the bad things about the special ed. kids," he says [155, ll. 38–39]), but his denial of his impairment is not just an attempt to avoid those stigmatizing effects. He is rejecting the biomedical understanding of impairment—according to which impairment is an inherent, pathological difference that makes someone abnormal—in favor of an alternative definition that takes account of social factors—particularly, given the reference to a job at McDonald's, his own working-class status, as David J. Connor, the author of the article recounting Michael's story, points out (2006, 159). Interestingly, Michael's definition also echoes the older view expressed in the working-class showman Norman's biography of Merrick (see chapter 2), which linked disability to the inability to work and be self-supporting.

As a result, to insist that when Michael denies that he is impaired he is merely trying to avoid the stigmatizing effects of being regarded as impaired, or to insist that he is really impaired, in spite of his claims to the contrary, is to *impose* a definition of *impairment* on him. The claim that people's denials that they are impaired (or disabled) are *always* an expression of "internalized oppression or false consciousness" is thus, as Shakespeare and Watson (2001) suggest, "patronizing and oppressive" (20). Michael is not internalizing oppression by agreeing that impaired people are bad and then denying his own status as impaired, or hanging on to a (supposedly) false belief about himself as not impaired; he is challenging the dominant (white, middle-class) culture's very definition of *impairment*.

Zola's observations can therefore be used to reinforce Tremain's suggestion that surveys or questionnaires intended simply to measure respondents' (supposed) impairment actually construct a definition of *impairment* and impose it onto respondents.

A GENEALOGICAL ARGUMENT AGAINST BIOLOGY

- Biology Is Tainted by Social and Political Interests

Tremain's suggestion that biological impairment is socially and politically defined and hence suspicious is further reinforced by the work of philosopher Ladelle McWhorter (2009), whose approach is also grounded in the genealogical method of Foucault. McWhorter argues that *biology*—a term first used in 1802—shifted how human beings were characterized in the West. Whereas the discipline of natural history, which preceded biology, focused on the morphology or visible structures of natural beings, biology defines living beings in terms of *functions* and *development* (97–98). The discipline of biology—and particularly the work of Georges Cuvier—went on to invent the science of functional and developmental norms (99–100). These norms were then used to characterize supposedly inferior races as developmentally stunted: "as retarded, as primitives or lifelong children constitutionally incapable of adult self-discipline or full participation as citizens in a democratic society, a developmental incapacity that was held to be physiologically and inevitably heritable" (101). McWhorter uses her analysis to suggest that the development of biology redefined racism as a form of prejudice and discrimination against the abnormal (32).

In 1854, for instance, McWhorter (2009) notes, Drs. Samuel George Morton and J. C. Nott, along with the Egyptologist George Gliddon, published the sixth edition of the book *Types of Mankind*, in which they suggest that civilization and morality were not products of environment, but of biological development. Members of (supposedly) inferior races were developmentally arrested or less well developed. They were like animals, (supposedly) primitive or savage ancestors, or like children, and "were best treated accordingly," as McWhorter describes the view (123). Differences in visible morphology between races were therefore no longer regarded as what defined race. Instead, those visible differences were merely outward markers of different degrees of development (123).

By the end of the nineteenth century, racial difference was now defined as biological or developmental difference. As McWhorter (2009) writes, "Integrated into the science of biology . . . racial difference was, essentially, developmental difference. Appearance was simply a manifestation of a developmental process" (139). Around the same time, "feebleminded" people, "idiots," or "imbeciles" also came to be defined, from a biological perspective, as "arrested in their development" (135). Differences in terms of physical and mental functioning or behavior were thus regarded as signs of a deeper biological and developmental difference, in which members of inferior races, mentally deficient people, and criminals "bore the stigma of arrested development" (139). Eventually, the class of (supposedly) developmentally stunted people, McWhorter says, included "imbeciles, criminals, prostitutes, consumptives, Africans, Asians, Mexicans, Jews, Irishmen, masturbators, deaf-mutes, epileptics, psychopaths, and shiftless Appalachian paupers" (139–40).

According to this new form of biologically based "racism against the abnormal," to use the phrase introduced by Foucault (2003, 316), unlike children, who were developmentally immature generally, members of biologically marked inferior races, criminals, and other groups of (supposedly) deficient people grew up to be sexually mature adults, even if they remained developmentally arrested in all other respects. This sexual maturity and ability, as adults, to reproduce (people like) *themselves* made them a threat to the superior, Nordic race. As McWhorter (2009) describes the view, members of these groups were "children in quasi-adult bodies, stunted and marked in various physical ways by their biological incompletion and deficient in reason and restraint but with all the drives and desires of sexual maturity" (139). And as "all children out of control, throwbacks, savages, and degenerates," they "posed a threat to the continued purity of highly evolved Nordic germ plasm" (140). This claim that (supposedly) abnormal people were threats to the Nordic race would not have been possible without the invention of biology. As McWhorter suggests, it would have been "unthinkable in the absence of the biological sciences, clinical medicine, and institutional psychiatry that arose in the last half of the nineteenth century" (140).

The invention of biology thus gives rise to worries about (supposedly) developmentally stunted populations generally, as well as to attempts by the eugenics movement (see chapter 2) to control the bodies and particularly the sexuality of such (supposedly) developmentally stunted populations—immigrants, women, blacks, "feebleminded" people, and sexually abnormal people (McWhorter 2009, 150–95). By the beginning of the twentieth century, McWhorter says, the primary method for managing bodies and protecting the "glorious Anglo-Saxon future" (199) was through sexuality: "sexuality was the invention, the technological apparatus, that would enable scientific racism to operationalize itself as the eugenics movement" (199). The whole, sorry, socially invented apparatus, McWhorter suggests, was made possible by the invention of biology and its emphasis on function and development: "Development was the fundamental concept in virtually every human science of the day," McWhorter writes. "Reality was development—patterns of change that could be measured, projected, and normed" (199).

Biology Is Tainted by Social and Political Interests

Because biology and its understanding of reality in terms of functions and development was invented as part of the questionable social practices of "racism against the abnormal" and the eugenics movement, McWhorter is suggesting, claims about biology should be regarded with suspicion. Tracing the development of biology and its role in these questionable social practices does not refute the claim that there is a purely objective, biological body, but, as McWhorter (2006) has said in an unpublished lecture, it does "undermine claims to definitive knowledge of the body by creating awareness—some might say a suspicion—that current claims are no more 'untainted' by power relations than the claims of previous generations and that they, too, may pass away" (4). By revealing that the discipline of biology was not only socially constructed or invented by a particular society in a particular time and place but also invented for particular, unjust, and hence suspicious social and political reasons, McWhorter's arguments cast doubt on the suggestion that the claims of biology are untainted by social interests and hence purely and objectively true. They suggest, instead, that biological beliefs are socially defined, and so may be supplanted by other beliefs.

ARGUING AGAINST AND POINTING BEYOND BIOLOGY

- A Yoruba Alternative to Western Body-Reasoning or Bio-Logic
- Biology Is Theory-Laden and So Is Socially Defined
- Western Sciences Are Socially Defined
- Scientific Descriptions Focus on a Restricted and Distorted Range of Facts

While McWhorter's argument does not definitively show that the claims of biology are socially defined, we can use the work of philosophers of science Norwood Russell Hanson and Jesse Prinz (see also chapter 4) to help establish the socially defined nature of biology. In his argument against those who hold that human beings have an innate conception of biology, Prinz (2014) suggests that infants' observations of people and animals moving around under their own power allows infants to draw a distinction between living beings and inanimate objects. However, it takes time for children to learn other biological facts (Prinz 2014, 95–96). It takes longer for children to learn that plants are alive, Prinz says, and they will sometimes continue to believe that some inanimate objects are alive, such as cars or even buttons. Another example of a biological mistake that Prinz offers is that children have mistaken beliefs about illness: "Four-year-olds think that bad moral behavior is as likely to make you vulnerable to getting sick as poor diet" (96). Some biological facts are difficult to learn by observation, and "do not come naturally," Prinz says (96). "Facts that are difficult to observe require instruction" (96).

However, facts that are difficult to observe and require instruction are also theory-laden, as Hanson would say, or presuppose commitments about what the world is like (see chapter 4), and hence are shaped by our cultures and languages. As Scheper-Hughes and Lock as well as some African philosophers have suggested, in cultures that do not make sharp distinctions between the natural and supernatural/spiritual, the body and mind, or the self and others, people often believe that bad moral behavior can make you sick. In many traditional cultures, bad moral behavior can lead to strained social relations, and strained social relations can make you sick. As Scheper-Hughes and Lock (1987) write, "Many ethnomedical systems do not logically distinguish body, mind, and self, and therefore illness cannot be situated in mind or body alone. Social relations are also understood as a key contributor to individual health and illness" (21). In belief systems that do not make a sharp distinction between body and mind or the natural and supernatural, bad moral behavior and poor social relations can make you sick.

African philosopher Godwin S. Sogolo (2003), who examines the belief in some traditional African cultures that bad moral behavior and poor social relations can make people sick (196–98), suggests that all cultures' concepts of (what we would call) illness are tied to their other, socially learned beliefs about the world. As he puts it, "In every culture, what counts as an acceptable conception of illness is tied to the people's general conception of health and disease. To a great extent, it is dependent on their overall world-view" (195).[4] Western claims that illness is biological and that bad moral behavior therefore cannot make you sick are no different. They are part of a socially learned and hence socially defined worldview that separates the body/nature from mind/spirit/supernatural and conceives of causes and the world in terms of socially isolated bodies or bodies-alone and biology. The assumptions of biology then lead us, as Hanson would say (see chapter 4), to construe the facts one way rather than another. Like Western societies' body- and biologically based racism against the abnormal and eugenic beliefs, Western beliefs about illness are thus part of a form of, to use terms borrowed from Oyěwùmí (1997), "body-reasoning" or "bio-logic" (5, 11).

A Yoruba Alternative to Western Body-Reasoning or Bio-Logic

Oyěwùmí (1997) has criticized the Western emphasis on "body-reasoning" or "bio-logic," or on what she describes as "the ubiquity of biologically rooted explanations for difference in Western social thought and practices," as well as "the extent to which biological explanations are found compelling" (8). Oyěwùmí's criticisms are directed primarily against Western feminists, who, she suggests, have tended to assume that sex and gender are culturally universal categories (15, 31–32). But because the social model of disability's distinction between impairment and disability (see the introduction) closely mirrors the traditional sex/ gender distinction, Oyěwùmí's criticism of body-reasoning or bio-logic and claim that sex is not a universal category can be used to call the concept of biological impairment into question as well.

Like the sex/gender distinction, as scholars of disability have noted (e.g., Tremain 2001, 623; Shakespeare and Watson 2001, 10), the impairment/disability distinction also rests on a division between supposedly biological characteristics (impairment, sex) and socially constructed characteristics (disability, gender). Oyěwùmí's claim that there can be worldviews that are not based on the body or on biology and in which there is no biological concept of sex therefore suggests that there can be a world in which there is no biological concept of impairment. Her discussion also points toward what a world without biologically rooted distinctions between people might be like.

Oyěwùmí (1997) maintains that, unlike under Western body-reasoning or bio-logic, the traditional Yoruba social order "is not focused on the body" (14), or is not based on the body at all (36, 42). Because the terms *obinrin* (the ones who have babies) and *okùnrin* (the ones who do not have babies) applied only to adults, being an *obinrin* or *okùnrin* was not conceived of as a biological or sexual essence that determined an individual's identity.[5] Instead, she suggests, traditional Yoruba society defined people not in terms of bodies or biology, but in terms of social relations (12–13, 36). The most important determinant of someone's identity in traditional Yoruba society was seniority (42), which was defined by when someone joined (came inside) the compound or lineage, either through birth or marriage (46). The Yoruba conception of seniority was thus "relational and situational," rather than bodily or biological, since whether one is senior or junior depends on social relations as well as on who happens to be present at any particular time (42).

Because traditional Yoruba society does not use the body or biology to define people, against the assumptions of Western feminism, Oyěwùmí (1997) suggests, "the Yorùbá social order requires a different kind of map, not a gender map that assumes biology as the foundation of the social" (13). Similarly, we could say, our social order could use a different kind of map, not a disability map that assumes biology or biological impairment as the foundation of the social.

Biology Is Theory-Laden and So Is Socially Defined

Not only was the Western concept of biology invented during a particular time period for particular social and political purposes about which we should be suspicious, as we saw, then, but it is also theory-laden, or presupposes commitments about what the world is like. It is inextricable from a series of *that* clauses of its own that are learned by instruction and expressed in language, and so is itself part of a socially shared worldview and hence is socially defined. Our biology says that animals are alive, that plants are alive, that living beings and bodies are defined in terms of functions and development, that there is a sharp distinction between the natural and supernatural, between self and others, and between the natural and the social, that bad moral behavior cannot make you sick, that human beings have sexual essences, and so on. There may be some *that* clauses human beings will agree on—for example, that people need to eat—but to conceive of *people* or *eating* as "biological" bodies or functions is already to invoke a whole conceptual apparatus that is specific to Western culture and hence socially defined. As Oyěwùmí (1997) puts it, "biology itself is socially constructed, and therefore inseparable from the social" (9).

Western Sciences Are Socially Defined

If the discipline of biology is socially defined and shapes the facts that we perceive, so are the other Western sciences. As Hanson (1969) concludes about scientific inquiry more generally, then, "the logical and grammatical traits of our several scientific languages, notations, and symbol-clusters may affect how we see the world, or what we understand about the world" (183) by leading us to see the world one way, rather than another.[6] Hanson's work suggests that an appeal to *biological* facts in an attempt to avoid suspicions about the concept of impairment fails to avoid the socially constructed nature of biology that makes it suspicious in the first place. If facts are, as Hanson says, determined by language and, we can add, by instruction, then that claim cuts into every language and all societies' instruction, including our sciences. If our languages and instruction were different, then, to paraphrase Hanson, we might come to see different aspects of the world, to think differently about it from the way we do, and to know different facts (182–83). "We" must, as we saw Zola (1991) telling his fellow medical sociologists (chapter 3), "accept at least the metaphor of Foucault and turn our gaze on the body ever more inward" (8), by questioning "further some of the most taken-for-granted and cherished assumptions that allowed us to put the word 'scientist' after our name" (8). Scientists must question the ways in which Western sciences have understood people as well as what (and how) those sciences regard (as) the body.

Scientific Descriptions Focus on a Restricted and Distorted Range of Facts

Indeed, Hanson's claim that languages shape the facts that we perceive by leading us to notice some things but fail to notice others (see chapter 4) explains why, as disability activists would remind us, the scientific descriptions and diagnoses of Western medicine and biology are so unhelpful: by focusing attention on (supposed) biological facts or physical conditions, on individual deficits or dysfunctions, we fail to notice what people can do, or what they could do, given different environments or social practices.

Claire McElvaney (2011), for instance, has suggested that placing the diagnosis of a child's disability at the top of client evaluations and summaries in rehabilitation practice shapes the descriptions of the child's skills as well as the facts that are reported, and leads counselors to assume that a deficit is the result of a disability, whether or not the disability is relevant (203). As McElvaney notes (204), Michael L. Wehmeyer and Nancy W. Garner (2003) found, for example, that the social environment, particularly the ability to make choices, and not IQ, had the largest impact on whether people with intellectual or developmental disabilities were self-determining and autonomous. In these cases, Western scientific languages lead professionals to notice some things and view the world one way, rather than notice other things and view the world in a way that might improve the lives of disabled people.

CONFRONTING SOME OBJECTIONS

- Are Western Science's More Definite Words about the Body or Impairments an Advantage?
- Do Other Cultures Simply Not Have All the Facts?
- Can Individuals Believe Whatever They Want?

Are Western Science's More Definite Words about the Body or Impairments an Advantage?

Perhaps someone will argue that, even if it is true that languages shape the facts that we perceive, Western languages and learning, which have more definite words—words for numbers, for instance—should be regarded as offering a better perception of the world, while languages such as that of the Pirahã people—which, since it does not have words for numbers (see chapter 4) has less definite words—offer worse perceptions. The language of the Pirahã people, for instance, with its less definite words, cannot express the fact that, to use Hanson's example, a gallon has eight pints. Having more definite words, on this view, allows Western languages and learning to perceive facts—including facts about the body and impairment—better than do languages with less definite words.

Hanson (1969) warns, however, that Western languages may not always have more definite words. We must think, he suggests, of the twentieth-century philosopher Ludwig "Wittgenstein's conjecture that there might be people who thought much more definitely than we, and used a variety of words where we use only one" (181). If having more definite words is always an advantage, then non-Western languages with more definite words related to some topic would provide more accurate perceptions of the relevant facts. Indeed, as we saw (in chapter 4), the concept of impairment is a highly abstract and so very indefinite concept.

But Prinz's (2014) work also suggests that there might be situations in which having more definite words may not be an advantage. Research into cross-cultural color perception suggests that the linguistic boundary that English draws between blue and green makes English speakers unable to correctly determine which color chips are more similar to one another, while members of Tarahumara culture, which has only one word for both blue and green, are able to do so (186–87).

For another example, African philosopher Kwasi Wiredu (2003a) has suggested, for instance, that Western philosophy's attempts to offer theories explaining what truth and knowledge are like are sometimes led astray by the distinction in English between *fact* and *truth*—a problem that will not occur in languages, such as Akan, that lack a word for, or concept of, *fact* (240). Philosophers who work in English have sometimes offered theories of truth that say, in effect, that something is true if and only if it corresponds to (or is) a fact. But in a language such as Akan—in which both *fact* and *true* would be translated by the same words,[7] namely, *te saa*, which means "is so"—such a theory of truth amounts to a tautology. It says essentially that something "is so" if and only if it "is so" (Wiredu 2003a, 240).[8] Wiredu grants that explaining the relationship between the concepts of "fact" and "truth" is a philosophical problem for any English speaker, but since other natural languages do not have both these words, "this task is not inescapable for the human mind" (241). He suggests that examining other languages would allow philosophers to distinguish fundamental philosophical issues—such as giving an account of what it is for something to "be so," which is a problem in many different languages—from philosophical issues that might arise in only one language or another (242).

For us, Wiredu's discussion illustrates another way in which having more definite words might not be an advantage. Although English has separate and more definite words about knowledge than does the Akan language (i.e., *fact* and *truth*), Wiredu's analysis suggests that having more definite words does not seem to help English-speaking philosophers explain what it is for something to "be so," which is a widely shared and hence, perhaps, fundamental philosophical question about truth and knowledge. In a similar way, as we saw, the definite words used by Western scientific languages to conceive of biological impairments focus attention on a distorted range of facts and block us from engaging with what disability activists would regard as more fundamental questions about how to alter social environments to make disabled people more self-determining and autonomous.

Do Other Cultures Simply Not Have All the Facts?

Oyěwùmí used an examination of traditional Yoruba culture to argue that claims about biology—including about biological sex—are not purely objective, but socially constructed. Since people in traditional Yoruba culture, unlike in Western cultures, she suggested, lived in a world in which children had no sex and there was no concept of biological sex, Western claims about biology and biological sexes are socially defined. Because the distinction between impairment and disability parallels the distinction between sex and gender—the first term (*impairment, sex*) is supposed to refer to a purely objective body or biology, while the second term (*disability, gender*) is taken to be socially defined—her reasoning implies that claims about biological *impairment*, too, are socially defined.

Perhaps someone will object to Oyěwùmí's argument by saying that, although the Yoruba may not regard babies or children as having a biological sex, as she claims, it does not follow that babies and children have no biological sex. Some cultures and their languages may simply not notice or recognize the *fact* that babies and children have biological sexes. Biological facts—including facts about biological sex or impairment—are still facts, on this view, whether or not a culture recognizes them.

However, insisting on facts does not escape the socially defined nature of those facts. As we saw Hanson (1969) remark (in chapter 4), "Given the thesis that changes in our language (and, *ipso facto*, changes in our conceptual framework) can change our appreciation of the nature of the world, the notion of *fact* is no antithesis, antidote, or corrective to this thesis" (198). Besides, on what basis would we insist that children have sexes? Even in our own view, little girls and boys do not share all of the "sexual" characteristics of women and men—pubic hair, breasts (in the case of women), for instance, or the ability to play a role in reproduction. Why give more weight to the characteristics that girls *share* with women, and boys with men, and insist that little girls and boys have "sexes," rather than to the characteristics that girls do *not* share with women, and boys do *not* share with men—such as having a role in reproduction—and say that girls and boys have no sex? Our view seems to presuppose that the world should be cut up or determined in terms of development—the presupposition of biology, as McWhorter might point out. Since most girls develop into women, and most boys into men, we say that girls are little women, and boys are little men. That presupposition leads us to see the world our way, rather than the way the Yoruba do, as Hanson might say. But since, even in our own view, all babies and children can play no role in reproduction, would it not also be fair, on those grounds, to say that all babies and children belong to the same category as one another in relation to questions of reproduction, and are neither female nor male? Our society might even be better off if we cut up the world differently in this way, and perceived different facts.

Can Individuals Believe Whatever They Want?

The claim that different languages and learning lead to different facts (or different propositions about what "is so") does not mean that individual people can believe whatever they want. Given a certain way of cutting up or perceiving the world, some things will simply "be so," even if there may occasionally be borderline cases. In some societies, unlike in most Western societies, it will simply "be so" that bad moral behavior made someone sick, that some individual is more (or less) *onipa* (a person) than he/she was before, that this adult here is *obinrin* (one who has babies) while that adult there is *okùnrin* (one who does not have babies), while this child is neither *obinrin* nor *okùnrin*, or that a certain color splotch is blue/green (but not blue or green), and so on. Within the worlds created by languages and learning, individuals cannot simply believe whatever they want. Some claims are just facts or "so." To come to believe different things, we, together with our shared social and language groups, would have to remake our social worlds, cut up the world differently, and perceive different facts. We will explore ways we might begin to do so in chapters 6 and 7.

CONCLUSION

Altogether, this chapter along with chapters 3 and 4 suggests that the first dimension of embodiment or personal body is socially defined. Chapter 3 suggests that, although there is something it is like to be Irving Kenneth Zola from the inside, or to *experience* the world as Irving Kenneth Zola, for instance, that *something*, the *being* of Irving Kenneth Zola, is socially defined. There is no given, purely objective, pre-social, natural personal body *in experience*, because the phenomenologically *experienced* personal body or the feel of one's own body is always socially defined.

Chapters 4 and this chapter suggest that the personal body, insofar as it is an object *out there*, is also socially defined. Chapter 4 suggests that, although there is *something* Irving Kenneth Zola is like from the outside, what Irving Kenneth Zola *is*, as an object out there—what identity he has, what facts we assert about him, whether he is impaired, has an impairment, smaller facts of impairment, or a bodily condition—also cannot be defined outside of the social, outside of language. Indeed, since there are cultures in which people do not regard themselves as individual bodies (see chapter 3), even to describe Zola as an individual body is already to have invoked a society's theory about what people are like and how they are defined.

This chapter adds that claims about personal bodies having *biological* impairments or facts are also socially defined. The concepts of biology and biological impairment as well as the belief in a biological reality were invented beginning in the late eighteenth century in Europe for specific social and political purposes—a history that casts doubt on the suggestion that the concepts or beliefs succeed in capturing an objective reality independent of the social. Instead, biology is just one of the concepts and sets of beliefs that shapes the facts that we perceive. Nonbiological conceptions of bodies and of persons, such as can be found in traditional Yoruba society, focus attention on different ranges of facts, or, as Hanson would say, lead people to notice some things rather than others (see chapter 4). At the same time, it does not follow that individuals can believe whatever they want. Within belief systems established by societies' learning and languages, some things are simply so. Still, we must be humble. Even though we cut up the world our way, the world can be cut up and perceived differently, and there can thus be different facts. As chapter 7 will suggest, cutting up the world differently and perceiving different facts might even be better for people we currently regard as impaired.

Taken together, then, this chapter along with chapters 1–4 suggest that the body, and hence also impairment and disability, is therefore always socially defined, along all three dimensions of embodiment (see the introduction). Along the third dimension of embodiment or institutional body, institutions and structures in a society define not only what categories of people there are *out there*, such as the category of disabled people, but also the *experiences* that people so categorized are likely to have (chapters 1 and 2). Along the second dimension of embodiment or interpersonal body, the social capital and roles that are available *out there* (and to whom), as well as how social roles are *experienced* are socially defined (chapter 3). Along the first dimension of embodiment or personal body, there is *no purely objective, pre-social, natural*, biological, or physical individual body—no impairment, facts of impairment, or biological impairment—either in *experience* (chapter 3) or *out there*, as an object (chapters 4 and 5). How the personal body is experienced and what it is as an object out there are always socially defined. In short, disability and impairment are *made*. Chapters 6 and 7 will explore how impairment and disability may begin to be *unmade*.

6

Beyond Individual Accommodation

In an article published in 1993, medical sociologist and disability studies scholar Irving K. Zola (1993), whose work we already explored (chapter 3), described a public bathroom he once encountered in Japan. In the United States, he said, we will typically encounter public bathrooms with one or two "handicapped" stalls that have grab bars bolted to the wall on one or the other side—a design that permits, as he points out, either "a right or left-side transfer, but not both." Or the grab bars in the "handicapped" stalls will be bolted to the floor close to the toilet, which permits "only a straight ahead up and over transfer." He contrasts this typical, U.S. design with public bathrooms he encountered in Japan. "Imagine my surprise in Japan," he wrote, "where I encountered in some public men's rooms the following:"

> [O]ne toilet is typical Japanese (common in much of the Far East) where to use it one squats over a tiled hole. The second features the same squatting arrangement but with grabbars. The third is Western style; the fourth is the same but with grabbars. Then came the indicated handicap toilet with an expansiveness in size and features I have never encountered outside of a private home. The space itself was quite large with the toilet in the middle. The grabbars were movable up and down with little effort, allowing for all manner of transfer with and without assistance. Equally astonishing were the urinals. Though generally fond of high technology, I am very wary of urinals that flush automatically, for often they have no external plumbing fixtures to hold onto. Here amazingly were urinals of at least two sizes and with grabbars all around for gripping wherever needed. The point is that these Japanese designers, having accepted the necessity of disability, did so on a continuum—thus humbling at least one "overdichotomizing" advocate. (24)

As Zola points out, while the Japanese bathrooms accommodated a variety of mobility needs in the handicapped-designated stalls, they also included various mobility aids in the non-"handicapped"-designated toilets and urinals. The Japanese bathrooms even accommodated different cultural choices, since they included both North American–style toilets as well as squatting toilets, which, Zola tells us, were common in parts of Asia at the time he was writing. The squatting toilets might even work better for some disabled people.

Zola uses this example to suggest that we should stop treating disability as a fixed and static status or as a dichotomous category. Since people can flow into and out of disability and become more or less disabled during the courses of their lives, it is not a static category. It is also not a dichotomous or either/or category. We tend to think that people are *either* nondisabled *or* disabled. But, Zola is arguing, disability is a continuum, along which people are always more or less disabled. Unlike U.S. bathrooms, which have *either* bare-bones, non-handicapped-designated stalls with no mobility aids for *nondisabled* people, *or* handicapped-designated stalls with some mobility aids for *disabled* people, the Japanese bathrooms treated disability as a continuum by providing a range of mobility options in all of the stalls.

But there is more. Instead of just loosening up the way we understand and apply the category of disability by defining it as fluid and continuous, rather than as fixed and dichotomous, as Zola maintains, the Japanese bathrooms do not rely on categorizing people at all. Although they still offer officially designated "handicapped" stalls, the presence of a variety of styles of toilets with various moveable grab bars in all the stalls suggests that, rather than a classification of *people*, the bathroom design is based on a rethinking of *access*. By including mobility aids in the non-"handicapped"-designated stalls and offering different styles of toilets popular in different parts of the world, the Japanese bathrooms provide a wide variety of combinations of *types of access*, without focusing on categorizing *people* at all.

In this chapter, I will begin to argue for a similar move in more theoretical terms. Instead of classifying individual people and providing certain "special" individuals with accommodations to meet their special needs, we can begin to unmake disability by revising structures and social arrangements in a way that focuses on classifying *access*, rather than people. If, as I have suggested so far, disability has been socially constructed or *made* along each of the dimensions of embodiment, in terms of both what it is *out there*, as an object, and how it is *experienced* (see the introduction for more on this distinction), then it can be *unmade*. But it must be unmade by addressing the structures and social arrangements that have constructed it in the first place. Reconstructing those social arrangements, systems, and institutions will require moving away from an emphasis on classifying *people* toward an emphasis on classifying and working on *access*—as the Japanese bathrooms do.

We began the analysis of how disability has been *made* by looking at the third dimension of embodiment or institutional body (see the introduction), which captures how institutions and structures—including the economic system of capitalism—have defined disability (chapters 1 and 2). We will begin the analysis of how to *unmake* disability with the third dimension or institutional body as well. However, because the system of capitalism that we have now is not the same as the system of industrial capitalism that emerged in the late eighteenth century, this chapter starts by examining how changes in the capitalist system, particularly deindustrialization, are reconstructing disability today.

You might think that deindustrialization, with its more flexible work arrangements, would make it easier for disabled people to participate in the wage market. But deindustrialization has actually reduced the participation of disabled people in the wage market. In fact, deindustrialization is reconstructing disability today. Changing work conditions, particularly the loss of control over work and time, are defining more people as disabled. Unmaking disability along the third dimension of embodiment will therefore require not changing individuals, which is the usual strategy for addressing the disadvantages of disability, but changing the employment environment and context to increase disabled people's access to work. Unmaking disability will actually require going further: it will require remaking the structure of work, including expanding what counts as work or as genuine economic activity beyond the current focus on wage labor. Because capitalism has been accompanied by a structure of public attitudes that tied citizenship to participation in wage labor, unmaking disability along the third dimension will also require changing those attitudes. But because disabled people will be able to fully participate only if their civil rights are also promoted, increasing access to genuine economic activity—even in an economy with an expanded definition of work—will also require rejecting the structure of cultural attitudes, developed during the nineteenth century (see chapter 2), that tied citizenship and civil rights to the ability to embody the norm.

Chapter outline:

➤ Capitalism, Deindustrialization, and Disability Today
➤ The Reconstruction of Disability under Deindustrialization
➤ Unmaking Disability along the Third Dimension of Embodiment or Institutional Body, Including under Capitalism
➤ Expanding the Definition of What Counts as Work or Genuine Economic Activity
➤ Unmaking the Structure of Attitudes
➤ Conclusion and Future Prospects

CAPITALISM, DEINDUSTRIALIZATION,
AND DISABILITY TODAY

- Deindustrialization Has Reduced Disabled People's Participation in the Labor Market
- Flexible, Deregulated Labor Markets Have Not Increased Labor Market Participation for Disabled People

As we saw in chapter 1, the long shift in Europe from a feudal economic system to a capitalist economic system, and particularly to industrial capitalism, increasingly excluded some people from work, thereby defining or categorizing them as "disabled" or as "un-able" under the new, dominant economic regimes. In much of the Middle Ages, there was a more rural definition of work in which people were valued based on the tasks, pieces, or projects they could complete—often in their homes—rather than on the time they worked. This economic structure meant that there was an expanded definition of *work* or of what counted as genuine economic activity that people who we would classify as disabled today were able to do and so were not "disabled" or unable to work. There is also evidence that work during the Middle Ages was often adjusted to people's abilities (or disabilities), such as in the distinction between heavy harvesting work and the lighter work of reaping, which was reserved for children and adults who were unable to do the heavy work. Under rural conditions of work during the feudal era in Europe, then, people were expected to engage in what was a wider variety of genuine economic activities to the best of their abilities.

However, the shift to an urban definition of work under mercantile and industrial capitalism, which valued people in terms of the time they worked, progressively excluded those who were regarded as less efficient or productive, creating a class of people defined as "disabled" or unable to work. Industrial capitalism's increased productivity requirements and invention of the factory also produced a demand for standardized bodies that could function like machines as well as a greater separation between the home and the workplace—a shift that excluded people with nonstandard bodies or less mobility from the labor market. These time- and factory-based working arrangements under industrial capitalism narrowed the definition of what counted as work, progressively excluding nonstandard people from engaging in genuine economic activity. Anthropologist Ida Nicolaisen noted that there was a similar constriction in the definition of work and corresponding reduction in the economic contributions and social value of people we would regard as disabled among the Punan Bah people of the central region of the island of Borneo in Malaysia during the 1980s, as the community came to rely increasingly on wages for its economic support (see chapter 1).

Since some of the economic structures that disabled people, such as the factory, were invented by industrial capitalism, you might think that recent processes of deindustrialization or "tertiarization" (Standing 2016, 44)—the development of capitalist economies based on providing services rather than on industrial manufacturing—would improve the labor-market participation of people we define as disabled. The economist Guy Standing (2016) has observed that the tertiary sector of the economy is characterized, for instance, by "a blurring of workplaces, home places and public places." On the one hand, work places have blurred into home and public places. More "teleworkers" work from home, in both the private and public sectors (45, 62), and more people do their work in cafés or cars (139). On the other hand, home places have also blurred into work. As Standing suggests, "What was once the preserve of the home is done in or around workplaces," such as showering or grooming at work (138). If industrial capitalism's distinction between home and work places helped to exclude disabled people from the labor market, blurring that distinction might help to include them. The "globalizing open market economy" is also now characterized, Standing suggests, "by informal contracts, part-time and temporary jobs, project orientation and myriad personal services" (67), a flexibility that might seem as if it could also benefit at least some disabled people and help them gain access to the labor market.[1]

Deindustrialization Has Reduced Disabled People's Participation in the Labor Market

However, deindustrialization has not helped disabled people at all. In fact, studies suggest that the process of deindustrialization as well as increasing global competition has produced a greater emphasis on economic growth and efficiency that has fueled higher requirements in terms of skill and education for workers and has driven more people with chronic health conditions and disability out of the labor market (Holland, Burström, et al. 2011, 397–98). Economist Paula Holland and her colleagues (Holland, Burström, et al. 2011) conducted an international comparison of the employment rates for disabled and chronically ill people aged 25–59 years in Canada, Denmark, Norway, Sweden, and the United Kingdom to test whether educational and health-related inequalities in the labor market have increased under deindustrialization. Those countries are comparable because they all have advanced social welfare systems, universal health care, and significant gaps in employment rates between people with and without disability and chronic health conditions. In all five countries, the employment rates of disabled and chronically ill people were lower than were the employment rates of nondisabled people, indicating that disabled and chronically ill people had an overall weaker position in the labor market, although the rates were different for the different countries (407). Moreover, because all five countries had experienced at least one economic downturn during the period studied, which ranged from the early 1980s to 2005, depending on the country, the researchers were also able to assess the effects of recessions on the employment of disabled and chronically ill people. Holland and her colleagues found that, during economic downturns, the inequality in the employment rates between nondisabled people and people with chronic illness and disability increased (410). However, unlike the rates for nondisabled people, the employment rates for disabled and chronically ill people did not *rebound* during periods of economic recovery, but continued to decrease during the 1980s, 1990s, and 2000s (410). This finding suggests that deindustrialization has *reduced* the overall participation of disabled and chronically ill individuals in the labor market.

Flexible, Deregulated Labor Markets Have Not Increased Labor Market Participation for Disabled People

Holland and her colleagues (Holland, Nylén, et al. 2011) went on to use the cross-country comparison to examine whether "flexible, deregulated labor markets with greater opportunities to work part-time or with flexible working hours" (416)—precisely the kind of labor market that, as we saw Standing suggest, tends to characterize today's deindustrialized or tertiary capitalist economies—would help people with chronic illness or disability gain entry into the labor market and hence raise their employment rates. Holland and her colleagues used an assessment of the five countries that ranked them according to their degree of employment deregulation or flexibility (vs. employment protection). According to the ranking, the UK had the highest score for deregulation or flexibility in the labor market (or lowest rating for employment protection or regulation), and so had the most flexible, deregulated labor market, followed, in order, by Canada, Denmark, Norway, and then Sweden (Holland, Nylén, et al. 2011, 417). If a deregulated labor market helped chronically ill and disabled people obtain jobs, then the UK and Canada should have had the highest employment rates for these groups in the five countries, and Norway should have had the lowest. Holland and her colleagues found, however, that the UK had the lowest employment rate for chronically ill and disabled people (59 percent for men, 50 percent for women), while Norway had the highest (74 percent for men, 67 percent for women). They also found that the *difference* in employment rate between nondisabled and chronically ill or disabled people was largest in the UK and smallest in the Scandinavian countries, and that "overall, the level of employment among people with a limiting illness was higher in the Nordic countries than in the United Kingdom and Canada" (420, cf. 427). This study suggests that, contrary to what one might have predicted, the kinds of flexible and deregulated labor markets that tend to characterize deindustrialized economies have not helped disabled and chronically ill people gain entry into the labor market.

THE RECONSTRUCTION OF DISABILITY
UNDER DEINDUSTRIALIZATION

- Changing Work Conditions, Particularly the Loss of Control over Work and Time, Are Increasing the Number of Disabled People
- Diminishing Welfare Benefits Also Increase Economic Precariousness and Reduce Access to the Labor Market
- Disabled People as the Canaries in the Coal Mine of Deindustrialization's Unsustainable Working Conditions

In fact, deindustrialization is *reconstructing* what counts as disability today, as Standing (2016, 100) suggests, by *increasing* the number of people who are disabled under capitalism. Changes in working conditions as well as recent attempts in some countries to cut the social safety net and welfare benefits have reduced more people's access to the labor market and pushed them into disability status. As sociologist and social policy analyst Ben Baumberg Geiger (2014)[2] points out, the number of applications for disability or incapacity benefits has been increasing in many countries that belong to the international Organization for Economic Co-operation and Development (OECD)—a fact that is puzzling on its face, because overall health is improving and work is becoming less physically demanding (Baumberg 2014, 289). Baumberg quotes a comment made in 1994 in the British House of Commons by the apparently exasperated prime minister at the time, John Major: "It beggars belief that so many people have suddenly become invalids, especially at a time when the health of the population has improved" (290; the quote is from Anyadike-Danes and McVicar 2008, 432).

Most explanations for this puzzle, Baumberg says, have suggested either, first, that although everyone agrees that more disabled people could work, the fact that they are not working is due to policy choices or failures, or, second, that many benefit recipients belong to a class of unemployed people—the "hidden unemployed"—who would be pulled into the labor force in an economy with full employment (290). The "hidden unemployed" are people with health problems, who, in a better economy with higher overall rates of employment (or lower unemployment rates) and hence more competition for workers, would be regarded as more desirable employees by potential employers and so would be absorbed into the labor market (290, 291–92).

Changing Work Conditions, Particularly the Loss of Control over Work and Time, Are Increasing the Number of Disabled People

Baumberg (2014) offers an additional explanation, however, namely, that there has been a genuine increase in disability—not because people are getting less healthy, but because changes in working conditions mean that, as he puts it, "work has become more difficult for people with health problems" (290). As he explains, "Working conditions can be disabling without damaging health—if working conditions deteriorate, then it can be harder for a person with an impairment to stay in work, even if their underlying health is unchanged" (294). Changes in working conditions under deindustrialization, he suggests—particularly a loss of decision-making freedom or control over work and time—are making it harder for many people to work, increasing the number of people who are now disabled under capitalism.

Baumberg uses the UK as his test country, because it has seen the highest increase in incapacity claims of all OECD countries aside from Korea, and because it has also seen a sharp rise in the number of jobs that make high demands on employees or require employees to work hard, but in which employees also have less decision-making freedom or control over their work and time—a rise in "high-demands, low-control jobs" (290). He suggests that the loss of control is caused partly by technology, which not only, as he puts it, "allows managers to monitor workers more closely," but also disproportionately increases the productivity "of harder-working, better-skilled workers" (294). Computer systems not only make it possible for some workers to process, for instance, more customer phone calls or insurance claims per hour, but also allow companies to track precisely the number of calls or claims each employee processes, even if the employee is working from home. The loss of control is particularly sharp in the UK, Baumberg suggests, because labor unions, which might have pushed back against the increasing surveillance and reduced autonomy of employees, as well as the regulation of technology are both weak there (294).

Because people's reports about their own working conditions are often biased, Baumberg collected data in the UK on the working conditions that people say others who share their occupational group have. He constructed scales that ranked different occupations in terms of their levels of demand, control, and physicality, and then imputed those scales (295) into another survey that tracks incapacity benefits, to see if working characteristics in one year "affect the chances of claiming incapacity benefits in the following year" (296). Baumberg found that people in occupations in which employees have a high level of control over their work had the lowest chances of claiming incapacity benefits the following year, regardless of the occupation's level of demand (298).

He also determined, however, that the general decline in the control that people have over their work that took place in the UK from 1992 to 2006 was increasing the number people who were receiving incapacity or disability benefits. Without that general decline in job control, Baumberg found, fewer people would have been receiving those benefits. One model he developed suggested that "if job control had not deteriorated since 1992," then one-sixth *fewer* people would have shifted from working to receiving incapacity benefits in 2006. Numerically, he says, "0.39 per cent of the sample would move from work to incapacity benefits during the following year, as opposed to the actual 2006 figure of 0.46 per cent" (299, cf. 302). These results suggest that changing work conditions under deindustrialization, particularly the loss of control over work and time, have increased the number of people who are now disabled under capitalism. Baumberg quotes from an article by social policy researcher Annie Irvine: "Perhaps the key question should not be whether an individual is fit for work, but whether the work is fit for the individual" (Baumberg 2014, 306).[3]

Deindustrialization is thus *reconstructing* the category of disability by excluding more people from the labor market. As Baumberg (2014) notes, his study reinforces Standing's claim that deindustrialization, with its more flexible, unregulated labor markets, is pushing more people into economic precariousness (306). Standing (2016) argues that deindustrialization has produced "the precariat," a new class of workers who are forced to accept informal contracts, part-time, and temporary jobs and are consequently subjected to a risk-strewn or precarious existence. This precariousness is combined with new systems of indirect control over work—particularly through technological mechanisms (45). The result is that workers have less control over how they use their labor power (40, 44), over their occupational potential (46), and over their time (136, 139, 147, 148, 151) than they did under industrial capitalism.

In a deindustrialized, tertiary economy, Standing suggests, more people who are regarded as different or as nonstandard workers are denied access to or pushed out of full-time jobs into more economically precarious and insecure part-time and temporary jobs as well as into jobs governed by informal contracts. "This is how disability and the precariat come together," Standing (2016) explains (101). "In today's electronically charged world of instant diagnosis and communication, it is easier to identify and categorise an individual's impairment and to tag that person for eternity. This means that many more are sized up for classification, for treatment or for neglect" (101), including through discrimination. Discrimination targets people for poor treatment or exclusion based on characteristics that may not even impact their abilities on the job. "Those identified as different are not only more likely to find life opportunities restricted to precarious options but they are also more likely to be pushed that way" (101). In a flexible, unregulated labor market, without the labor unions and protections of the old industrial era, employers are "reluctant to recruit and eager to dispense with the 'performance impaired,'" Standing suggests. As a result, even people with episodic disabilities, for instance, such as epilepsy, are drifting "into precarious jobs and a precarious cycle of disadvantage and insecurity" (101).

Disability studies scholars who have been inspired by Marxist theory have also noted the worsening position of disabled people in the labor market under deindustrialization. Colin Barnes and Geof Mercer (2005) as well as Paul Abberley (2002), for instance, suggest that the shift to less stable employment under globalization makes participation in the labor force more problematic for many disabled people (Abberley 2002, 131–32; Barnes and Mercer 2005, 539–40). As Abberley puts the point, for instance, "As technological advances and increased globalization combine to make permanent full-time employment an increasingly rare phenomenon for the majority of the work-force, disabled people will continue to be in the forefront of those groups who cannot provide the versatility and work rates demanded by the labour market" (131).

Diminishing Welfare Benefits Also Increase Economic Precariousness and Reduce Access to the Labor Market

Standing (2016) suggests that the precariousness experienced by different or nonstandard workers is being exacerbated by the fact that many governments, beginning in the twenty-first century, have been looking for ways to reduce the cost of disability benefits by pushing people into jobs. As a result, at the very moment that such people are being pushed out of the labor market or "*dis*-abled" by deindustrialization, they may also be denied welfare benefits on the grounds that they are able to labor (Standing 2016, 101). The reconstruction of their status as both disabled and nondisabled by these two conflicting structures only pushes them further into economic precariousness. The film *I, Daniel Blake*, directed by Ken Loach (2016)—which won the Palme D'Or at the Cannes Film Festival— depicts the struggles of the character Daniel, who has been told by his doctor that the stress and physicality of his job is too much for his weakening heart and has been advised to stop working, but is categorized as able to work by Britain's social services system and denied income support. Although the film is fictional, *The Guardian* (2016) newspaper created a short documentary film, titled *Meet the Real Daniel Blakes*, profiling people in Daniel's situation. Melvin Newton, for instance, who was out of work with (what we would call) high blood pressure, was, like Daniel in the film, having financial problems and fighting with the British social services system for support.

According to Standing (2016), community help or support, a form of social income, has also become increasingly insecure under global capitalism (52, 57). This economic shift might further exclude and isolate disabled people, who may rely more on community support. Indeed, the disability activist community's emphasis on the value of *inter*dependence, rather than independence (see, e.g., Longmore 2003, 222; Barnes and Mercer 2005, 529–30; White et al. 2010), a theme we will return to in chapter 7, may reflect such a reliance.

At the same time, we must keep in mind that this reliance, too, is socially structured and defined. African philosopher Kwasi Wiredu (2003) describes the Akan belief in what he characterizes as "the essential dependency of the human condition." According to Wiredu, the Akan hold that all individuals are essentially dependent on others. An individual's "growth and acculturation" as well as

acquisition of "skills and abilities will reduce this dependency but will never eliminate it altogether" (293). While self-reliance is encouraged in Akan society, they
also understand, he says, that the very possibility of self-reliance "is predicated
upon this ineliminable residue of human dependence" (293). Human beings always need the help of others—even to be self-reliant. In the West, the difference
between nondisabled and disabled people, as defenders of the human variation
model of disability might point out (see the introduction), is that the structures
and institutions of Western societies routinely accommodate the main dependencies of most nondisabled people, while the interdependent needs of some
disabled people fall outside of what those structures and institutions routinely
accommodate. That, too, is one of the ways in which, as political scientist and
disabilities studies scholar Harlan Hahn might say, Western societies are *designed*
for nondisabled people (see chapter 1). The increased economic precariousness
that disabled people may experience as a result of the loss of social income under
deindustrialization is therefore also socially structured and defined.

Policy-makers often *deliberately* push people into economic precariousness.
They believe that "decommodification" or passive labor market policies in
which people are provided with a high level of security when they fall outside
of the labor market will increase the number of people who leave or remain
outside of that market. Relatively generous welfare policies that are easy to
qualify for make it possible for people with reduced work ability to leave the
workforce without serious economic consequences and discourage those people
from seeking jobs. The converse hypothesis is that making it harder for people
to qualify for benefits and making benefits less generous—or ensuring that
people are more economically precarious—will force such people into working
(Holland, Nylén, et al. 2011, 418).

Holland and her colleagues (Holland, Nylén, et al. 2011) used their five-
country comparison to examine whether "more generous social protection will
act as a disincentive to work" for people who are disabled or chronically ill (418).
They used the OECD's "decommodification index" to rank the five countries
according to the generosity of the countries' entitlement programs, including
pension programs, sick-pay, and unemployment compensation. According to
the index, the UK had the least generous or expansive welfare benefits programs,
followed, in order, by Canada, Norway, Denmark, and then Sweden (417). Holland and her colleagues found, they said, "no evidence of a disincentive effect
of more generous welfare benefits" (427). If the generosity and expansiveness of
welfare benefits served as a disincentive for people with chronic illness or disability to work, then the Scandinavian countries, which had relatively generous
welfare and entitlement benefits (higher decommodification), should have had
lower employment rates for chronically ill and disabled people. The employment
rates for chronically ill and disabled men and women, however, as they report,
"were higher in the Nordic countries than in Canada and the United Kingdom."

Indeed, Holland and her colleagues found that illness and disability had the greatest impact on employment in the UK, "which, along with Canada," as they point out, "offers the least generous levels of welfare benefits" (427).

Holland and her colleagues went on to speculate about why less generous welfare benefits seem to harm the employment prospects of disabled and chronically ill people. They suggest that reducing the economic and material resources that are available to disabled and chronically ill people outside of the work force may make it more difficult for such people to reengage with the workforce later. Poor welfare benefits may send people on what Holland and her colleagues call a "trajectory of cumulative disadvantage," in which "financial worries and material shortage" exacerbate the effects of health problems and disability, thereby increasing the barriers, rather than creating an incentive, to work (427–28). In other words, less generous welfare policies further disable people by making getting a job even more difficult.

Disabled People as the Canaries in the Coal Mine of Deindustrialization's Unsustainable Working Conditions

The claim that changed working conditions under deindustrialization have increased the number of people who are disabled by capitalism might lead us, perhaps, to think of disabled people, as Anna Stubblefield (2009) suggested in a different context, as similar to the canaries in the coal mine whose deaths warned the miners of dangerous levels of poisonous gas. People who are being increasingly excluded as disabled from the labor market under deindustrialization, are, like the canaries, the warning sign of—or merely the first to be defeated by—unsustainable working conditions overall in today's deindustrialized or tertiary, capitalist economies. As Stubblefield observes about the United States, when disabled people "suffer from inadequate education, inadequate employment, and inadequate healthcare—we should recognize that as a sign that our society is failing" (110). Overall, in terms of employment as well as social welfare support, access for disabled people has decreased in the present phase of capitalism.

UNMAKING DISABILITY ALONG THE THIRD DIMENSION OF EMBODIMENT OR INSTITUTIONAL BODY, INCLUDING UNDER CAPITALISM

- Changing Individuals versus Changing the Employment Environment or Context
- The Employer Practice of Using (Supposedly) "Essential" Tasks or Skills to Limit Access to Jobs
- Beyond Changing the Employment Environment or Context

We can begin to unmake disability under capitalism by focusing not on individuals but on *structural conditions*. As we will see, individualistic policies that aim to help disabled individuals look for work or receive training, for instance, will not improve their access to the labor market, though structural policies that aim to change the employment environment or context can help. One change to employer practices that might be particularly helpful would involve forcing employers to carefully construct and justify the lists of tasks or skills they regard as "essential" for doing particular jobs. However, unmaking disability under capitalism will ultimately require going beyond merely changing the current employment environment or context. It will require redefining what counts as work or as genuine economic activity altogether.

Changing Individuals versus Changing the Employment Environment or Context

To see why individualistic solutions will not work, let's return to the article by Holland and her colleagues (Holland, Nylén, et al. 2011) discussed above, in which they use the comparison between the UK, Canada, Denmark, Norway, and Sweden to examine whether unregulated and flexible labor markets are *worsening* the position of chronically ill and disabled people in employment. In that same article, they also examined what the five-country comparison could tell us about how the employment prospects of chronically ill and disabled people could be *improved*. They ranked the five countries according to the percentage of gross domestic product (GDP) that each country spent on active policies and programs aimed at helping chronically ill and disabled people in employment. In this ranking, Canada spent the lowest percentage of its GDP on such active labor market policies, followed, in order, by the UK, Norway, Sweden, and then Denmark (417). The fact that the UK and Canada had the lowest employment rates for chronically ill and disabled people, while Denmark and Sweden had the highest, suggests that greater investment in active labor market policies for chronically ill and disabled people does help to improve their employment rates.

However, Holland and her colleagues go on to suggest that the study also pointed toward what *kinds* of active labor market policies might be most helpful. Not only did the countries spend different percentages of their GDP on active labor market policies for chronically ill and disabled people, but they also enacted *different kinds of policies*. Whereas policies in the Scandinavian countries focused on making the employment environment or context more "disability friendly," as Holland and her colleagues put it (428), policies in the UK and Canada focused on making individual disabled or chronically ill people more employable. In other words, the Scandinavian countries focused on changing employment structures and arrangements, while the UK and Canada focused on classifying and changing individuals. The fact that Canada had among the lowest employment rates for chronically ill and disabled people out of the five countries—even though its rate of deindustrialization or loss of industrial employment was more limited than in the other countries (Holland, Burström, et al. 2011, 410)—suggested, preliminarily, that policies aimed at classifying and changing *individuals* are less effective at improving the employment rates of chronically ill and disabled people than are policies aimed at changing the employment environment or context (Holland, Nylén, et al. 2011, 428).

In two follow-up studies, Stephen Clayton and his colleagues (2012) examined the effectiveness of these two types of active labor market strategies for improving the employment of chronically ill and disabled people. The first study examined the effectiveness of employment-context strategies[4] in the UK, Canada, Denmark, Norway, and Sweden. Clayton and his colleagues found that the most promising interventions were wage subsidies—if the subsidies were generous enough, but not so generous that they created a segregated form of employment—as well as financial support for employers to take measures that make the work environment more accessible and flexible and promote return-to-work planning for people who had taken sick-leave. Focusing on improving disabled people's *access* to jobs, then, did increase their employment. However, Clayton and his colleagues found that none of these interventions was used on a wide enough basis "to make a population-level impact" (438).

Strategies that focused on assisting or changing *individuals*—their jobs searches, skills, motivations, or physical/medical conditions—by contrast, did *not* succeed in increasing the employment of disabled and chronically ill people. The second study examined the effectiveness of individualistic strategies that had been employed only in the United Kingdom.[5] Clayton and his colleagues found that, although individualized case management for vocational and job-search assistance did help people return to work, case managers or advisors tended to select people who were already close to being work-ready. Case managers or advisors regarded the time they were given to work with clients as too short to deal with clients who were further from the labor market or had more complex health conditions.

On the other side of the desk, clients of the programs complained that the programs did not address "what they perceived as primary barriers to work—weak local labour markets, attitudes of employers" (Clayton et al. 2011, 6).[6] Clayton and his colleagues agreed. They suggested that the UK's emphasis on policies aimed at individuals has meant that the "real barriers" to employment have not been addressed. As they put it, there had been "a relative neglect of the environmental orientation which would address real barriers to employment of disabled people and people with long-standing health conditions, including attitudes and practices of employers and agencies, as well as access to work issues" (10).

The Employer Practice of Using (Supposedly) "Essential" Tasks or Skills to Limit Access to Jobs

One employer practice that excludes many disabled people from jobs involves requiring employees to have skills that are not really needed to do the relevant job. In 2016, philosopher and scholar of disability Shelley Tremain (2016) described two job postings for philosophy professors at American institutions that said the job required the "ability to stand and deliver a lecture" and "full sight and hearing capacity." Tremain (2016) also notes an article in which history professor David M. Perry (2016) reports that the University of Arkansas at Little Rock regularly included a clause in its job advertisements for professors that listed the following skills as "essential": carrying, pushing or pulling 10 pounds, kneeling, climbing stairs or ladders, sitting or standing for long periods of time, hearing, vision, distinguishing colors, depth perception, close vision, and frequently walking short distances. Several people Perry interviewed pointed out that such ads violate the Americans with Disabilities Act (ADA), which prohibits employers from using criteria to screen candidates if the criteria are not in fact job-related (Perry 2016).

Requiring all applicants to possess these skills excludes many disabled people from applying for the jobs, of course. But the skills are not really needed to be a philosophy professor. One can deliver a lecture without standing, for instance, and one can teach without delivering lectures. Political scientist Theresa Man Ling Lee (2006), for instance, reported that, after the onset of speech difficulties, she was able to continue teaching with accommodations from her university. There are also professors who do not have "full sight and hearing capacity," such as disability studies scholar and bioethicist Adrienne Asch (2001; 2004), who was blind (2001, 3, 16; 2004, 11–12, 28). One does not even need to be able to breathe unassisted to be a university professor. As history professor and disability studies scholar and activist Paul K. Longmore (2005) pointed out in one of his articles, "The author of the article you are reading is a university professor who uses a ventilator in the classroom" (39).

Unfortunately, Western societies often seem more interested in classifying people than they are in carefully scrutinizing the standards employed to limit access to jobs. Asch (2001; 2004) points out, for instance, that, in court cases in the United States in which people challenged their treatment by employers under the ADA, the courts focused primarily on whether the people suing their employers were "sufficiently impaired" to qualify as disabled and be covered by the law. She suggests that courts should focus not on whether the person is correctly classified as disabled but on whether employers' claims that tasks or skills that exclude the person are truly essential for the job (2001, 10; 2004, 20).[7] In other words, instead of classifying *people*, courts should focus on classifying skills needed to *access jobs*. Forcing employers to screen candidates or exclude employees based only on tasks or skills needed to do a job would certainly improve the employment environment and context—and employment access—for many disabled people.

Beyond Changing the Employment Environment or Context

However, even policies aimed at changing the employment environment and context may not go far enough. As Baumberg (2014) points out, if the increase in disability is caused by deteriorating working conditions, particularly the loss of control, then any solution has to address those working conditions. But addressing those working conditions has to take account of the structural roots or macro-level causes of those conditions. From the employers' perspective, as Baumberg puts it, "if the 'ideal worker' has to work harder and more rigidly, then what counts as a 'reasonable' adjustment [or accommodation] may still be insufficient to enable disabled people to continue working" (304). In a context in which the "ideal worker" works harder and is more controlled, changing the working conditions only for disabled people through reasonable accommodations or adjustment—one of the types of programs that addresses the employment environment or context that Clayton and his colleagues examined—is likely just to fuel resentment among colleagues. Even providing employers with incentives to hire and retain disabled employees, Baumberg suggests—another program addressing the employment environment or context that Clayton and his colleagues examined—will, as Baumberg put it, "only deal with the symptoms of a deeper problem" (204). Exhorting employers to create better working conditions will also have little effect, Baumberg says, without paying attention "to the wider forces that make employers act in particular ways; if it makes sense to compete using low-autonomy, high-demands jobs, then this is what employers will do" (305).

Baumberg suggests that Scandinavian countries, for instance, continue to have better working conditions not only because they have an employee population with a high level of skill and because these countries' governments have exhorted businesses to maintain better working conditions, but also because the continued strong role of labor unions as well as less deregulated and flexible labor markets (or more labor protections) mean that, in those countries, providing good work is still "a sensible business strategy" (305). As long as excluding less ideal workers remains a sensible business strategy, employers will continue to do so.

It is important to keep in mind that the belief that disabled people are not ideal employees is at least in part an ideology or assumption (see also chapter 1). A 2014 survey of 230 businesses (Parrey et al. 2014, 30) that employ people with intellectual and developmental disabilities (IDD) conducted by the Institute for Corporate Productivity found, for instance, that "the profile of an employee with IDD reads like that of an ideal employee" (3, 10). More than 80 percent of the employers surveyed said that their employees with IDD are dependable, engaged, motivated, integrate well with co-workers, and have great attendance records. More than 75 percent reported that their employees pay strong attention to work quality and are highly productive (10). Seventy-three percent of the surveyed employers reported that hiring a person with IDD was either a positive experience or a positive experience that exceeded expectations, and a full one third of the employers whose businesses were classified as "high-performance organizations" said that hiring employees with IDD had exceeded expectations (12).

At the same time, the study also suggests that including people with IDD in the workforce may require redefining jobs and work—a topic for the next section. The survey found that, although people with IDD worked in "a broader spectrum of jobs than most people expect" (Parrey et al. 2014, 12)—including clerical work, data entry, janitorial work, cleaning, general maintenance work, food preparation and service, materials management, retail, health care, and line or manufacturing work—the surveyed employers reported that 11 percent of their employees with IDD were engaged in a job that belonged in the category of "other." Parrey and her colleagues, who wrote the report, suggest that the fact that the employers categorized 11 percent of the jobs their workers with IDD were doing as "other" "may indicate that more mature organizations are thinking creatively to discover roles for workers with IDD or using job coaches to carve out pieces of jobs that call for the talents of individuals with intellectual and developmental disabilities" (13).

Carol Salter, the assistant vice president of workforce development for the Easter Seals organization, told the story of a man with IDD she knew who worked in a sheltered workshop and said he wanted to build truck engines. She went to visit a company that built truck engines and saw people who were earning $30 per hour "hauling in boxes of equipment and oil, cleaning spills and breaking down boxes" for recycling, as the report puts it. Salter convinced the company to hire John, the name she gave the man for the purposes of the report, to do those jobs, "thus allowing $30/hour employees to do $30/hour work." Hiring John increased the productivity of the whole staff. As the report explains, "Not only was John excited to work around truck engines, other employees were excited that his presence allowed them to concentrate on what they were trained to do" (Parrey et al. 2014, 15).

Still, if, as Baumberg (2014) suggests, deteriorating working conditions generally are excluding more people from the paid wage market and hence disabling them, then improving the economic position of people so classified will require restructuring the economy more broadly. In particular, it will require "changing the nature of work" (Baumberg 2014, 304). As Baumberg explains, his study suggests that "high levels of disability in the twenty-first-century are to some degree 'genuine', and that policies to reduce incapacity claims should cast their eye on the world of work" (306).

EXPANDING THE DEFINITION OF WHAT COUNTS
AS WORK OR GENUINE ECONOMIC ACTIVITY

- Expanding the Definition of *Work*
- Beyond Work: A Broader Pattern of Exclusion for Disabled People

If *disability* has been defined under capitalism in part by a constriction in what counts as work or genuine economic activity (see chapter 1 and above), then one solution would be to expand what counts as work. For such an expansion to work for disabled people, however, I will suggest, it will have to take account of their particular social circumstances.

Expanding the Definition of *Work*

"Every age has had its peculiarities about what is and what is not work," Standing (2016, 137) says. The problem with capitalism today, he suggests, is that much of what counted as work in other ages, particularly what the ancient Greeks considered work as praxis as well as what they called *schole*, are not considered work. Work as praxis is the work that people do "with relatives and friends around the home, in caring for others—reproducing them as capable of being citizens themselves," Standing says. This work "was about building civic friendship" (137). *Schole* was leisure and learning, centered around public participation in the life of the community (15, 137). While ancient Greek society was flawed, Standing says, their distinction between productive labor, work as praxis, *schole*, and play as relaxation is useful. Today, we emphasize productive labor and play, while work as praxis or care work and *schole* are not considered genuine economic activity.

I think, for instance, of the difference between my mother's life and mine. I was raised at a time when a white, middle-class, Canadian man could earn enough to support a family. My mother was a homemaker. She engaged in a great deal of work that helped the family economically, such as clipping coupons, comparison shopping, cooking, and baking, as well as sewing, knitting, or crocheting clothes, mittens, dish clothes, doll clothes, and so on. Because she did this work as part of her care work for the family, however, the capitalist system did not regard it as genuine economic activity, and so it was unpaid. My mother also spent time doing other kinds of work as praxis or social work. She planned and hosted social activities with friends and neighbors, for instance—activities that, as a working mother, I have not had time to do. Compared with my parents' social life, my own family's social life has, in my view, been relatively impoverished.

My mother also did most of the direct care work for her children as well as for her parents later. The issue of care work is complicated, however. As Barnes and Mercer (2005) note, disabled people have often been critical of an emphasis on care because "it raises the spectre of traditional assumptions of inadequacy and dependence" (540), or tends to reinforce the assumption that people who may need assistance with daily living are dependent and hence inadequate.

Discussions of care have also led to conflicts between nondisabled and disabled women. As feminist disability studies scholar Alison Sheldon has pointed out, disabled and older people often support community-based care. The independent living movement, for instance, lobbies for the right of disabled people to live independently in homes in the community.[8] In spite of that support, however, Sheldon (1999) notes, feminist scholars have criticized the deinstitutionalization movement, or the shift from institutionalized to community-based care, because women are often the ones who must perform most of the increased, unpaid, informal caring and domestic work that is required once care has been shifted out of institutions and into the community (652). As Sheldon points out, however, it is society that causes the conflict that this shift sets up between mostly younger, nondisabled women and some disabled and older people, including disabled and older women (653). I would add that the conflict is caused particularly by capitalism's exclusion of work as praxis or care work around the home from what counts as genuine economic activity, as Standing (2016, 137) notes, and by a division of labor that requires women to do most of that work.[9]

In terms of *schole*, my mother could also afford to pursue various educational programs at community colleges—programs that have now become increasingly expensive—both for her own interest and to improve skills, such as secretarial skills that she used in other activities, including her civic-minded volunteer work for a radio program ("Call for Action") that helped people pursue consumer complaints against companies and government agencies. It is an unnoticed irony, Standing (2016) suggests, that, after the Great Recession of 2008, there was a growth in "work that was not labour" (190), or in work that would not be regarded as productive labor under capitalism. The rush to answer former president Barack Obama's call for people to engage in public service through volunteer work and community service, for instance, testified, Standing says, "to a desire to work on socially worthwhile activities. Losing jobs can be liberating." As Standing concludes, then, "We must stop making a fetish of jobs" (190).

Expanding the kind of work that is regarded as genuine economic activity not only could help disabled people receive more care in the community, when needed, but could also help them do meaningful and socially valuable *work*. Disabled people are capable of a great deal of different kinds of work (see chapter 1). In an article calling for a reformulation of the concept of work and hence disability, Barnes and Mercer discuss Andre Gorz's and Ulrich Beck's descriptions of what moving "beyond the wage-based society," to use Gorz's (1999, 73) phrase, to an economic system less focused on jobs might look like. As Barnes and Mercer note, Beck, for instance, proposes a "counter-model to the work society" that Beck describes as "a multi-activity society in which housework, family work, club work and voluntary work are prized alongside paid work" (Barnes and Mercer 2005, 540; Beck 2000, 125). Such a society, Beck proposes, could be designed on a model of "civil labour" in which people would engage in organized and creative, self-determined and self-fulfilling, project-oriented, cooperative labor "for others, which is performed under the guidance of a public welfare entrepreneur" (130). Beck suggests that this labor could be "rewarded both materially and nonmaterially" with civic money (public money paid through the public welfare organizations, company sponsorships, or local government money [for community work, for instance]), with qualifications or certificates (which could then be used to help obtain paid labor, pension entitlement) and with what he calls "favour credits" (such as entitling someone to send his or her child to childcare for a certain amount of time) (127, 130).

Philosopher, critical theorist, and feminist Nancy Fraser (1994) imagines a similar new kind of economy as part of her argument for the claim that feminists are well placed to offer solutions to the problems produced by less stable employment and more diverse family arrangements in a post-industrial economy—particularly solutions that "appreciate the importance of care work for human wellbeing and the effects of its social organization on women's standing" (Fraser 1994, 593). In this economy, "all jobs would assume workers who are caregivers too; all would have a shorter work week than full-time jobs have now; and all would have employment-enabling services" (612), such as (well-paid) daycare services. This imagined economy would allow some informal care work to be supported on a par with paid work through social insurance programs, but there would also be state-funded, local organizations in which men and women who did not personally have care responsibilities would join others in providing care through civic organizations, thus deconstructing the traditional distinction between public and private settings. As Fraser puts it, "The trick is to imagine a social world in which citizens' lives integrate wage earning, caregiving, community activism, political participation, and involvement in the associational life of civil society—while also leaving some time for fun" (613).

Beyond Work: A Broader Pattern of Exclusion for Disabled People

Barnes and Mercer (2005) suggest, however, that these sorts of "attempts to re-conceptualize the meaning of work beyond waged labour" must not ignore "the specific circumstances or implications of social change for disabled people" (541). As Beck (2000), for instance, admits, his notion of civil labor "presupposes civil rights" (126). Barnes and Mercer (2005) point out, however, that many of the barriers that disabled people face in the labor market are a result of a broader pattern of exclusion, including the denial of civil rights and access to public goods generally. As they put the point, "The position of disabled people in the labour market is located within a broader pattern of social and environmental barriers such as access to education, information, transport, the built environment, as well as cultural and media representations" (536). Disabled people will be able to fully participate *as workers* in an economy with an expanded notion of work, then, only if their civil rights are also promoted, including access to public transportation, to the sites (physical or technological) where such civil labor is to take place, to ongoing educational opportunities to develop skills and abilities and so on. As a result, such a post-wage-labor society will only *work* for disabled people if the structure of attitudes that has excluded them from fully accessing other public goods is also addressed.

UNMAKING THE STRUCTURE OF ATTITUDES

- Reject the Capitalist Connection between Citizenship and Wage Labor
- Quirky Citizenship: Rejecting Citizenship Based on Normalcy

The structure of attitudes, or set of "values, expectations, and assumptions about the physical and behavioral attributes that people ought to possess in order to survive or to participate in community life" (Hahn 1988, 40), as we saw Hahn put it, that has excluded disabled people in many Western societies has been closely linked to capitalism. Valuing people based on their participation in the paid labor force and punishing people who do not do so, including many disabled people, with exclusion and impoverishment helps to ensure that less-disabled people hide and deny any suffering or disease they may be experiencing as long as possible so that they can continue functioning in the capitalist system. Less-disabled people get the message: "Be able, or else" (see chapter 1).

In this chapter, I have argued that deindustrialization is reconstructing the category of disability by defining more people as disabled. A person must be even more "able," these days, to be employed in the tertiary or service-based economy. As "ability" is defined upward, demanding a greater variety of skills, more energy, more health, and so on, additional people are being disabled and hence subjected, under the current structure of attitudes, to the corresponding exclusion and precariousness with which the category of disability has been associated. But perhaps, as more people come to be defined as disabled and hence to be potentially excluded and impoverished, more people will reject the structure of attitudes toward disability, not only for themselves, but also for others.

Reject the Capitalist Connection between Citizenship and Wage Labor

We can begin to see what rejecting the current structure of attitudes might look like. As Barnes and Mercer (2005) suggest, if exclusion is defined by the denial of the rights of citizenship, such as civil, political, and social rights, then inclusion is connected to the concept of *citizenship*. Concern with citizenship, they say, "has a specific resonance for disabled people precisely because it presumes inclusion" (532). In recent capitalist societies, participation in the system of wage labor has determined not only one's income but also one's citizenship rights and social standing (540). As a result, they suggest, citizenship has been "associated pre-eminently with being an active economic agent, with the linked assumption that paid employment is privileged over other forms of work activity" (532). Expanding the definition of what counts as work or as legitimate economic activity beyond wage labor or having a job means that the structure of attitudes will have to reject the traditional connection that capitalism has drawn between wage labor or having a paying job and citizenship (541).

Barnes and Mercer (2005) note that feminist scholars have often responded to (white, middle-class) women's traditional exclusion from the paid wage market by recommending that the kind of work that is recognized as a basis for citizenship should be expanded to include domestic and care work.[10] However, they suggest, such an expansion will be of limited use for many disabled people (541). If care work is defined solely as care "for others," as Beck puts it, for instance, it will fail to take account of other forms of unrecognized domestic or care work that disabled people often do. Barnes and Mercer point out that disabled people are often required to do other kinds of unrecognized work, such as spend additional time and effort to complete everyday tasks.

When my daughter uses the shared-ride, door-to-door accessible bus system in New Jersey, for instance, which is called Access Link, she is given a forty-minute window for each pick-up. Since drivers only wait five minutes for people to board the bus, she is forced to sit in the living room (with her coat on, when needed) to wait for sometimes up to forty minutes (or even more) for the ride. The bus often takes ninety minutes (and occasionally up to two hours) to get to her destination, which is but a 25-minute drive from where we live. As the New York City comptroller Scott Stringer is reported to have once said about that city's paratransit system, which is called Access-a-Ride, "There's a reason Access-a-Ride passengers call the service 'Stress-a-Ride'" (Altamirano 2016).[11]

Barnes and Mercer (2005) suggest that disabled people also often do work that medical sociologists have identified as "patient work," such as organizing and administering medications, attending therapies, and dealing with professionals—professionals such as, I would add, support coordinators, care staff, doctors, and medical transportation organizations and staff. Disabled people are also required to do "biographical work," or work to incorporate impairment and disability into their everyday lives and to explain that work to others (537). As Barnes and Mercer suggest, then, "Disabled people have argued that living with impairment in a society organized around non-disabled lifestyles involves additional time and effort, as well as specialized skills" (537). I bet that if everyone had to use Access

Link, the pick-up windows and time spent during trips would be shorter.[12] Simply expanding the kind of work that is recognized for citizenship to include the sort of domestic and care work that women have tended to do will still not take account of other forms of work that disabled people living in a society designed for nondisabled people are often required to do.

Quirky Citizenship: Rejecting Citizenship Based on Normalcy

During the nineteenth century in many Western societies, the structure of attitudes under capitalism came to define disabled people not only as an economically excluded and impoverished group but also as a despised group of outsiders (see chapter 2). The invention and growing importance of the concept of normalcy as well as the eugenics movement and the ugly laws employed a concept of abnormalcy to restrict the civil rights of disabled people, such as the right to have a job, to marry, to bear children, or to live in the community rather than in an institution. Fully including disabled people in a post-wage-labor society will require the structure of attitudes not only to reject the association between citizenship and wage labor, but also to reject the association between citizenship and being "normal." Political scientist Kristin Bumiller (2008) notes that many "feminist theorists have emphasized how in modern capitalist societies the privileges of citizenship are contingent on one's ability to embody the norm" (982–83). The opposite is also true, she suggests: we often measure normality in terms of being a good citizen in the capitalist system. The "good citizen is an avid consumer in the market," does not make too many demands on the government or the government's coffers, and "conforms to conventional family forms." From this point of view, Bumiller says, disabled people, who are disproportionately impoverished (see chapter 1), are "a variant of citizen outside the norm." As she adds, they "are often seen as presenting an unwanted drain on the market economy like other groups that are considered undesirable because of their class, race, or criminal record" (983).

Bumiller (2008) suggests that the neurodiversity movement founded by autistic people undercuts the connection that capitalist societies have drawn between citizenship and being normal (984). The neurodiversity movement promotes a notion of what she calls "quirky citizenship" (980), or a notion of "citizenship outside the norm" (984). Although autism is typically medically defined "by an inability to understand social conventions," Bumiller says, it is "a form of bodily difference that interferes with the person's ability to process information (sensory, language, tactile, and visual) in a typical fashion" (976). Autistic people experience their environment and perceive reality differently, "particularly in terms of how they process sensory information or social knowledge," she suggests. "For example," Bumiller writes, "autistic persons may actually hear noises as louder or with enhanced frequencies, recognize atypical patterns of visual information from faces or pictures, and register unusual tactile sensibilities like feeling soft touch as painful" (974). These differences in sensory and social experience and perception produce the "manifest differences" in behavior that nondisabled people notice or recognize in social situations and use to mark or define autistic people as disabled. Some autistic people also disidentify with their genders, a phenomenon that Bumiller calls "one of the most costly behaviors" (977).

Because, as Bumiller (2008) puts it, "autistic persons' lives are replete with situations where their differences matter" (977), parents of autistic children are pressured to seek intensive behavioral training, particularly applied behavioral analysis (ABA) therapy, which essentially trains autistic children to imitate normal behavior (976). Children are taught to understand social cues and respond in ways that would be considered normal, such as smiling when happy to see someone. They are also taught to eliminate repetitive behaviors and adopt behavior considered gender appropriate, even when such training disregards "the child's own conception of gender relevance" as well as the fact that the child may be using repetitive behaviors to reduce anxiety (977).

Against these oppressive, normalizing strategies, the neurodiversity movement insists that autistic people should be appreciated for their individual differences, afforded the same personal dignity as everyone else, and have their differences respected in everyday situations. As Bumiller (2008) puts it, one of the core assumptions of the neurodiversity movement is that autistic people "are empowered by constructions of their identity that are individualized, affirming of difference, reinforcing of personal dignity, and dynamically interpreted in the context of everyday living situations" (971). Psychologist Kathryn Boundy (2008) says, for instance, that autistic people active in the neurodiversity movement often advise nonautistic people to regard autistic people as if they are aliens, with their own systems of cultural meaning. "Calls to be seen as alien beings and to be treated with the respect which would be extended towards treasured visitors from a vastly different culture proliferate wildly in neurodiversity literature," Boundy writes (section titled "'There Is No Madness but That Which Is in Every Man': Notes Towards a Manifesto," para. 1).

Bumiller (2008) argues that the neurodiversity movement also makes "a powerful case for recognizing how many of the unique qualities of individuals with autism are potentially an asset to the human condition" (980). As she explains it, if the "influence of social conventions, bureaucracy, and compulsion toward conformity are seen as a threat to the vibrancy of democracy, then groups who possess tendencies to resist the pull of the social realm are well positioned to enliven citizenship" (980). For many activists, then, neurodiversity is "the foundation of an understanding of identity that promotes more inclusive citizenship" (Bumiller 2008, 982) and contributes "to a culture of citizenship that fosters equality without sameness" (980). The neurodiversity movement's support for "quirky citizenship" therefore "has the potential to transform how persons with unique characteristics are valued in society" (982).

If Western, capitalist societies came to have a new structure of attitudes based on a notion of "quirky citizenship" that separated the concept of citizenship, not only from paid work but also from the requirement that one be normal, then being normal would no longer be a prerequisite for inclusion and participation in the life of the community. Under a structure of attitudes shaped by a notion of "quirky citizenship," we would expect disabled people to be included broadly in all public interactions and spaces. There would be broad public support and expectation for public bathrooms to have a wide variety of types of access, all subway stations to have working elevators, all new apartments to have wheelchair accessible doorways, disabled people to live, work (all kinds of work), learn and play in our communities, disabled students to be included in and benefit from the public education classroom and so on. Instead of classifying *people*—as workers or shirkers, as normal or abnormal, as nondisabled or disabled—we would focus on classifying and improving access for the widest possible range of quirky people.

CONCLUSION AND FUTURE PROSPECTS

Because impairment and disability are socially constructed or *made*—both in terms of what they are, as objects *out there*, and in terms of how they are *experienced* (see chapter 3)—they can be *unmade*. I began this chapter with a vignette from Zola's work about Japanese bathrooms that illustrates how impairment and disability can be unmade. Instead of classifying *people*, we can begin to unmake disability by classifying and then opening up structures and *access*.

This chapter examined what unmaking disability in this way would be like along the third dimension of embodiment or institutional body, which refers to how institutions and structures in societies, including economic systems, regulate, survey, and control people. The economic shift from industrial capitalism to a tertiary capitalist system based primarily on providing services appears to be restructuring how disability is defined by making it more difficult for people to have jobs in the paid labor market. In effect, deindustrialization is expanding what counts as disability under capitalism. In an economy increasingly dominated by, as Standing (2016) puts it, "informal contracts, part-time and temporary jobs, project orientation and myriad personal services" (67), one must be even more "able," these days—one must have a greater variety of skills, more energy, more health and so on—to have a stable, paying job in the tertiary or service-based economy.

The economic position of disabled people under deindustrialized capitalism today—which is generally weaker than the economic position of nondisabled people (see chapter 1)—will not be improved by individualistic strategies designed to help individual people get jobs, receive training to increase skills, or improve their physical/medical conditions, for instance. Instead, we can improve the economic position of disabled people only by addressing the structures and institutions of capitalism in a way that increases access to jobs. At the very least, this will require improving the employment environment and context for disabled people by, for instance, providing employers with wage subsidies to hire disabled people or with grants or funds to increase accessibility and provide accommodations, or by forcing employers to prove that tasks or skills that screen out disabled candidates or exclude disabled employees from jobs are in fact essential to doing the job.

However, merely improving the employment environment or context may not be enough. As long as employing only the most ideal workers—or those who are regarded as the most ideal workers—remains a good business strategy, as we saw Baumberg put it, then that is what employers will do. Under these circumstances, improving the economic position of disabled people will require restructuring the economy more broadly. Since disabled people's increased exclusion from what counted as genuine economic activity during the shift from a feudal economy to industrial capitalism in Europe was defined in part by a contraction in the types of activities that counted as work or as genuine economic activity (see chapter 1), then improving the economic position of disabled people—and perhaps everyone else as well—will require expanding what counts as work under a restructured, deindustrialized capitalist economy. In particular, it will require a definition of *work* that goes beyond mere wage labor or merely having a job. However, the shift to a post-wage-labor economy will be of limited use to disabled people unless the unique types of work that they are required to do, such as spending more time on daily activities or doing what medical sociologists have called "patient work," is not recognized and rewarded, or if the broader sources of exclusion or denial of civil rights, such as the lack of access to transportation, housing, education, and so on, are not also addressed.

Addressing the broader sources of exclusion or denial of civil rights will require changing what I called, borrowing from Hahn, the "structure of attitudes" that excluded disabled people from accessing public goods (see chapter 1). At the very least, the structure of attitudes will have to stop defining people's citizenship or inclusion in terms of having a paying job. However, because the invention of normalcy, freak shows, the eugenics movement, and the ugly laws in the nineteenth century came to define disabled people not only as excluded and impoverished but also as despised outsiders (see chapter 2), the structure of attitudes will also have to stop defining citizenship or inclusion in terms of being normal. It could come to embrace what Bumiller (2008) calls, drawing on the neurodiversity movement endorsed by many autistic people, a notion of "quirky citizenship," or a notion of "citizenship outside the norm," that, as we saw Bumiller put it, promotes "a culture of citizenship that fosters equality without sameness" (980).

Under such a notion of citizenship, we would come to expect disabled people to be included in and welcome them into all public interactions and spaces in all of our institutions and structures. In other words, just as Fraser (1994) argues that taking full account of domestic and care work will require, at the least, "subverting the existing gender division of labor and reducing the salience of gender as a structural principle of social organization" or, at best, "deconstructing gender" (612), so including disabled people fully as citizens will require, at the least, subverting the division of labor in which disabled people are regarded as dependent and unable to work and reducing the salience of disability "as a structural principle of social organization," to use Fraser's phrase, or, at best, *deconstructing* disability.

Deconstructing disability, however, will require unmaking disability not only along the third dimension of embodiment or institutional body, which captures the way in which bodies are regulated, controlled, and surveilled by the institutions and structures of societies, including capitalism, as we saw in this chapter, but also along the first and second dimensions of embodiment. In chapter 7, we will see how to deconstruct or unmake disability for the second dimension of embodiment or interpersonal body, which captures how cultures use the body to conceive of social roles, society, or the world (cf. Scheper-Hughes and Lock 1987, 18–23), as well as for the first dimension or personal body (see also the introduction).

7

Diversifying Access, Remaking Worlds

In an article arguing against legalizing physician-assisted suicide, Paul K. Longmore (2005) tells the story of David Rivlin, a quadriplegic ventilator user who petitioned the courts to allow him to commit suicide with medical help. As Longmore tells the story, Rivlin wanted the same things in life that many other American men wanted. "I wanted a wife, children, to be able to do lots of things," Rivlin told one reporter. "Life is more than surviving. It's interacting with other people, it's having a family, it's having a career, it's having a wife. It's all of those things and I can't have them," he told another. "I've tried to figure out other ways but there is none." Media reports claimed that Rivlin's dreams of fulfilling those social roles—of being a friend, an employee, a parent, a sexual partner—were killed by his impairments. As one put it, according to Longmore, "His dreams disappeared as he was pounded and torn by the churning surf in his 1971 accident." But it was not Rivlin's impairments that prevented him from fulfilling those social roles, Longmore argues; it was *society* (39).

Rivlin tried to live independently in the community, have friends, and have a career. He had been a philosophy major in college and hoped, according to various accounts, to be a philosophy teacher or psychotherapist. After his accident, he continued to pursue his education, attending university from 1974 to 1979. Still, Rivlin remained socially isolated. Even though he was living independently at the time, Longmore writes, "His life was 'mostly . . . just school and home." Rivlin told reporters, "I didn't have much of a social life" (Longmore 2005, 39). Moreover, although Rivlin "employed personal assistants to live with him," Longmore says, his attempt to live independently did not last.

Once again, the media blamed this failure on Rivlin's impairments and health conditions. *People* magazine reported, for instance, that repeated infections while living independently forced Rivlin into the hospital over and over. But this explanation is incomplete. "*People* did not explain why independent living was so hard for Rivlin," Longmore says. "It did not report the meager support the state of Michigan offered disabled people who wanted to live in their own homes or apartments" (Longmore 2005, 39–40). While the state of Michigan "gave Rivlin less than $300 per month to live in his own home, it paid a nursing home $230 a day to warehouse him" (40). That $300 per month "averaged out to a mere $10.00 a day, or a meager 41 cents an hour." As Longmore points out, "At that rate, no quadriplegic person could find a competent and responsible, personal assistance worker. No wonder David Rivlin kept getting sick. No wonder his repeated attempts at independent living failed" (40). Since Rivlin was already socially isolated, however, being forced into the nursing home "simply deepened the segregation he had already suffered. But at least when he was trying to live independently, he could have some hope that he might somehow realize his dreams for a different kind of life" (39).

Rivlin tried again to realize his dreams for a different kind of life. While in the nursing home in Dearborn, Michigan, he met and fell in love with Zoe Dixon, an office worker, and they got engaged. In 1980, Rivlin moved into her home. But this attempt at a different kind of life also failed. As Rivlin explained, Longmore reports, "It lasted about a year. The burden of my being a quadriplegic broke us up." Here again, the media did not question Rivlin's suggestion that it was his impairments or quadriplegia that made it impossible for him to fulfill the role of being a lover and companion. "None of the reporters who covered the story asked what Rivlin meant when he called himself a 'burden,'" Longmore writes. "Neither they nor any of the nondisabled people around him had enough knowledge about the experience of people with significant physical disabilities" to question the assumption that Rivlin and Zoe's relationship had failed because of his impairments (39). If Michigan had provided more money for David to live in his own home or if David and Zoe had had the help of paid workers who would have given her some respite and made David less reliant on her, would their relationship have lasted? In other words, how did government policies, Longmore asks, "affect their relationship and plans?" (39) We can add more questions: If David and Zoe had lived in a place or time in which disabled people could engage in genuine economic activity to the best of their abilities and so come to have social worth (chapter 1), or in which disabled people were not segregated (see chapter 2) and lived together with family or community members who could provide additional support (see chapter 3), would their relationship have lasted? In a different social context, would Rivlin's impairments have been the "burden" he took them to be? But no one asked any of these sorts of questions. "None of the reporters, nor the attorney who petitioned the court for Rivlin's right to doctor-assisted death, nor the physician who facilitated his suicide, nor anyone close to him in his final days," Longmore says, "had enough knowledge about David Rivlin or physically disabled people to raise any of these questions" (39).

Longmore's account suggests that, under different social arrangements, Rivlin could have had the roles he valued and lived in his own home in a loving relationship. "The truth was that David Rivlin might have enjoyed the life he yearned for," Longmore says, "but society blocked his efforts, and government policies forced him into a nursing home." Rivlin decided to die when he realized that he, as Rivlin put it, "would have 'to spend the remainder of my life in an institution. . . . What pushed me over the edge," Rivlin told reporters, "was the realization that I was anchored to one spot" (39). While society would not help him live, it did help him die. Rivlin won his case in court and went ahead with what Longmore says was "the medically assisted suicide of a disabled person who could no longer endure his mistreatment by society" (41).

In chapter 6, I suggest that, instead of classifying people and providing certain "special" individuals with accommodations to meet their particular needs, we can begin to unmake disability by revising social structures and arrangements in ways that focus on providing *access*. Chapter 6 explores how this strategy can be applied to the third dimension of embodiment or institutional body. Here, we will explore how to unmake disability in a similar way along the second and first dimensions of embodiment, the interpersonal body and the personal body (see the introduction for a discussion of the three dimensions of embodiment). Unmaking disability along the second dimension or interpersonal body will require redefining social contexts in ways that dismantle Western societies' emphasis on bodies and bodily capital and facilitate disabled people's access to *social* capital and to valued social roles and activities, including the roles of sexual partner and parent. Since social contexts define not only social relationships but also the very facts and identities that we perceive (chapters 4 and 5), unmaking disability along the first dimension of embodiment or personal body will require getting out of our perceptual bubble and remaking our world. At the end of the chapter, I point toward what remaking the world of education in the way that I suggest might look like.

Chapter outline:

➤ Unmaking Disability along the Second Dimension of Embodiment or Interpersonal Body
➤ Remaking the Social Roles of Sexual Partner and Parent
➤ Unmaking Disability along the First Dimension of Embodiment or Personal Body
➤ Case Study: Unmaking "Special" Education
➤ Conclusion

UNMAKING DISABILITY ALONG THE SECOND
DIMENSION OF EMBODIMENT
OR INTERPERSONAL BODY

- "Disability Spread" or Disability as a Master Status
- A Western Emphasis on Sight or the Visual Sense
- Unmaking the "Sick Role" or "Handicapped Role"

Recall that the second dimension of embodiment or interpersonal body, according to Nancy Scheper-Hughes and Margaret M. Lock (1987), captures how cultures use the body to conceive of society, the world, and social roles or people's places in the social, technical order (18–23). In societies in which having what is defined as a normal body determines one's access to income and civil rights, the normal body becomes a form of privately held capital—"bodily capital"—that one can work on and convert into value in interpersonal contexts (chapter 3). Since, as the discussion of political scientist and disability studies scholar Harlan Hahn's work (chapter 1) and the ugly laws (chapter 2) suggests, Western societies regard people as disabled for both aesthetic and functional reasons, people defined as disabled because they have aesthetically or functionally different bodies have a devalued bodily capital that has to be managed (chapter 3). Disabled people often try to manage this devalued bodily capital and improve their places in the social, technical order by, for instance, dressing meticulously or fashionably (chapter 3) or by appearing and behaving as normally as possible (chapter 6).

Having bodies that look and behave normally may be even more valuable today under deindustrialization. The economist Guy Standing (2016) has suggested that another effect of the shift to a deindustrialized or tertiary economy based on providing services (see chapter 6) is that what he calls "personal deportment skills" have become more important for employment. "The ability to look good, produce a winning smile, a well-timed witticism, a cheery 'good day' greeting, all become skills in a system of personal services," Standing says (144). He points out that the demand for these skills tends to disadvantage people with less education or income, who may have had fewer opportunities to hone such skills, and to benefit women ("Customers like pretty faces; bosses love them," he says) as well as good-looking youths over "less attractive middle-agers" (144). This demand would also disadvantage many people regarded as disabled on the grounds that they have bodies that appear different, function differently, or interact differently in social encounters with others.

As we have seen, however, it is possible to have a society in which people are not classified by their bodies. Feminist scholar and sociologist Oyèrónkẹ́ Oyěwùmí (1997) suggests that members of traditional Yoruba society in Africa, for instance, did not classify people in terms of their bodies or biologies, but in terms of social

relationships (see chapters 3 and 5). Indeed, Oyěwùmí criticizes the Western tendency to organize society around bodies. In Western thought, she says, "society is
constituted by bodies and as bodies—male bodies, female bodies, Jewish bodies,
Aryan bodies, black bodies, white bodies, rich bodies, poor bodies"—where the
term *bodies* here, she says, refers to both physicality (or what I have been calling physical conditions) and to biology (1). In modern Western societies, then,
Oyěwùmí says, "the body is the bedrock on which the social order is founded" (1).

Sociologist Ken Plummer (2011) has suggested that, even today, many of the
moral conflicts in the United States, such as the conflict over abortion, "centre
over the body, as a key symbol of the wider social order" (246). As Oyěwùmí
(1997) points out, using the body as the bedrock for social order affects both "the
social body" as well as "the body politic" (2), to use Scheper-Hughes and Locke's
terms, or both the second and third dimensions of embodiment, the interpersonal
and institutional bodies, as I am calling them (see the introduction). Body-based
categories are used to assign social roles (the second dimension) and are used by
large structures and institutions to regulate and control people, such as under sexist, racist, classist, and, we can add, ableist laws and social policies (see chapters 1
and 2 for examples of ableism under this third dimension of embodiment).

"Disability Spread" or Disability as a Master Status

Disability activists and scholars have noted that when nondisabled people use
the body to classify people as disabled, the disability status comes, in the minds
of the nondisabled people, to dominate the entire disabled person. In a project
originally completed in 1948 for Stanford University and several federal agencies,
such as the War Department, Gloria Ladieu Leviton, Dan L. Adler, and Tamara
Dembo (1948) describe a "spread of evaluation" (60) in which, in the minds of
nondisabled people, a person's physical disability comes to characterize the whole
person. For nondisabled people, disability status spreads, as it were, over the
whole disabled person, shaping how nondisabled people evaluate the disabled
person's other characteristics. As Beatrice A. Wright (1960), also a member of
that original research team, explained later, "Physical deviation is frequently seen
as *the* central key to a person's behavior and personality" (118). Disability activist and stand-up comedian (Sutherland 1989) Allan T. Sutherland (1984) writes
that "one thing of which all of us are conscious is that we are seen to be different
from other people, in ways that go far beyond the actual facts of our disabilities"
(58, cf. 61, 65). Dembo, Ladieu Leviton, and Wright (1975) speculate that this
"disability spread," as it came to be called (see, e.g., Liesener and Mills 1999),
provides nondisabled people "with an excellent reason for excluding the injured
from participation in activities" (39).

Other scholars of disability describe the same phenomenon using the concept of a "master status." Psychologist Michelle R. Nario-Redmund (2010), for

instance, who links the notions of "spread" and "master status," suggests that, for many disability groups, disability functions as "a 'master status' classification" that leads "assumptions about disability [to] 'spread' across all aspects of a person's identity" (474). Sociologist Kathy Charmaz (2003) connects disability's role as a master status with having a devalued identity: "A defined difference from ordinary peers separates a person and confers an actual or potentially devalued identity," she writes. "That difference often becomes a master status, such as 'disabled person,' 'leper,' or 'AIDS victim,' that floods all statuses and identity" (284). Bodily deviation (in terms of function, behavior, or appearance) from what counts as normal leads to a devalued identity or bodily capital as disabled that, in the minds of nondisabled people, functions as a master status and spreads across the entire person or floods the disabled person's other statuses or identities.[1]

A Western Emphasis on Sight or the Visual Sense

Oyěwùmí (1997) suggests that the emphasis on bodies in Western societies is rooted in the fact that these societies privilege sight or vision over the other senses. As she explains the point, the "differentiation of human bodies in terms of sex, skin color and cranium size is a testament to the powers associated with 'seeing'" (2). Cultures that understand reality according to other senses or other combinations of senses, however, will come to have different kinds of knowledge, to know different things (2). Such cultures will also not use the body to organize society: "In cultures where the visual sense is not privileged . . . the body is not read as a blueprint for society" (9). The visual sense focuses on bodies, Oyěwùmí suggests, because it privileges the physical world. But it misses nonphysical or unobservable aspects of the world. "A concentration on vision as the primary mode of comprehending reality promotes what can be seen over that which is not apparent to the eye," Oyěwùmí says, "it misses the other levels and the nuances of existence" (14).

In traditional Yoruba society, for instance, people's social roles are primarily determined not by their bodies but by social relationships based on seniority determined according to when a person joined (came inside) the traditional living compound or lineage, either by birth or through marriage (see chapter 5). Because this notion of seniority is a social relationship that is not connected to age or sex, it is neither physical nor written on bodies.

We can begin to unmake disabled people's devalued "bodily capital" as well as disability's tendency to spread and function as a master status by abandoning Western societies' focus on the visual sense and on bodies, and by emphasizing, instead, social relationships and other aspects that are not apparent to the eye. As philosopher Naomi Zack points out,[2] the phenomenon of disability spread or of disability as a master status is a part/whole fallacy in which nondisabled people assume that impairment or disability, which capture only part of a person, define the whole person. But the fallacy need not be accepted as an inevitable social reality.

We can begin to unmake this element of disability by learning to pay attention to aspects that may not be readily apparent to the eye and to the "other levels and the nuances of existence," to use Oyěwùmí's phrase. Bioethicist and disability studies scholar Adrienne Asch (2001; 2004) suggests, for instance, that, for her, her blindness was only one facet of her character, along with, as she put it, all the "intellectual and personal interests that define me" (2001, 16; 2004, 28). People are also characterized by nonvisible social roles and relations, as Oyěwùmí's discussion of traditional Yoruba society suggests. If what mattered to us was whether a person is a member of our living compound or lineage, our neighbor, an expert on bioethics, or a lover of horror movies, then impairment and disability would not necessarily imply a devalued bodily capital and would not spread over or come to dominate, in the minds of nondisabled people, a disabled person's identity. Paying attention to aspects that are not apparent to the eye and to the other levels and nuances of existence would also help people with nonvisible disabilities, who often have to manage others' presumptions that their bodies are normal (see chapter 3). Once we accept that people's characters and situations cannot be read off their bodies, we would stop assuming that people who appear to be normal could not possibly be disabled.

I am not recommending that bodies be ignored.[3] As Oyěwùmí (1997) suggests, ignoring the body is merely the flip-side of a culture that is obsessed with bodies. "Paradoxically, in European cultures, despite the fact that society was seen to be inhabited by bodies, only women were perceived to be embodied; men had no bodies—they were walking minds," Oyěwùmí says. "Two social categories that emanated from this construction were the 'man of reason' and the 'woman of the body,' and they were oppositionally constructed" (6). Both roles—being a body or being no body at all—assume that people are defined primarily by their bodies, whether they are regarded as mired in, or as having escaped from, their bodies.

In most Western societies, however, people both *are* and *are not* their outwardly visible, bodily identities at the same time. The African American poet Pat Parker (2000) has a wonderful poem titled "For the White Person Who Wants to Know How to Be My Friend" that perfectly captures this idea. The poem begins with the lines: "The first thing you do is to forget that I'm Black. Second, you must never forget that I'm Black" (73). White people who want to be Parker's friend should forget that she's black, but, in a society inundated with racism, they must also never forget that she is black.

I once had a physically disabled student who used a walker and said she had wonderful friends who invited her to participate in their activities. But her friends also sometimes forgot to ensure that the activities were in places that were accessible to her. It was good, she said, that her friends forgot that she is disabled and enthusiastically included her in all their activities. But they also needed to remember that—in this society, given the way in which it is structured and the facts that its members perceive—she is disabled.

To say that people both are and are not their outwardly visible bodily identities is to say that we need to focus, not on bodies, but on socially defined *embodiment* along all three dimensions—people's social positions in relation to large social structures and institutions, including racism, sexism, ableism, and so on (the third dimension; see chapters 1 and 2), their socially defined roles and identities or places in the social, technical order (the second dimension; see chapter 3), and their socially defined, individual experiences (the first dimension, as experienced; see chapter 3) as well as identities (the first dimension, as objects out there; see chapters 4 and 5). Unmaking disability along the second dimension of embodiment thus involves recognizing that people are not bodies, but socially defined *embodiments*. Instead of classifying people or their bodies, we should focus on ensuring that socially defined embodiments—social contexts and identities—provide people who we currently classify as disabled with access to positive *social* (rather than bodily) capital.

Unmaking the "Sick Role" or "Handicapped Role"

In terms of the second dimension of embodiment or interpersonal body, one of the social roles that disabled people have often been assigned is the "sick role" or "handicapped role," which assumes that disabled people are helpless, dependent, and passive, and exempts them from the obligations of age-appropriate social roles or, in many cases, from any adult social roles whatsoever. This role is rooted in the medical model of disability (see the introduction), which conflates disability with a sickness. As we saw psychologist and education scholar Michelle Fine and bioethicist and disability studies scholar Adrienne Asch (1988) explain the reasoning, "The nonhandicapped person equates having a disability with a *bad and eternal* flu, toothache or broken leg" (12), which are sicknesses that would ordinarily lead nondisabled people to be out of sorts and exempt them from their usual responsibilities (see chapter 3). When such conditions are temporary, Fine and Asch suggest, it may be appropriate for someone to be unsteady and out of sorts and to receive help and suspend his or her usual social responsibilities. But the "sick" or "handicapped" role mistakenly assumes that people with long-term disabilities will have the same difficulties. Unlike nondisabled people with temporary sicknesses or conditions, however, Fine and Asch suggest, people with long-term disabilities "have learned to use alternative methods to accomplish tasks of daily living and working" (12). The "sick" or "handicapped" role's assumption that disabled people are sick and therefore incapable of carrying out the responsibilities of age-appropriate or adult social roles is therefore unwarranted.

REMAKING THE SOCIAL ROLES
OF SEXUAL PARTNER AND PARENT

- Changing Social Structures to Increase Access to Sexuality: Beyond the Public/Private Distinction
- Does Sexual Freedom for People with Intellectual and Developmental Disabilities Lead to a New Form of Forced Sterilization?
- From Sexuality to Worries about Reproduction and Parenthood
- Redefining What Makes Someone a Competent Parent
- From Independent Living to Interdependent Living

Among the adult social roles that disabled people have often been denied are the roles of sexual partner and parent. This denial has also routinely been translated into a general denial of their sexuality (see chapter 3). As sociologist and disability studies scholar Russell P. Shuttleworth (2012) notes, however, disabled writers and their allies have recently been producing work that explores disabled people's sexuality (55). Shuttleworth (2002) himself, for instance, conducted an in-depth, interview-based study with fourteen men with cerebral palsy to explore how the men diffuse society's construction of them as asexual and undesirable to establish intimate relationships with partners.

In an aptly titled book, *Already Doing It: Intellectual Disability and Sexual Agency*, Michael Carl Gill (2015) explores the sexuality and reproduction of intellectually disabled people as well as how society has controlled their sexuality and reproduction. "Individuals are 'already doing it' in the midst of limited sex education, discourses of risk, and active efforts of desexualization," Gill concludes. "Uncovering, or claiming, or even acknowledging that intellectually disabled individuals have sexual desires highlights the naïveté of the individual doing the uncovering and claiming, not that of the disabled person" (193).[4]

Changing Social Structures to Increase Access to Sexuality:
Beyond the Public/Private Distinction

Because social roles are both socially constructed and experienced as socially constructed (chapter 3), liberating the sexual lives of disabled people will require changing the social structures that prevent access to sexuality. Literature and art professor and disability studies scholar Tobin Siebers (2012), for instance, suggests that sexual identities are not identities that we each construct all by ourselves, but are, as he puts it, "theory-laden constructions" that combine both subjective and objective elements (40). This phrase echoes philosopher of science Norwood Russell Hanson's claim that facts are theory-laden in the sense that they presuppose commitments about what the world is like—commitments that are embedded in cultures' languages and learning (see chapters 4 and 5). Cultures' languages, concepts, and beliefs determine the facts—and hence the identities— that we perceive (see chapter 4), including, as Siebers is suggesting here, sexual identities. Because sexualities and sexual identities are socially constituted, liberating disabled people's sexuality will require developing what Siebers calls a "sexual culture." He uses the term *sexual culture* to contrast it with the term *sex life*, which, he says, implies that sex is private or belongs purely in the private sphere. Because sexual identities are "theory-laden constructions" and hence socially defined, however, Siebers says, liberating sexuality requires rejecting the distinction between the private and public spheres or the assumption that sex is purely private. Paying attention to the ways sexuality and sexual identities are socially defined is particularly important for disabled people, Siebers suggests, for whom opening up greater sexual access will require developing social structures around sex or a sexual culture (rather than a "sex life") that transgress(es) the distinction between the public and private (39–40).

Siebers examines several ways in which liberating sexuality and sexual identities for disabled people will require transgressing the distinction between the public and private. First, as he puts it, "the stigma of disability may interfere with having sex" (39). In a society ruled by "the ideology of ability" shaped by the eugenics movement (see chapter 2), in which the "preference for ability permeates nearly every value" (40), Siebers says, "any departure from sexual norms reads as a disability, disease or defect. Moreover," he says, "the equation runs in the other direction as well: disability signifies sexual limitation, regardless of whether the physical and mental features of a given impairment affect the ability to have sex" (42). In such a social context, liberating disabled people's sexuality will require major changes in public and social attitudes toward disability or, as he puts it, will require a "sea change in current scientific, medical, political, and romantic attitudes" (42).

Second, Siebers says, disabled people tend "not to judge their sexuality by comparison to normative sexuality" but "think expansively and experimentally about what defines sexual experience for them" (49). They often discover forms of eroticism that are not focused on penetrative sex, for instance, and as a result do not necessarily need to separate sex time or lives from everyday time or lives (48). The sexual eroticism of a neck bite (49), for example, need not take place in private at some special time.

Third, disabled people's sexuality also undercuts the public/private distinction insofar as disabled people embrace "new formations of gender and sexed identities" that challenge conventional sexual identities and so are political and hence public (Siebers 2012, 51). Finally, for many disabled people who live in group homes (see chapter 3) or use personal attendants, there is no real distinction between public and private time or places (Siebers 2012, 45–46). As Siebers says, "The myth that sex must be spontaneous to be authentic does not always make sense for people who live with little privacy or whose sexual opportunities depend on making arrangements with personal attendants" (49).

Because liberating sex for disabled people requires abandoning the notion that sex is a purely private activity or requires transgressing the distinction between public and private, Siebers suggests, liberating sexuality for disabled people will require bringing "rights to the places where disabled people want to have sex" (50). As disabled people demand access to sexuality and claim "a sexual culture based on different conceptions of the erotic body, new sexual temporalities, and a variety of gender and sexed identities," according to Siebers, the "emerging sexual identities" have two characteristics. First, these identities "represent disability not as a defect that needs to be overcome to have sex but as a complex embodiment that enhances sexual activities and pleasure," Siebers says, and second, "they give to sexuality a political dimension that redefines people with disabilities as sexual citizens" with a right "to create new modes of access for sex" (47). Instead of focusing on classifying *people* (scientifically, medically, or politically), liberating the sexual lives of disabled people will require redefining disabled people as sexual citizens with a right, as Siebers puts it, "to create new modes of access for sex" (47).

Does Sexual Freedom for People with Intellectual and Developmental Disabilities Lead to a New Form of Forced Sterilization?

As we have seen, the sexualities and reproduction of people with intellectual and developmental disabilities have often been curtailed and denied (chapter 3), and the eugenics movement led to the enactment of state laws prohibiting marriage and permitting the forced sterilization of people with intellectual and developmental disabilities as well as members of other groups (chapter 2). There is some evidence that society may be becoming more accepting of the sexualities of intellectually disabled people than it once was. One fairly recent study with parents of intellectually disabled adults, for instance, suggests that parents may be less opposed to the sexuality or sexual expression of their adult children with intellectual disability today than such parents were in the past. The psychologist Michel Desjardins (2012) conducted an in-depth, interview-based study with fifteen parents (twelve mothers, three fathers) of twelve adult children (aged between fifteen and twenty-five years) with intellectual disability in the greater Montreal area of Quebec, Canada, and found that the parents supported their children's sexual expression (73–74).

However, Desjardins also found that the parents actively engaged in a conscious strategy to persuade their adult children to "choose" to become sterilized. Desjardins says that this finding suggests that society's earlier policy of forced sterilization has been reshaped into a new process with the same outcome (i.e., the mass sterilization of intellectually disabled people as a group) except that now intellectually disabled adults are sterilized one by one, supposedly according to their own wishes and consent (80–82). As a result, Desjardins says, although the parents support their adult children's sexual expression, the adult children were still forced into an "extraordinary" or "adapted" sexuality that was different from the sexuality that parents would anticipate for other children, whose sexuality would be expected to progress or mature toward reproduction. In contrast, parents of the intellectually disabled adults in the study did not consider their children mature enough for sexuality until *after* they had been sterilized (81–82).

From Sexuality to Worries about Reproduction and Parenthood

As Desjardins (2012) points out, however, these parents' practices should not "be judged without regard to the global social context" (83). The parents in his study opposed their children's reproduction on grounds that were largely social. Desjardins found that the parents had three main reasons for wanting to prevent their adult children from reproducing. First, they worried that the grandchildren would be harmed because the intellectually disabled parent would be unable to look after the grandchild appropriately. Second, the parents worried that the intellectually disabled adult would be harmed by having the grandchildren taken away. Third, the parents of the intellectually disabled adults worried that they themselves would be forced to become the primary parents of the grandchildren, a social role that they did not want to adopt (77). As Desjardins suggests, these worries are shaped by the social context, particularly, I would say, by the fact that, in most Western societies, parents are expected to raise children largely on their own in nuclear families. Parents with intellectual disability may fail to take proper care of their children, and grandparents may be required to raise grandchildren without much support, only if they are each expected to care for the children largely on their own in nuclear families.

In other social contexts, other decisions would be more attractive. Ida Nicolaisen's work with the Punan Bah people of the central region of the island of Borneo in Malaysia suggests that the Punan Bah are an example of a society that, because they regard having children as necessary to achieving full personhood, not only expect people who we would regard as disabled to have children, but also take steps, within families, to help disabled family members have children (see chapter 3).

In an article exploring experiences of disability in Botswana, however, anthropologist Benedicte Ingstad (2007) worries about the burden that such definitions of personhood may have on children who are born to, and then are often expected to care for, disabled parents. "To what extent should the right of a person with a disability to have a child," Ingstad writes, "be weighed against the need of the child to have a secure childhood and an adult life in which obligation toward a disabled parent does not become too much of a disability in itself" (251). However, I worry not only that Ingstad's concern presupposes that caring for disabled parents is a burden (and that the parents have little to contribute) but also that the concerns may only apply under standard, Western social arrangements. In traditional Punan Bah society, where communities live together in longhouses, any needed tasks of caring for disabled parents might be spread out fairly evenly among a number of community and family members, and so might not fall primarily on disabled parents' children.

Worries that the grandparents or the children of disabled parents would have to bear the (supposed) burden of caring for grandchildren and/or disabled parents are therefore themselves constructed by social arrangements. In particular, they presuppose that children of disabled parents must live, as in many Western societies, primarily in nuclear families with either the parents or grandparents, in which case either the children (when they grow older) or the grandparents would have to assume the bulk of any tasks that may be needed to care for the disabled parents and, in the case of the grandparents, the grandchildren (when they are young). Under other social arrangements, however, this would not be the case.

Redefining What Makes Someone a Competent Parent

As Asch (2001; 2004) suggests, although it may seem impossible, in many Western societies today, people with characteristics such as "quadriplegia, autism, or limited ability to use or understand verbal language" are studying, working, and caring for children. They are able to do these things because "they have found or constructed arrangements in which they can contribute based on their capacities and receive assistance with facets of life that are difficult. Arguably," Asch continues, "that is what everyone does." We are all dependent on others to help us complete tasks. Lawyers do not fix their own cars, Asch points out, but "society does not degrade them for being dependent on mechanics." Similarly, people should not be devalued or patronized for obtaining spoken language through an interpreter or captioning, for getting ready for work with the help of a personal attendant, or for working with support staff to run errands. If environments do not "accommodate [someone's] mix of talents and needs," Asch says, "the problem may be the lack of imagination or the lack of will on the part of others" (2001, 10; 2004, 20–21).

Once we recognize that no one raises children by him- or herself, we can redefine what makes someone a competent parent. In a study with twenty-five Polish women who had various physical disabilities, Agnieszka Wołowicz-Ruszkowska (2016) found that the women were able to be successful mothers by redefining *competence* in terms of interdependence and building relationships. "The women made clear that independence does not mean the exercise of care without help," she writes. "The inability or limited ability to perform physical tasks related to parenthood has little to do with the ability to be a competent parent." Instead, Wołowicz-Ruszkowska says, "the women perceived those in supportive roles as helping in the background while they built a relationship between mother and child" (89).

As Chris Norton, who uses a wheelchair, has limited use of his arms and hands and is raising five children aged 8 and under with his wife, Emily, recently told

CNN reporter Christina Zdanowicz (2018), "with the kids, I know that there wasn't a lot I could do with helping them put a shirt on. . . . I can be more of a cheerleader and helping them grow as a person rather than being physically active." Chris also handles the finances and supervises people who "clean the house, do laundry and wash dishes."

A study conducted by Tim and Wendy Booth (2000) with thirty adults who had had at least one parent with learning difficulties found that their lives were more or less the same as the lives of other people from the same socioeconomic backgrounds ("Discussion," para. 2). Contrary to what Booth and Booth refer to as the "damage model," which holds that growing up with a parent with learning difficulties will damage a child, Booth and Booth found that the adult children in their study had developed resiliency, continued to maintain good relationships with the parent with learning difficulties, and had experienced disadvantages that came largely from others—such as bullying, harassment, and so on—rather than from dysfunctional parenting. Booth and Booth also found that "the strength of the parents' support system had an important bearing on their children's experience of growing up" and recommended redefining parental competence "as a distributed feature of parents' social network rather than as an individual attribute" (para. 6).[5] Kitty, the study participant whose family had had the most social supports, according to Booth and Booth, for instance, grew up with neighbors who helped her mother with chores such as shopping and cutting the grass and frequently stopped in to check on her mother. Kitty considered the neighbors a "second family," and the neighbors' daughters were like sisters. Kitty and her mother also had friends through their church ("Relationships and Support Outside the Family," para. 4).

From Independent Living to Interdependent Living

If we define parental competence, as Booth and Booth (2000) suggest, "as a distributed feature of parents' social network rather than as an individual attribute," then our society should find ways of redefining social relationships and arrangements to make it possible for disabled people to have access to the social role of parenting. One way to help disabled people become successful parents would be to supplement rehabilitation services with services that focus on *interdependence*. Although this research is not specifically about the role of parenting, rehabilitation and independent living scholar Glen W. White and his colleagues (2010) suggest that the core *in*dependent living skills that are currently addressed during rehabilitation and in centers for independent living (CILs)—peer counseling, training in daily living skills such as cooking or writing checks, advocacy services to help disabled people "fight for their rights and obtain benefits," and information and referral services (235)—need to be supplemented with *inter*dependent living services. Focusing purely on independent living skills, White and his colleagues say, leads some clients to become overdependent on the CILs for their social support (237).

Instead, professionals should help clients learn to build social capital and become "interdependent in communities" in ways that increase community participation (White et al. 2010, 238). As White and his colleagues suggest, "Rather than these [disability related] programs and services trying to be the social support for their consumers, they should be the facilitator of these social supports, teaching consumers how to create their own support system" (236). *Inter*dependent living services would help people become more competent in relationship building, in political advocacy, and in "interdependent community roles," such as the roles of friend, neighbor (236), and, we could add, sexual partner and parent.

If Rivlin—whose history we saw in the vignette at the beginning of the chapter—and his wife had lived interdependently with others in a supportive environment, perhaps their marriage would have lasted. And if we define *parental competence*, as Booth and Booth suggest, "as a distributed feature of parents' social network rather than as an individual attribute," then helping people build social networks would increase parental competence. Interdependent living would also call on us all to be part of such social networks.

Unmaking disability along the second dimension of embodiment or interpersonal body thus requires the same strategy that unmaking disability along the third dimension of embodiment requires (see chapter 6). To unmake disability along the second dimension, we should stop focusing on classifying *people* or their bodies, and focus instead on constructing social relationships and contexts that allow disabled people to access valued social (rather than bodily) capital and social roles, including the roles of sexual partner and parent.

UNMAKING DISABILITY ALONG THE FIRST DIMENSION OF EMBODIMENT OR PERSONAL BODY

- Should We Presuppose the Standard Environment to Specify Person-Level Activities?
- Presupposing the Standard Environment Misses How Barriers Are Constructed by Social Context, Including by Our Sciences
- Bursting a Socially Shared, Perceptual Bubble
- Acknowledging Corporeal Powers
- Changing the Social Context to Construct People as Capable

As we saw, in terms of the first dimension of embodiment or personal body, the individual *experience* of the body is always socially defined (see chapter 3). What the personal body is, as an object *out there*—its physical conditions or impairments (chapter 4) and its biology (chapter 5)—is also socially defined. Once we acknowledge that both what the body is, as an object out there, as well as how it is experienced are socially defined, then it follows that unmaking disability along the first dimension of embodiment or personal body will require not classifying people's bodies, physical conditions, or impairments but changing the social context that defines them in the first place. Since social context, including a society's language, concepts. and learning, shapes the facts and identities that we perceive, changing the social context will require changing society's language, concepts, and learning. Besides, diagnosing a person's medical/physical conditions or (biological) impairments tells us little about what a person can do (see chapters 4 and 5).

Should We Presuppose the Standard Environment to Specify Person-Level Activities?

Perhaps someone will grant that impairments cannot be specified outside of social contexts and practices, but still insist that we have to find some way to specify what someone's objective impairments are like for the purposes of political action, international research, and rehabilitation. Bioethicist and disability studies scholar Jerome Bickenbach and his colleagues (1999), for instance—who helped to develop the International Classification of Functioning, Disability and Health (ICF) for the World Health Organization (which was ratified in 2001)—criticized the original social model of disability on grounds very similar to the arguments by David Wasserman (against the minority model) and by Tom Shakespeare and Nicolas Watson that we saw in chapter 4. Bickenbach and his colleagues argue that the original, Marxist-inspired social model's sharp distinction between *impairment* and *disability* and insistence on defining *disability* only in terms of the restrictions on activity that are socially caused (see chapter 3) ignores what they call "person-level activities" (1177). They suggest that we need to consider person-level activities, not only to make international, cross-cultural research into disability and rehabilitation possible, but also to provide evidence for the social model's claim that environments disable people. Whether something is a barrier that blocks a disabled person's access has to be established empirically, but we cannot show what part of an environment is a barrier unless we can distinguish the environment from what a person is able to do (Bickenbach et al. 1999, 1178). That means that we have to be able to characterize "person-level activities" or what an individual person can do in a given environment. Bickenbach and his colleagues ultimately endorse an account of disability—the "'biopsychosocial' model" (1183, 1184)—that, like Wasserman's as well as Shakespeare and Watson's accounts, combines the medical and social models.

However, unlike Wasserman as well as Shakespeare and Watson (see chapter 4), Bickenbach and his colleagues grant that no human activity can be specified without reference to socially defined environments, practices, and customs. Although attempts to specify all activities "refer to the world and socially-created physical objects such as steering wheels, cars and roads, we can—and rehabilitation therapists regularly do—characterize a person's disabilities solely in terms of his or her person-level activities," Bickenbach and his colleagues write. "For classification and assessment purposes, the therapist asks what the individual can do, given the way steering wheels, cars and roads are usually constructed" (1178). Even if we want to say that the environment—such as the standard design of steering wheels—is a barrier, we have to be able to provide evidence for that claim, and we can only provide such evidence if we can specify what a person can or cannot do in a standard environment. As they put the point, "We are only justified in concluding that a physical or social barrier exists—and that standard steering wheel construction is such a barrier—when we know what is being prevented from happening by that barrier. And we can only find this out by assessing the person's abilities and disabilities, given the standard environment" (1178). We can determine what a person can and cannot do and whether some socially defined environment is a barrier, they are suggesting, only if we presuppose a standard environment.

Presupposing the Standard Environment Misses How Barriers Are Constructed by Social Context, Including by Our Sciences

Medical sociologist and disability studies scholar Irving K. Zola offers an argument against a focus on individual, "person-level" characteristics that can be used to reply to Bickenbach and his colleagues' points. Zola is not criticizing Bickenbach's and his colleagues' argument directly. Rather, he is criticizing the traditional emphasis in the United States generally on individual conditions and so-called "person-centered" planning, which, Zola says, has proven to be stubbornly persistent and, we can add, is still very much in vogue today (Taylor and Taylor 2013). These approaches are attractive, Zola (1993) suggests, because they are in line with other Western cultural assumptions, particularly Western culture's emphasis on individualism. As he puts it, "To shift away from the traditional condition/person-centered perspective meets with much resistance. Medical practitioners and researchers are not only wedded to this paradigm, but it is one reinforced by a tendency of U.S. culture to individualize medical and other social problems . . . including responsibilities . . . and interventions" (25). Zola criticizes approaches that emphasize individual conditions on the grounds that they are overly individualized, deficit-oriented, and invoke a notion of "'typical normal users' applied to any product, place or environment" (26). Such approaches will continue to focus our attention on individual deficits and interventions—on one person's inability to turn the steering wheel, for instance, and on a solution to that problem for that one person—rather than on trying to design more universally accessible devices. The approach also continues to take "typical normal users"—

the people who can turn the wheel of the car, given how the steering wheel is currently designed—as the standard of measurement.

In effect, Zola's argument suggests, Bickenbach's and his colleagues' approach advises us to ignore the role that socially constructed designs and environments play *before* we begin our measurements to determine what individual people can or cannot do. But the cost of this strategy, Zola (1993) says, will be that it will lead us not to notice the ways in which individual "conditions" are already socially structured (26). Because older people tend to be uncomfortable with using assistive devices, for instance, Zola suggests, individualistic systems of distribution that require older people to self-identify as needy and specifically request devices end up discouraging them from using the devices. When the systems are designed to provide assistive devices automatically, however, older people use those devices. For example, Zola says, when older people were provided with closed captioning on their television sets as part of their regular service, the usage "zoomed," as Zola puts it, but when they had to request the service and pay a small fee, few used it (27). In this case, a system whose design was modeled on our scientific assumption that the need for closed captioning is an individual condition different from the "typical normal person"—or is "special" (27), Zola says—made closed-captioning essentially inaccessible to older people. As Fine and Asch (1988) remark, we need to "cease considering the environment— whether physical or attitudinal—as given" (8).

If we start our studies—our science—by presupposing the standard environment, as Bickenbach and his colleagues suggest, then we will fail to notice, as Hanson argues (see chapters 4 and 5), the subtle and complex ways in which barriers are constructed by our languages and learning, even by the claims and assumptions of our biology or "science" itself. In Zola's example, it is the scientific assumption that a need for closed captioning is an individual condition that deviates from the "typical normal person" that constructed the very social context that made television inaccessible to many older people. We must, to return to Zola's (1991) point in chapter 3, "accept at least the metaphor of [Michel] Foucault and turn our gaze on the body ever more inward," by questioning "further some of the most taken-for-granted and cherished assumptions that allowed us to put the word 'scientist' after our name" (8).

We can still work to determine when medical interventions are appropriate (see the introduction), but deciding which interventions are appropriate will not be helped by treating either embodiment or the body as capable of being defined— even if only artificially, as Bickenbach and his colleagues suggest—outside of social contexts, concepts, and practices. Decisions to work on narrowly defined physical goals with questionable significance as part of rehabilitation therapy, for instance—such as on how to swing one's arm in the "biologically normal" way while walking, as one therapist worked on with my daughter (see the preface)— do have social implications. At the very least, they distract people from other goals that might be more socially efficacious as well as from an emphasis on changing the ways we structure our world in the first place. After all, our medical, physical, and biological ways of understanding the world are just one way of constructing reality and the facts we perceive (chapters 4 and 5).

Bursting a Socially Shared, Perceptual Bubble

In *A World without Words: The Social Construction of Children Born Deaf and Blind*, sociologist David Goode (1994) describes coming to notice, through his work with Christina (or "Chris"), a deaf and blind child who did not have language, how his reality is constructed. "My eyes and ears, once I had been socialized to use them 'correctly,'" he writes,

> provided me with a relatively coherent gestalt of experience, experience based upon these seeing-hearing beliefs and practices. These were the gifts of my family and their forefathers and allowed me to produce a stock of practical knowledge about my life world. But this body of knowledge had taken on a *sui generis* character, an existence of its own that I had to take into account. I had had no control over this learning how to see and hear reality, since the activities I had been taught were the same activities by which the knowledge was "validated." (29–30)

The body of knowledge that Goode created with his ears and eyes, in light of the gift of the rules for their use or the seeing and hearing beliefs and practices he learned from his family and foreparents, took on a *sui generis* (literally "of its own kind") character in the sense that he came to regard that knowledge as if it were its own kind of thing, as if the reality he knew was simply there on its own. We could say, for instance, that he was socialized to perceive and know *disability, impairment, mental illness* (cf. chapter 4), *biological sex* (cf. chapter 5), *rattle*, and so on. (my use of the *rattle* example will become clear shortly). But rather than regarding these "things" as a function of his learning and language, he took them to be "of their own kind": to be "reality," separate from him, out there in the world on their own. His belief in this "knowledge" was also self-reinforcing, because he had been taught to engage with the world in ways that validated the belief in them.

But the seeing and hearing beliefs and practices and knowledge he learned from his parents and foreparents were actually a "perceptual bubble" in which he "was trapped," Goode said. "I had been taught the work of making this bubble, this 'reality,' not the work of unmaking it. Yet it was a bubble I had to burst in order to discover Chris's 'own terms'" (30). Goode had to burst or *unmake* this perceptual bubble—the bubble determining how he perceived the world that he had learned from his family and foreparents, including when he learned language—to try to understand Christine's interactions on their own terms. In a similar way, unmaking disability and impairment along the first dimension of embodiment or personal body and coming to see people we define as disabled or impaired on their own terms will require bursting the dominant, perceptual bubble(s) of Western societies, including the one(s) created by our sciences. We have to come to see (hear, touch, smell, taste) the world differently, and perceive different facts.

Acknowledging Corporeal Powers

Besides, characterizing people we call disabled or impaired only in terms of what they *cannot do*, given standard, socially defined environments—or characterizing people only in terms of their *vulnerabilities*—fails to take account of their corporeal *powers*. In a critique of philosopher Eva Kittay's attempt to redefine personhood in terms of dependence, rather than independence, which is the criterion favored by traditional Western political philosophy and liberalism, the philosopher Shiloh Y. Whitney (2011) suggests that the problem with defining personhood in terms of pure vulnerability or dependence is that it fails to take account of "powers that are inseparable from vulnerabilities, powers we have failed to affirm" (569). Whitney cites Kittay's own example of the comedian Richard Pryor, who said that after multiple sclerosis took away his old capacities, he had to learn new ones, such as how to trust people (Whitney 2011, 569; Kittay 2002, 248). Whitney points to disability activist Sunaura Taylor's ability to carry her coffee in her mouth, an ability or power Taylor says she often does not use in public because other patrons are, as Whitney puts it, "usually uncomfortable with seeing a mouth plied to the task of carrying coffee." Whitney also mentions the ability that blind people have to navigate the world using hearing and touch (569, n. 22, 573).

Similarly, Goode (1994) points to what he calls Chris's "demonstrated skill in 'alternative object readings'" (35). Because Christine did not use language and was freed from our intentional meanings of what objects, such as musical rattles, are "for," Chris was able, Goode says, "to constitute a rattle as an object that could provide for her a number of different experiences" (35). She used it, for instance, as a tongue thumper and as something to bang on her front teeth. "I had to ask myself," Goode writes, "Who was getting maximum mileage out of that rattle? Is it we, who use it singularly and for specific purposes, or Chris, who uses it in a variety of ways?" (36). Goode grants that Chris's "not knowing how to use a rattle is problematic." In particular, he says, "it disqualifies her from membership in the category of persons who know how to use a rattle. However, it also *qualifies* her as a member of a category of persons who, by virtue of their not knowing how to use a rattle, do things with it that are inaccessible to persons who 'know' its proper use" (37). Christine's lack of language and hence of "knowledge" about what a "rattle" *is* gave her the power to read, define, and use the object in alternative ways that were more creative.

As Whitney (2011) suggests, these sorts of powers are not just consistent with people's vulnerabilities, dependencies, or with what people cannot do, but also complicit with those vulnerabilities—they are "powers whose development is inseparable from the adaptation and cultivation of specific vulnerabilities" (570). Unmaking disability along the first dimension will require acknowledging these corporeal powers.

It is because vulnerabilities have corresponding powers that disability scholars and activists object to the strategy of trying to show nondisabled people what it is like to be disabled by having nondisabled people wear blindfolds or pretend they cannot move their lower limbs while using wheelchairs, for instance. As Asch once said to me, putting a blindfold on a sighted person will simply scare the person, since the person has not acquired the skills that Asch acquired during years of negotiating life without vision.[6] Siebers (2008) explains that such simulations are problematic because they fail to give nondisabled pretenders "a sense of the embodied knowledge contained in disability identities" and thereby lead only to "emotions of loss, shock and pity at how dreadful it is to be disabled." Under these conditions, the pretenders "become so preoccupied with sensations of bodily inadequacy that they cannot perceive the extent to which their 'disability' results from social rather than physical causes" (28).[7] Nondisabled pretenders who have not developed the corresponding "embodied knowledge" or corporeal powers, Siebers is suggesting, will be so frightened by the bodily aspects of the simulations that they will be unable to notice the ways in which, as the social models of disability suggest (see the introduction), their (artificial) disability is socially caused.

Changing the Social Context to Construct People as Capable

As Zola and Siebers note, characterizing people we call disabled only in terms of what they cannot do, given standard socially defined environments, fails to take account of the ways social contexts construct people's incapacities. Jenny Morris (2001) recalls visiting a young man who had been at the same residential school since the age of four and who, according to his parents, teachers, and the care staff, had no way of indicating "yes" or "no" responses to communicate his preferences or choices. When Morris visited him in his home and at school, she says, "he had no discernible interaction with others; indeed, he spent a large part of each day asleep." After returning to live with his parents, however, Morris observed him at a new day program "actively participating in relationships with the care staff and other disabled young people. He 'said' yes by looking straight at you, and looked away for no," she writes. "His smile was so broad it took up all of his face and he never slept during the day—he was too interested and involved in what was going on." Morris suggests that this transformation was a result of a caring relationship that "started with his human right to communicate and which sought ways to make this possible" (14). It was thus the social context—in this case, the absence of a certain kind of social relationship—that constructed the young man as unable to say "yes" or "no" or to indicate his preferences and choices. As soon as the social context constructed him as able to do these things, he turned out to be able to do many other things as well.

Acknowledging the ways in which social contexts, including our languages and learning, our "science," shape the facts and realities we perceive as well as people's capacities and incapacities means that unmaking disability along the first dimension of embodiment or personal body requires remaking our worlds. Instead of focusing on classifying *people*, we need to remake socially defined environments—including our languages and learning and sciences—in ways that construct the widest variety of people as capable and as able to access our socially defined—and our *social* world. Talking with and reading about the experiences of people we define as disabled, examining history and talking with people from non-Western cultures and subcultures to explore how people from other times, places, and cultures construct(ed) those who we would define as disabled, takes an important step toward remaking our social world and perceiving different facts.

CASE STUDY: UNMAKING "SPECIAL" EDUCATION

- The Investigative Science Learning Environment (ISLE) as an Example of an Inclusive Teaching Approach

The profession of "special" education, which is supposed to serve students who are classified as disabled, is firmly rooted in exactly the kind of individualistic approach focused on classifying *people* that I have been criticizing. In their book, *Rethinking Disability: A Disability Studies Approach to Inclusive Practices*, special education and disability studies scholars Jan W. Valle and David J. Connor (2011) point out that special education is heavily invested in a medicalized approach to disability that sees disability as "a pathological condition intrinsic to the individual." School psychologists administer a battery of tests to determine whether an individual student "meets criteria for one or more of 13 disability categories" that would make him or her eligible for special education (41). All thirteen categories, Valle and Connor say, "focus on the pathology of disability" (65).[8] The results of the tests and evaluations then "form the basis of a treatment plan"—a student's Individualized Educational Plan (IEP)—which is "intended to remediate the individual's deficits." The supposedly scientific practice of special education thus, as Valle and Connor put it, "spins around the notion of normal/abnormal" (43), according to which the average, normal, or typical student is tracked into general education, while children diagnosed with deficits and hence defined as disabled—as "special"—get tracked into a parallel system of special education (10–12). As education scholars Dimitris Anastasiou and James M. Kauffman (2011), who defend the separation of general and special education, suggest, the "general education system matches the needs of assumed 'average' students" (379–80), while special education, "as a scientific field . . . allows the delivery of appropriate instruction geared to the individualized needs of atypical students" (379).

However, Valle and Connor (2011) suggest, the tests used to determine eligibility for special education ask students to complete tasks under scientific conditions that, from the point of view of the students, strip the tasks of any meaningful context. "We might consider what an unnatural social situation it is," they write, "for a child (who is typically caught unawares) to accompany an unfamiliar adult (who offers minimal explanation) to a small room where timed and untimed questions (of the adult's choosing) are presented for the duration of at least two hours." Although this routine may be familiar to the professional adult, it "may be experienced by a child as something akin to being 'taken in' for police interrogation" (47).

The problem is, Valle and Connor suggest, context helps to determine what people can and cannot do. Valle uses the example of her husband, Paul, whose progressive hearing loss looks increasingly severe on audiology tests, but, because Paul has developed "ingenious ways of his own invention to cull meaning from visual context," has not really affected his ability to move, as Valle and Connor describe it, "competently and confidently through the world as he does every day." Paul's ability to move through the world based on visual context allowed him to navigate Paris during a vacation just as well as he would have navigated an English-speaking area, even though he had no competence in the French language. "You know what?" Paul said during the trip, "I can't hear in English. And I can't hear in French. It really doesn't matter where I am, now does it?" (48). While the audiology tests measure Paul's pure, "auditory acuity," Valle and Connor suggest, it does not measure his "'hearing behavior' within the context of daily life." Paul's disability can therefore be "constructed differently" depending on whether we focus on the former, which is used to calibrate his hearing aids, or the latter (49).

"If context matters—and we believe it does—what might we be missing," Valle and Connor ask, "by evaluating children using decontextualized, standardized, and objective methods of science? Is it possible that children appear less able when asked to perform under conditions that remove everyday contextual cues?" No wonder there are often discrepancies, they suggest, between the way parents describe their "child-in-context" and the psycho-educational tests (49). As Valle and Connor ask, "How might the very *practice of standardization* influence test performance as well as the construction of disability?" (47). The scientific practice of removing children from everyday social contexts for psycho-educational tests constructs the students as less able or as dis-abled.

The result is that the scientific profession of "special" education, which employs an individualistic and medicalized approach that regards disability as an individual "deficit," Valle and Connor suggest, has led to the creation of a separate but unequal educational system (64) with negative outcomes for students, including rising dropout rates, underemployment, unemployment, and an overrepresentation of students of color in segregated, special education settings (31–35, 46, 59).

Other scholars have also found that "deficit thinking" helps to explain the disproportionate number of students of color in special education. Education scholars Roey Ahram, Edward Fergus, and Pedro Noguera (2011) found that what they call "cultural deficit thinking" about race and socioeconomic status together with misguided beliefs about disability on the part of teachers explains why students of color are overrepresented in special education classes. In their study, which was conducted in two, multiracial suburban school districts in New York state, Ahram, Fergus, and Noguera found that when teachers combined a faulty "cultural deficit thinking," particularly the assumption or belief that poverty affects cognitive ability (even though the teachers could not explain how poverty could cause a learning disability), with a misguided view of disability, according to which being normal is the same as being able (or being unable is the same as being abnormal), they pathologized, as disabled, low-income black and Latino children who were struggling in school relative to white students and referred those students for special education (2238, 2245–47, 2256). Cultural deficit thinking also allowed teachers to shift the blame for academic problems onto the students—the students' socioeconomic status, families, and cultures—rather than examine ways in which they themselves might reach struggling learners (2256–57).

As Valle and Connor (2011) tell the audience of young teachers at which their book is aimed, what one believes is how one teaches—or, we could add, what one believes is how one does not teach, in the case of students one believes one cannot reach. A teacher who reads a student's IEP documenting a student's deficits with skepticism about whether the student will fit into his or her classroom, Valle and Connor suggest, will spend time documenting student behaviors that support the belief that the student does not fit; a teacher who "reads the IEP with an eye to what the student needs in order to succeed in [the] classroom" will "work on developing organic strategies" to support the student's "inclusion within the class community." Note, Valle and Connor say, that the disabled student "remains constant. What shifts is the *conceptualization* of that student, depending on who is doing 'the looking'" (13). Deficit thinking thus *constructs* and hence *defines*, not only lower-income black and Latino students, as Ahram, Fergus, and Noguera found, but also students with disabilities, as Valle and Connor (2011) suggest, as less capable learners (69).

Besides, Valle and Connor say, the idea that there is an average or normal group of students is itself a myth, and they ask their graduate students "to rethink the 'myth of homogeneity' that drives the unending pursuit of new methods for sorting children according to their sameness." They say they hear teachers complaining year after year "about the number of students who fall outside of defined 'grade level' performance" and about failing to encounter a "grade level" class (52). But "to believe that homogeneity exists (presumably out there somewhere, in someone else's classroom) is to forever be disappointed—and to miss the point of teaching," Valle and Connor suggest (52–53). Indeed, they say, the main challenges that students with disabilities face—challenges in reading, written and oral language, and math—are common among students *without* disabilities as well (67–68). Instead of seeing students as normal or abnormal, as "belonging" or "not belonging," teachers should expect diversity, rather than homogeneity, in their classrooms and adopt inclusive practices that address the "academic and social needs of *all* students" (53).

Before we blame teachers, however, we must keep in mind, as Valle and Connor point out, that teachers' beliefs and practices, too, have been "shaped by patterns of human behavior and social structures" (14). To address the needs of all students, then, teachers have to be provided with conceptual and theoretical resources to question dominant beliefs and assumptions about impairment and disability as well as practical strategies that will help teachers make their instruction accessible to the widest possible variety of learners (Valle and Connor 2011, 68–69, 73).

The Investigative Science Learning Environment (ISLE) as an Example of an Inclusive Teaching Approach

What might an inclusive teaching approach look like? I would like to use the Investigative Science Learning Environment (ISLE) for teaching physics developed by physicist and physics education scholar Eugenia Etkina and her colleagues as an example of an inclusive learning system. Etkina (2015) says she first began to rethink how she taught physics after she had been teaching in Moscow schools for some years and ran into a former student who had been one of her best. The student was now studying to be a theater director and excitedly recounted how his class had built a *camera obscura* "to model a medieval theatre." Etkina asked him if he remembered building a *camera obscura* in a lab session for her class. "His answer stuck in my brain forever," Etkina writes. "Honestly," he said, "I do not remember anything from physics, except X-rays. Remember, I did a presentation on X-rays? I learned about X-rays by myself." "All my years of brilliant teaching and intriguing demonstrations did nothing for him," Etkina comments, "and the only thing that made an impression was what he learned on his own." This encounter led Etkina to adopt a new approach to teaching focused not *"on what I would do to teach my students, but on what they would do to learn"* (669).

One way in which ISLE is inclusive is that it is built in part on a constructivist theory of education (Etkina 2015, 669), according to which students acquire new knowledge by actively connecting it to already-existing knowledge. Under constructivist theories of education, teachers become not the imparters of wisdom that students are expected to absorb, but facilitators in students' self-driven learning processes (Fosnot 2005, ix). ISLE therefore shares several characteristics with other reformed curricula, such as an emphasis on, as Etkina (2015) describes them, "active engagement, group work, authentic problem solving, and reconciling students' original ideas with conventional ideas" (673).

ISLE's use of a constructivist approach gives it the potential to reach students with a variety of abilities. Education and disability studies scholar D. Kim Reid and Valle (2005) have suggested that a nonconstructivist teaching approach, or what they call "'transmission-infused' instruction," constructs students as less capable learners. Expecting students simply to copy the thoughts of the teacher and giving them no opportunity to think aloud or collaborate with peers eliminates the ability to use language as a "tool for thought" and positions students "as passive learners and astrategic thinkers" who have no "legitimate experiences on which to draw or the capability to do so" (156). If a student has difficulty producing a specific word that the teacher is thinking of, for instance, the student's "diagnosis" as disabled (e.g., as having word-finding difficulties) and as less able to learn may be reinforced in the mind of the teacher (Reid and Valle 2005, 158). Strategies rooted in transmission-infused instruction thus construct students as less capable learners.[9] By contrast, teaching strategies in which all students are constructed as "active, valuable and contributing member[s] of a vibrant classroom community," or in which "all children contribute to each other's meaning-making in the world" foster inclusion (Reid and Valle 2005, 161). ISLE's emphasis on "active engagement, group work, authentic problem solving, and reconciling students' original ideas with conventional ideas," to use Etkina's description, constructs students as capable learners and fosters inclusion.

ISLE has three additional components, however, Etkina says, that make it different from other reformed approaches. First, ISLE is aimed at helping students acquire certain kinds of reasoning skills, in particular, the kinds of skills that physicists use. In other words, it is intended to help students learn "how to think like physicists" (Etkina 2015, 670). Classes are structured so that students begin by observing a phenomenon, such as a laser hitting a mirror and reflecting in a dispersed pattern (Etkina 2015, 671), or a streak of alcohol smeared on, and then disappearing from, a sheet of paper. The students are expected to work together in groups to find patterns in the observation and then construct possible explanations, even "crazy" ones, for those patterns, which students typically do by drawing analogies to other things they already know (e.g., the alcohol parts are still there but have become invisible, or the alcohol parts were absorbed by the air, fell off the paper, or floated away).

Students are then expected to design experiments to test their explanations (Etkina 2015, 673). Teachers thus create a "mistake-rich environment" in which students are encouraged "to think like a physicist and not to be afraid to throw in ideas that later might be rejected" (674). Students read the textbook only after they have developed their ideas in class (672). By practicing how physicists come up with ideas and test those ideas, students not only learn how to think like a physicist, Etkina suggests, but also develop critical and independent thinking skills that "will be useful for them no matter what they chose to do in the future" (670).

The second additional component of ISLE, according to Etkina, is that it requires students to use a variety of tools to analyze the patterns and data they develop—tables, graphs, and different sorts of charts and diagrams, in addition to mathematics. These tools provide students with a variety of ways to make sense of information and make it part of their own reasoning processes (Etkina 2015, 674).

Third, the labs allow students not only to practice reasoning skills in "authentic" contexts that mirror those encountered by physicists, but also to become aware of *how* they came to know the things they know, or *why* they know what they know (Etkina 2015, 674). Follow-up studies suggest that "students who can adequately describe how they learned something do learn more than those students who think that they learn by reading a book or by watching somebody solve a problem on the board" (Etkina 2015, 675).

These three components reinforce ISLE's ability to be an inclusive teaching practice. Reid and Valle (2005) suggest that, unlike decontextualized, direct instruction, contextualized, cooperative, child-initiated instruction is more effective and elicits an enhanced response from disabled students (159). By offering students opportunities to develop knowledge in authentic (physics-like), cooperative, and student-initiated contexts, ISLE thus provides precisely the kind of learning environment that has the potential to reach disabled students. ISLE also satisfies two of the core principles—"equitable use" and "flexibility of use"—of universal design for learning (UDL) strategies, which are a set of guidelines intended to help create learning environments that are accessible to all students. Valle and Connor (2011) explain the principle of "equitable use" as the principle that instruction must be "designed to be useful and accessible to people with diverse abilities" (77); "flexible use" is the principle that instruction must be designed in a way that "accommodates a broad array of individual abilities and preferences" (78). Because ISLE requires students to use a variety of tools to build and analyze information as well as to read the textbook only after developing ideas in class, it provides opportunities for students with different strengths, abilities, and preferences to actively participate in developing knowledge.

Etkina and her colleagues (2017) also suggest that good physics teachers must develop several "habits of mind and practice." Some of these habits grow out of ISLE's roots in a constructivist approach to teaching, such as the idea that teachers should develop the habit of helping students connect new ideas to the students' existing ones, of encouraging students to test their ideas experimentally rather than wait for approval from an authority, and of listening to students and building instruction on students' ideas in the moment. Other habits reinforce

ISLE's emphasis on making instruction contextual, such as the idea that teachers should develop the habit of being guided by the belief that "cheap, readily-available materials can serve as the basis of a good physics lesson" and be aware of aspects of the environment—the natural environment, current events, or developments in science, for instance—that can help students learn (Etkina, Gregorcic, and Vokos 2017, 010107–7).

One of the habits Etkina and her colleagues (2017) recommend, however, is crucial to an inclusive teaching approach. Teachers, they suggest, should develop the habit of "treating all students as capable of learning physics and contributing to the generation of physics knowledge (as opposed to treating learning physics as a weed-out competition)" (p. 010107–7). Physics is not an exceptional form of knowledge accessible only to an elite few.

Indeed, as education and physics professor David Hammer (2000) points out in an article cited by Etkina and her colleagues, physics teachers often complain about the misconceptions about physics that students bring to the classroom. Hammer advises physics teachers to regard the naïve ideas about physical phenomena that students bring to the classroom as resources to build on, rather than as misconceptions to correct (p. S53). By developing the habit of treating all students as capable of learning physics and of contributing to the generation of knowledge about physics in the classroom, teachers will avoid the kind of "deficit thinking" that, as Valle and Connor (2011) suggest, constructs some students as less capable learners (69). Treating all students as capable of learning physics and of contributing to the advancement of knowledge in the classroom will also help to reach a wider variety of students by reducing the likelihood that students will develop what scholars call a "'fixed' mindset," or the belief that they do not have the capacity to learn something—a belief that can undercut students' motivations to learn that topic (Ormrod, Anderman, and Anderman 2017, 386–87).

As Etkina points out, there are aspects of ISLE that may not be able to be replicated in other disciplines. In physics, for example, she says, "it is often easy and highly productive to say, 'Go ahead and try it; set it up (bulbs, cart, magnet) and see what happens.' In chemistry, that may not be true, and in biology, it is very unlikely to be true" (Etkina, Gregorcic, and Vokos 2017, 010107–7). I have images in my head of the bad things that could happen if students decided to mix up a number of chemicals and see what happens. Still, there are many aspects of ISLE that can be replicated in other disciplines. Even philosophers, for instance, engage in "thought experiments."

ISLE thus provides an example of an approach to teaching that avoids classifying *people*, and worries instead about classifying and developing ways in which people with a variety of skills and abilities can *access* the content. In this case, ISLE focuses on creating a learning environment that produces a variety of ways for students with different skills and abilities to engage in socially meaningful, cooperative, and student-initiated activities to build on what they know and access new knowledge about physics.

I am not suggesting that no student ever needs special education. As Valle and Connor (2011) write, "Certainly there are children whose severity of disability *may* require special instruction outside the general education classroom." The trouble is, they say, "it has become more and more naturalized to construct struggling learners as *belonging* in special education." This is the stance that is "increasingly challenged by proponents of inclusive educational practices who contend that all children are far more alike than not, and that general education teachers, in fact, already possess a rich repertoire upon which to draw in teaching everyone" (43).

Education scholar Thomas Hehir (2002) distinguishes the notion of special education from the notion of *specialization* in education. Teaching some students with disabilities may require specialization or specialized skills that we cannot assume regular education teachers will have, such as reading Braille, knowing how to help students use communication devices, or knowing how to develop positive behavioral interventions for students with autism (24). What should be rejected, however, Hehir says, is the assumption that children who qualify for special education in virtue of needing teachers with such specialized skills should receive a *different* education from the one that other students receive (23).

CONCLUSION

Once we acknowledge that embodiment—what it *is* (as an object out there), and *is like* (in terms of experience), to move about in the world (see the introduction)—is socially defined, then we can acknowledge that the embodiment of impairment and disability is also socially defined (see chapters 1–5). From this point of view, unmaking disability will require reconstructing the social contexts and arrangements that define and construct impairment and disability in the first place. Unmaking disability along the third dimension of embodiment or institutional body, including under capitalism, will require remaking the world of work as well as the structures of attitudes that excluded people who we define as disabled from other large social structures and institutions as well as from social citizenship (see chapter 6).

This chapter has explored what unmaking disability would be like along the second and first dimensions of embodiment, the interpersonal body and personal body. Unmaking disability along the second dimension of embodiment or interpersonal body will require redefining social arrangements in ways that undercut Western societies' propensities to define people's characters in terms of visually observed, bodily appearances, functions, and behaviors—characterizations that tend, in the minds of nondisabled people, to spread over the whole person or become a master status—and come to define people in terms of social and other characteristics that are not apparent to the eye. We also need to redesign social attitudes and structures so that disabled people can access valued social roles, including the social roles of being sexual partners and parents.

Unmaking disability along the first dimension of embodiment or personal body will require remaking our worlds, including our languages, learning, and "science" itself. We need to reconstruct concepts, socially defined devices, and social contexts in ways that provide access to the widest possible variety of people, thereby constructing people as able, rather than as impaired or disabled. I used the example of the Investigative Science Learning Environment (ISLE) for teaching physics developed by Etkina and her colleagues to suggest that, instead of classifying people as nondisabled or disabled, as able or unable, as belonging or not belonging, we can design learning environments, for instance, that focus on providing students with a wide variety of skills and abilities access to social contexts in which they can build on what they know and develop new knowledge about physics.

Conclusion

Bodies and embodiment are socially defined both in terms of how they are *experienced* as well as in terms of what they *are*, as objects *out there*, along all three dimensions of embodiment or all three "bodies": the institutional body, the interpersonal body, and the personal body (see the introduction). Both *disability* and *impairment*—terms used in many Western societies to characterize bodies—are therefore also socially defined and constructed or *made*.

In this conclusion, I begin by summarizing the book's account of *how* both disability and impairment were *made* along all three dimensions of embodiment, starting (as the book did) with the third dimension or institutional body, as I call it. As disability studies scholars and social models of disability (see the introduction) have insisted, contrary to what most people in Western societies assume, disability is not a personal characteristic of individual bodies (the first dimension or personal body), but a category that has been defined by and embedded in Western societies' social institutions and structures (the third dimension or institutional body). In other words, disability has been defined, not from the *bottom*—the individual, personal body or first body—*up*, so to speak, but from the *top*—the institutional body or third body, or social institutions and structures—*down*. From this point of view, the third dimension or institutional body *is* the beginning of the story. The conclusion ends by summarizing the book's account of how disability may be *un*constructed or *unmade*.

193

Outline of conclusion:

➤ Making Disability
➤ Unmaking Disability

MAKING DISABILITY

• The Third Dimension of Embodiment or Institutional Body
• The Second Dimension of Embodiment or Interpersonal Body
• The First Dimension of Embodiment or Personal Body

The Third Dimension of Embodiment or Institutional Body

Along the third dimension of embodiment or institutional body, which captures how large structures and institutions in societies regulate, survey, and control people (see the introduction), the development of the capitalist economic system in the West defined the social category of disabled people. In the Middle Ages in Europe, there was no universal concept or understanding of what we today call "disability." People we would classify as disabled were part of a multiform category of people who needed the support of others, which included widows, sick people, pilgrims, economically poor people, and people with what we would call impairments. As the growth of capitalism spread urban economic arrangements in which people were paid for the time they worked rather than, as in rural systems of work, for the products or projects they completed, people regarded as having a lower level of productivity and as more expensive laborers were excluded from the capitalist wage market and came to be defined as *dis*-abled or as unable to work. Such people were also excluded and hence "dis-abled" by the capitalist wage market's narrowing of what counted as work or as genuine economic activity. Beginning in the middle of the eighteenth century, an increase in productivity requirements under industrial capitalism as well as a demand for standardized bodies (that could function like machines) further excluded and "*dis*-abled" people, including people with nonstandard bodies, in relation to the capitalist wage market (chapter 1).

Public values and beliefs also changed in ways that reflected the new system of work. Starting in the late thirteenth century and certainly after the spread of the Protestant work ethic beginning in the mid-seventeenth century, all social strata of urban society adopted the elite's discourse on the intrinsic value of labor (chapter 2). The capitalist economic system was accompanied by a new structure of public attitudes that took for granted the exclusion of people now classified as disabled—an assumption that, in turn, led to additional exclusion from other structures and institutions, such as the transportation, education, and health care systems, as well as common architectural designs (chapter 1).

In the nineteenth century, with the establishment of the power of the capitalist (middle and upper) ruling classes (chapter 2), the development of the disciplines of medicine and biology, as French philosopher Michel Foucault observed (chapter 7), and the invention of the concept of "normalcy," people classified as disabled came increasingly to be defined in many Western societies not only as excluded and disadvantaged but also as a despised group of outsiders (chapter 2). Freak shows, which first became common during the sixteenth century, had made it possible (albeit not in an ideal way) for many people who we would regard as disabled to be self-supporting and hence "able-bodied" under definitions of disability and impairment linking those terms to an inability to labor.

Beginning in the nineteenth century, however, there was a shift in how disability came to be defined. Ruling class values, the disciplines of medicine and biology, and the concept of "normalcy" came to define bodily differences in terms of disease, defect, or abnormalcy, and as a necessary barrier to work or as necessarily "dis-abling." People so defined were also increasingly segregated and confined in institutions—just as Joseph Merrick, who had exhibited himself in freak shows as the "Elephant Man" in the 1880s, was confined to the London Hospital by Dr. Frederick Treves. This new, biomedical understanding of impairment (see also chapter 5) and disability and new structure of cultural attitudes, which remained intertwined with the workings of capitalism, was reflected in, but also reinforced by, the eugenics movement, the enactment of so-called "ugly laws," and the increasing institutionalization of disabled people, often under inhumane and neglectful conditions.

In many ways, these cultural attitudes persist in Western societies, as disabled people continue to be the targets of negative, ableist attitudes, to be treated according to medical models, and to live in and experience segregated social contexts (chapter 2). Today, we use the concept of "impairment" in medicalized ways to refer to what we regard as biological diseases, defects, or abnormalities in people's bodies (along the first dimension of embodiment or personal body; chapter 5), and the concept of "disability" either is used to mean the same thing as "impairment," under the medical model of disability (introduction), or is defined, in Social Security law, for instance, as the inability to labor in the capitalist wage market (chapter 1).

The Second Dimension of Embodiment or Interpersonal Body

In terms of the second dimension of embodiment or interpersonal body, which captures how societies use the body to define social roles, society, or the world, disabled people have a devalued bodily capital or prestige in Western societies that they have to manage on a daily basis. While they have typically been assigned one *devalued* social role—the "sick role" or "handicapped role"—they have simultaneously been denied *valued* social roles, such as the roles of being a sexual partner and parent. The denial of the roles of sexual partner and parent has also meant that disabled people's sexuality generally has typically been denied and curtailed (chapter 3). During the eugenics movement, of course, these denials took legal form, as laws were passed permitting the forced sterilization of disabled people and restricting their rights to marry (chapter 2).

Today, marriage-restriction and forced-sterilization laws are no longer active or enforced, but nondisabled people in many Western societies still have difficulty acknowledging the sexuality of disabled people and regarding them as sexual partners and parents. Although parents of adult children with intellectual and developmental disability (IDD) may be becoming more accepting of their adult children's sexuality, they pressure their adult children with IDD into "choosing" to become sterilized—a pressure they would not bring to bear on nondisabled adult children, whose sexuality they would expect to mature to reproduction. Parents may thereby achieve the same end that forced-sterilization laws did (namely, the mass sterilization of people with IDD), but under a new guise in which sterilization is now (supposedly) freely chosen by individuals. Societies' difficulties accepting disabled people as sexual partners and parents also affects the ways in which disabled people experience these roles, when they do. Physically disabled people report experiencing shame about their bodies in sexual encounters with lovers, for instance. And disabled mothers often experience their social role of being a mother as tenuous (chapter 3).

The First Dimension of Embodiment or Personal Body

Along the first dimension of embodiment or personal body, which captures how individual bodies or selves are defined (in some cultures, however, people are not regarded as individual selves or bodies; chapter 3), although we tend to think of experiences of our bodies as simply given, even the *feel* of one's own body is socially defined. Disabled people's experience of their bodies is shaped by the same social structures, institutions, and structures of public and cultural attitudes that shape the second and third dimensions. Medical sociologist and disability studies scholar Irving Kenneth Zola's experiences of his body while traveling through airports, for instance—his experiences of arriving at his destinations sore, tired, and cramped—were shaped by the designs of airports as well as by the social assumption that one should be physically independent and always try to do things in as "normal" a way as possible. Similarly, the experience of intelligence by cognitively disabled people as well as the pain experienced by people with sickle-cell anemia are shaped by ableism (chapter 3). There is *something* it is like to *experience* the world as, say, Irving Kenneth Zola, but what that something *is like* can never be determined outside of social contexts and practices. There is *no* given, purely objective, pre-social, purely physical, or biological *experience* of the disabled body; the very *feel* of disabled, personal bodies or of the phenomenologically experienced, disabled body is always socially defined.

We must be careful, therefore, not to think of em*body*ment as being about the body, in the sense of a purely objective, pre-social, physical, or biological body, which is how the body is typically understood in the West today. For, just as there are no purely objective, pre-social, natural, physical, or biological bodies in *experience*, so there are also no purely objective, pre-social, natural, physical, or biological bodies *out there*, as objects.

The concept of "impairment," which is used to characterize bodies *out there*, is a highly abstract concept that does not exist in many traditional cultures. In the Middle Ages in Europe, there was no single term that was used to capture all and only what we would think of as impairment today. What we identify as "impairment," smaller "facts of impairments," or "bodily conditions" are all socially defined by our languages and learning (chapter 4). The concept of impairment has not even been trans-historical under capitalism in the West, as there was a shift to a new definition of impairment under industrial capitalism, in which it became a biomedical disease, defect, or abnormality that was an inevitable obstacle to work or was necessarily "dis-abling" (see chapters 2 and 5). But the discipline of biology and the practice of medicine to which it is connected are just one way of defining the world and the facts that we perceive.

Claims about *biological* impairments or bodies are therefore also socially defined. People at other times and in other cultures, such as in traditional Yoruba society, have defined what we call the biological body differently, and perceived different facts (chapter 5). There is *something*, some identity, that Irving Kenneth Zola *is*, insofar as he is out there in the world, then, but what that something *is* cannot be determined outside of the social, of learning, of language (chapters 4 and 5). Both *impairment* and *disability* are socially defined (see also the introduction).

UNMAKING DISABILITY

- Unmaking Disability along the Third Dimension of Embodiment or Institutional Body
- Unmaking Disability along the Second Dimension of Embodiment or Interpersonal Body
- Unmaking Disability along the First Dimension of Embodiment or Personal Body

Because disability has been made in ways that harm people, we should find ways to *unmake* it. It is always easier to describe how things are or have been than to describe how they could or should be, but I tried to point to ways in which disability might be unmade (chapters 6–7) in light of how it is made (chapters 1–5). In general, because *disability* is socially defined along all three dimensions of embodiment (chapters 1–5), unmaking disability will require not an individualistic approach focused on changing individuals or providing them with individual accommodations, but a structural approach that changes the social structures and institutions that have defined disability in the first place. We must change *all* of the social structures and institutions that define, exclude, disadvantage, and harm disabled people and deny them access to valuable social capital and roles—including the structures of public or cultural attitudes in many Western societies as well as those societies' concepts and beliefs (chapters 6–7).

Unmaking Disability along the Third Dimension of Embodiment or Institutional Body

Along the third dimension of embodiment or institutional body, although deindustrialization, or the shift to a capitalist economy dominated by providing services rather than by manufacturing, is redefining the structure of work in the West in ways that might seem hospitable to disabled people—including an increasing reliance on informal, temporary, and project-oriented jobs—this restructuring is in fact further disabling people in relation to the capitalist wage market. Changes in working conditions, particularly the loss of control over the kinds of work done as well as over how time is spent, are increasing disability today. Cuts in welfare benefits and an increase generally in economic precariousness are also reducing people's access to the wage market.

Unmaking disability in relation to deindustrialized capitalism will require addressing the structural conditions that disable people. Strategies aimed at changing *individuals*, such as help with job searches or training, are not very useful. By contrast, changing the employment context for chronically ill and disabled people in ways that increase their access to jobs, such as by offering wage subsidies for employers to hire them and financial support to help employers make work places more flexible and accessible, will help to improve the employment rates of chronically ill and disabled people. Forcing employers to screen candidates based only on the essential skills required to do a job would also be helpful. Still, changing the employment context will not be enough. As long as excluding people who are regarded as less ideal employees is a good business strategy, employers will continue to do so.

Ultimately, unmaking disability under capitalism will require changing the nature of work. Expanding the definition of what counts as work beyond wage labor would be a first step. Including what we can think of as social work or civil labor, such as work with civic organizations, work done with friends and family to care for others, and public participation in the life of the community—much of which is currently done for free or on a volunteer basis—would give disabled people not only access to more care, if needed, but also access to more *work* (chapter 6). Disabled people are capable of a great deal of work (chapters 1 and 6), and expanding the definition of what counts as genuine economic activity beyond current definitions of wage labor would increase their access to work. The notion of work should also be expanded to include other kinds of work that disabled people are often required to do, including the additional time and effort spent on everyday tasks, often because society is designed for nondisabled people (chapter 6). It takes additional time, for instance, to use a subway system in which many stations are inaccessible (see the introduction), or to use typically underfunded, paratransit systems (chapter 6).

Because disabled people will be able to access work—even under an expanded definition of *work*—only if their civil rights are also promoted, improving their access to work will require changing the structures of public attitudes, particularly notions of citizenship, that have underpinned disabled people's exclusion from other structures and institutions, including the transportation, education, and health care systems and the built environment. In many capitalist, Western societies, citizenship and the civil rights of citizenship have been tied to having a paying job. Unmaking disability will require decoupling the notion of citizenship from paid wage labor.

Since the development of the concept and system of normalcy in the nineteenth century, these societies have also based access to the civil rights of citizenship on the ability to be "normal" or to live up to the norm. Unmaking disability will require redefining the notion of citizenship to separate it not only from having a paying job but also from the requirement that one must be "normal" to be considered a citizen with civil rights. Political scientist Kristin Bumiller recommends adopting a notion of "quirky citizenship" that she suggests has been proposed by the neurodiversity movement founded by autistic people (chapter 6).

Unmaking Disability along the Second Dimension of Embodiment or Interpersonal Body

Unmaking disability along the second dimension of embodiment or interpersonal body will require giving up Western societies' tendencies to classify people based on the visual sense and bodily appearances and paying attention to aspects of people's characters that are not apparent to the eye. Such an approach would also help to overcome the current ways in which visibly disabled people have a devalued "bodily capital" and help them achieve social capital instead. It would also help invisibly disabled people by liberating them from other people's assumptions that they are not disabled. Because of the tendency in the minds of nondisabled people for disability status to spread over the whole disabled person, or because disability tends to function as a master status that comes to dominate, in the minds of nondisabled people, the whole disabled person, one must, as it were, forget that someone is impaired or disabled and focus on other aspects of his or her character. At the same time, one must keep in mind that, in societies structured around notions of impairment and disability and in which these classifications have serious social consequences, one must also never forget that someone is disabled. One must pay attention not to disabled people's bodies but to their *embodiment*, along all three dimensions of embodiment (chapter 7).

Unmaking disability along the second dimension will also require nondisabled people to resist assigning disabled people the devalued "sick" or "handicapped" social role that leads nondisabled people to regard disabled people as helpless, dependent, and passive and to deny disabled people access to adult social roles. Instead, we must remake the social structures in societies to provide disabled people access to sexuality and to the social roles of being a sexual partner and parent, as they do in Punan Bah society. Accessing sexuality for disabled people will require redefining them as sexual citizens with a right to sex as well as working to create social structures that facilitate access to sex. Accessing the social roles of being a sexual partner and parent will require reorganizing social structures and relationships to facilitate such social roles. Once we recognize that parental competence, for instance, is actually a feature of a person's social network, rather than an individual characteristic, we can organize and participate in social networks that define disabled people as competent parents (chapter 7).

Unmaking Disability along the First Dimension of Embodiment or Personal Body

Along the first dimension of disability or personal body, unmaking disability will require changing the very way in which we structure our world, all the way down to the concepts and beliefs that shape the facts that we perceive. Because presupposing our standard environments—including the ones created by our sciences—often misses the ways in which barriers are constructed by those very social environments and contexts, we will have to change the structures as well as the beliefs and practices that shape the perceptual bubbles from which we know the world. To understand disabled people on their own terms, we will have to come to see (hear, touch, smell, taste) the world differently, and perceive different facts. Instead of simply measuring what a disabled person cannot do, given how something is currently designed, for instance, we should rethink the way things are designed. Constructing people only in terms of impairments, *dis*-abilities, or what they cannot do also fails to recognize corresponding corporeal powers. Asking nondisabled people to pretend to be disabled as part of an exploration of experiences of disability is not helpful because they have not developed the corresponding skills and abilities or corporeal powers that disabled people develop over time.

We must also remake social contexts, including beliefs, in ways that construct people currently defined as disabled as *capable*. Instead of classifying individuals as "impaired" or "disabled" and shuttling them off to "special" education, for instance, we should redesign teaching and the educational system in ways that construct the widest possible variety of students as capable learners. Because our socially shared concepts and beliefs shape the very facts that we perceive, unmaking disability along the first dimension of embodiment will ultimately require remaking our socially defined worlds (chapter 7).

Notes

PREFACE AND ACKNOWLEDGMENTS

1. For a more thorough exploration of these issues, see Maybee (2011).

INTRODUCTION AND THEORETICAL OVERVIEW

1. For a brief description of the film, see www.tiff.net/festivals/thefestival/programmes/short-cuts-international/short-cuts-international-programme-5/midfield.

2. In her book *Perspectives on Disability and Rehabilitation: Contesting Assumptions; Challenging Practice*, for instance, which urges rehabilitation professionals to take seriously the ways in which work in disability studies challenges many of their assumptions, Karen Whalley Hammell (2006) writes that disability studies undercuts the assumption that rehabilitation professionals, who "demonstrate very little knowledge of what it means to live as a disabled person in the community," are the only "experts," proposing instead that "the term 'expert' must be broadened to respect the knowledge of people who have different positions and perspectives based on their experiences as users of health care and as experts concerning their own problems, needs and perceptions of life's quality" (8). Similarly, in his introduction to the second edition of *The Disability Studies Reader*, Lennard Davis (2006) notes that disability studies' focus on the political aspects of disability "is being organized by people with disabilities and other interested parties" (xv). Disability studies' emphasis on the perspectives of disabled people was also well expressed by the title of James I. Charlton's (1998) classic book, *Nothing About Us Without Us: Disability Oppression and Empowerment*.

3. Davis (2006), for instance, takes disability studies' criticism of the oppression and repression of disabled people to be central to its definition. "The exciting thing about disability studies is that it is both an academic field of inquiry and an area of political

activity" (xv). Hammell (2006) suggests that the field raises questions about "issues of power and privilege and of the systemic oppression of disabled people" (5).

4. Both Davis and Hammell, for example, compare disability studies to race, class, or gender studies (see Davis 2006, xv). Hammell (2006) suggests that, like gender or women's studies and other studies of social categories of difference, disability studies explores disability as a socially constructed category of difference "that is defined according to specific social, cultural and historical contexts" (4). Davis (2006) says that, in disability studies, disability "gains a new, nonmedicalized, and positive legitimacy both as an academic discipline and as an area of political struggle" (xv).

5. Philosopher and bioethicist John Harris (2000) has argued that social conceptions of disability in general are flawed because they cannot distinguish exclusion or discrimination conducted on the basis of disability from exclusion or discrimination conducted on the basis of gender or race. As he puts the argument, "If disability could be identified simply in terms of social conditions, for example, social exclusion, or discrimination, then all victims of racial and gender discrimination would count as disabled and Jews, Blacks and Women would be people with disabilities" (95). However, his argument ignores the fact that social conceptions of disability typically hold that impairment is the underlying marker used to identify those who are targeted for exclusion or discrimination on the basis of disability. That criterion—impairment—is different from the criteria used to identify those who are targeted for racism (i.e., certain skin colors, hair textures, bone structures) and sexism (i.e., certain sex organs), and so can be used by supporters of social conceptions of disability to distinguish ableism from other forms of social exclusion or discrimination.

6. A copy of the 1975 EAHCA (Public Law 94-142) may be found at: https://www.govinfo.gov/content/pkg/STATUTE-89/pdf/STATUTE-89-Pg773.pdf. The 1990 amended version (Public Law 101-476) may be found at: https://www.congress.gov/bill/101st-congress/senate-bill/1824. The IDEA of 1997 (Public Law 105-17) may be found on the Congress.gov website of the Library of Congress at www.congress.gov/105/plaws/publ17/PLAW-105publ17.pdf. The IDEA as amended in 2004 (Public Law 108-446) can be found on both the websites of the U.S. Government Publishing Office at www.gpo.gov/fdsys/pkg/PLAW-108publ446/html/PLAW-108publ446.htm and at Congress.gov at www.congress.gov/bill/108th-congress/house-bill/1350. The Americans with Disabilities Act of 1990 may be found on the website of the Equal Employment Opportunity Commission (EEOC) at www.eeoc.gov/eeoc/history/35th/1990s/ada.html. The ADA Amendments Act of 2008 (Public Law 110-325) may also be found on the EEOC's website at www.eeoc.gov/laws/statutes/adaaa.cfm. (All websites were accessed on July 26, 2019.)

7. For instance, Andrew I. Batavia and Kay Schriner (2001) have argued that, because the ADA's basic design means that violations of civil rights are addressed largely on an individualistic, case-by-case basis, the ADA will always have limited effectiveness. Melanie K. Jones (2008) reviews the early literature on whether the ADA helped or hurt disabled employees (414–17). Adrienne Asch (2001; 2004) criticizes how the courts' overemphasis on who counts as disabled undercuts the effectiveness of the ADA. Frank Cavaliere, Toni P. Mulvaney, and Marlene R. Swerdlow (2012) examined the ways in which U.S. Supreme Court decisions weakened the effectiveness of the application of the ADA, and they make some predictions about whether changes under the ADAAA will make the law more ef-

fective. John LaNear and Elise Frattura (2007) question the standard story according to which the education provided to disabled students has steadily improved, and they assess the overall effectiveness of special education law.

8. Not all of the critics who complain that the social model ignores the body would also criticize it for presupposing a pre-social, purely biological body. Sociologist Simon J. Williams (1999), for instance—whose work I quote in chapter 1—turns his complaint that the social model has written the body out into a call to bring the biological and pre-discursive body "back in" (805). I address this sort of argument—though not Williams's version of it—in chapters 3, 4, and 5. In chapter 3, I argue that there is no *experience* of a pre-social body, in chapter 4, I argue that there is no pre-social body *out there*, and in chapter 5, I argue against the claim that there is a pre-social, purely *biological* body.

9. The materialist position, Gleeson argues (1997), does not ignore "the real limits which nature, through impairments, places upon individuals"; instead, materialists simply separate, "ontologically and politically, the oppressive social experience of disability from the unique functional limitations (*and capacities*) which impairment can pose for individuals." Impairment, Gleeson says, is just "a form of first nature which certainly embodies a given set of limitations and abilities which then places real and ineluctable conditions on the social capacities of certain individuals" (194).

10. Disability activist and scholar Paul Abberley (1987), who embraces but extends the Marxist, economic analysis of disability by employing a wider conception of oppression (8), also defends the view that impairment and biological phenomena have social origins (12), and he criticizes theories that treat impairment as a given or natural property (14). Materialist theorists whose work focuses on other social categories, such as gender and race, have made similar points. Teresa L. Ebert (1996), for instance, argued against what she regarded as some feminists' tendencies to treat biology as a given, natural base (235), suggesting instead that bodies and bodily processes are always "mediated," or are "constructed, made intelligible, and experienced through the structuring of the symbolic order and the operation of the political economy of social relations according to the division of labor and demands of modes of production" (238). In other words, bodies and their parts and processes are not given, biological or natural entities, but are constructed, understood, and experienced through a structure of language, symbols, and concepts that is itself produced by the social relations that result from the division of labor and modes of production of an economic system. In our case today, bodies and their parts and processes are constructed by capitalism. Similarly, philosopher and materialist theorist Stephen C. Ferguson II (2017) has argued that race is a "phenotypic ascription," an act of regarding someone as having certain characters or qualities, such as "skin color, hair texture, eye shape, lip formation and so on," that have no value other than to provide a supposedly "empirical basis for identifying putative superior and inferior groups" as part of the social relations of capitalism. Race is therefore a social category through-and-through, Ferguson suggests, that "can only be correctly seen in abstraction of nature or natural (phenotypic or genetic) ascriptions." To treat race as if it can be separated from the systems of racism is thus a "reification," an act of making race and the supposedly underlying phenotypic or genetic characters or qualities into things (264). I am grateful for Stephen's help in bringing Ebert's work to my attention.

11. My argument for the view that the experience of the first or personal body is always socially defined will help to show what is wrong with Simon J. Williams's (1999) argument

for the view "that our identities are lodged in our bodies" (811). Williams argues that we can distinguish a concept of self—which is socially defined—from a "universal sense of self" (811)—which is not socially defined. This universal sense of self gives rise to a personal identity, which is the identity that is lodged in our bodies, or is the identity of the flesh (811). I will argue, however, that while there might be a universal sense of self in the sense that there is always *something* it feels like to be, say, Irving Kenneth Zola, that *something* has no definite character—or cannot be defined or *identified*—outside of the social. Williams's leap from a "universal sense of self" to *identity*, then, is unwarranted. There is no *identity* that is not already shaped by the social. Williams argues that there could never be selves capable of resisting the social unless there is such a pre-social self or personal identity (812). But we say "no" for all sorts of reasons, and one can say "no" to one's society in particular circumstances, I think, without presupposing that one must have a definite identity separate from one's society.

CHAPTER 1. DISABILITY AND CAPITALISM

1. The article by Anna Stone and Toby Wright (2013) just referenced, for instance, examines the degree to which employers discriminate against both people with facial disfigurements and people who use wheelchairs, finding that the discrimination against those with facial disfigurements was in their view surprisingly similar to the discrimination their study found against people who use wheelchairs (522).

CHAPTER 2. A NEW STRUCTURE OF ATTITUDES: NORMALCY, EUGENICS, THE UGLY LAWS, AND SEGREGATION

1. For an additional discussion of how the conception of "normalcy" was invented in the nineteenth century, see also, for instance, Ladelle McWhorter (2009).

2. It even dominates the Wikipedia entry about Merrick ("Joseph Merrick" 2018).

3. I note that it seems odd that Merrick could build models and weave baskets but could not work. Perhaps in an earlier time, during the Middle Ages (see chapter 1), when there was a greater variety of forms of labor, Merrick might well have been able to do what people at that time would have regarded as legitimate economic activity.

4. Magruder's textbook must have been enormously popular. It was first published in 1917 and then republished in new editions every year until a few years after his death in 1949, when it was taken over by William A. McClenaghan. A "Publisher's Note" on the back of the title page in a 1950 edition of the book says that the book was revised "at least once a year," to keep it "thoroughly up to date." The 1950 edition still contains the same arguments justifying control of the reproduction of feebleminded people as well as segregated education and institutionalization of "imbeciles and morons." The book argues that "feeble-minded persons usually have large families," which will "injure our race" and "contribute a large proportion of our criminals, drunkards and paupers." It goes on to note that some states prohibit the marriage of feebleminded people "unless treated to prevent offspring" and segregate "those having illegitimate children" (Magruder 1950, 663). Imbeciles and morons "do not develop initiative, and have weak will power," the

book says, "but they can be taught to lead a useful life within an institution. There they can be happiest because engaged in tasks at which they can succeed." In the 2004 edition, now called *Magruder's American Government* and advertised as "revised" by William A. McClenaghan, the section from Macgruder's editions in which those arguments had appeared, titled "The Betterment of Society," has been removed. Still, the only context in which disabled people are mentioned in the text is during a discussion of democracy, in which the text says that democracy "does not claim that all are born with the same mental or physical abilities" (Magruder and McClenaghan 2004, 19). Several photographs contain images of disabled Americans as examples of interest groups (237, 249) and Congress's commerce power (298). The Americans with Disabilities Act receives only one mention—on a timeline in a highlight box called "The Enduring Constitution" (307), and there is no mention of people with disabilities at all in the section titled "Diversity and Discrimination in American Society" (594–99).

5. The deinstitutionalization movement for people with mental distress has been controversial and uneven, as Braddock and Parish (2001) note. Although the emphasis on community treatment was positive, the declining overall number of people in institutions masked continued overcrowding as well as a revolving-door experience for many people. Deinstitutionalization has also been blamed for increasing homelessness among people with mental distress (45). However, more recent work has challenged this latter claim, suggesting instead that homelessness following the deinstitutionalization movement has been caused largely by social conditions and context, such as the state of local treatment services in the communities in which people came to live, budget cuts or lack of funding at the time that people were being released from institutions, poor delivery of services within community health systems, globalization, migration, increased individualism and less emphasis on traditional families, failures in family relationships, housing and labor market problems (including increased unemployment), increased illegal drug use, legal changes such as the War on Drugs, and changes in mental healthcare funding (Draine et al. 2002; G. Johnson and Chamberlain 2011; Winkler et al. 2016; Nishio et al. 2017). For a summary of these sources, see Maybee (forthcoming).

CHAPTER 3. THE EXPERIENCE
OF THE SOCIALLY DEFINED BODY

1. During a presentation of some of the ideas in this chapter for the Spring Lecture Series of the Women's Studies Program at Lehman College, music professor Janette Tilley pointed out that the onlookers' assumption that the disabled woman could not be the mother of the baby may have betrayed not only the assumption that the disabled woman could not be a mother, but also an assumption that she could not be an object of sexual interest.

2. In his book exploring the experiences primarily of physically disabled people (Sutherland 1984, 11), disability studies scholar and activist Allan T. Sutherland notes the common assumption by nondisabled people that, as he puts it in one place, "a person with a particular disability is mentally subnormal, or mad, or incapable of running their own life" (65).

3. Ladelle McWhorter (2006) argues that the medical doctor Benjamin Rush, who was one of the signers of the Declaration of Independence, not only believed that bodies

were machines, but also experienced and treated his own body as a machine to be kept in good working order (10).

4. Zola's call to "bring our bodies back in" caught on, though he is usually not given credit for having introduced the phrase. Williams (1999) uses the same sort of phrasing (805), for instance, as does M. Miles (2000, 606).

5. Zola's area of study was the doctor-patient relationship.

6. Interestingly, this notion of seniority is both material and socially constructed. Seniority based on birth affects what it is and is like to move around in the world because age affects personal characteristics such as size and understanding, but seniority based on marriage is socially defined. I am grateful to Christina Nadler for this point.

7. Rhoda Olkin (1999) has argued that the requirement to regulate one's affect is a common element of the disability experience in our society. Disabled people are subject, for instance, to what she calls the "requirement of cheerfulness." As she puts it, "Disabled people are supposed to smile" (77). This phenomenon would affect both the experience of the personal (the first body), insofar as it may lead people with disabilities to control how they feel, as well as the experience of the interpersonal body (the second body), insofar as disabled people might use smiling to negotiate a place of comfort in a world that expects them to be cheerful.

8. O'Toole (2002) notes the remarks of disability rights activist and assistant secretary of education (under President Clinton) Judy Heumann, who was reported to have said in 1982, "I don't know if I am offended by sexist comments or not as they have never been directed at me" ("Introduction," para. 1).

9. For an excellent exploration of the ambivalence of one disability scholar and activist about devotees, see Kafer (2012). Recent discussions in the popular press or on blogs about the controversies in the disability community surrounding devotees include Gander (2016), S. Williams (2016), Smith (n.d.), and Nguyen (2014).

10. I think also of the story of Oswaldo Martinez, who was born deaf in 1971 into an agrarian society in El Salvador, where he married and had two children. He followed his brother, Mario, to the United States, and lived with Mario until Mario kicked Oswaldo out of the mobile home they lived in because, Mario told *Washington Post* journalist Paul Duggan, "his newly arrived brother had uncouth living habits." Mario forced Oswaldo to live "in a side-yard shed with a mattress, power cord, space heater and camp stove." In 2005, Oswaldo apparently raped and strangled Brittany Binger, who was sixteen years old. He has spent the last thirteen years locked in a state hospital, because, since he is unable to speak any language, he has been declared incompetent to stand trial but has also been denied release (Duggan 2017). Thus, while he was able, in his home society in El Salvador, to be a husband and father, in the United States, he has been defined as criminally insane.

11. Other scholars who reject the Marxist approach but, like the Marxists, take seriously the idea that large structures and institutions, especially the economic system, systematically disadvantage disabled people, have also been critical of the civil rights approach. They agree with the Marxists that disadvantages produced by large institutions and structures cannot readily be addressed by laws that presuppose that disabled people are disadvantaged primarily by discrimination perpetrated by government agencies or businesses or by morally corrupt individuals who have bad attitudes toward disabled people (see, e.g., Bickenbach et al. 1999, 1181; Scotch and Schriner 1997, 151–54).

CHAPTER 4. THE SOCIALLY DEFINED BODY IN SOCIETY

1. Details for this story have been stitched together from several sources, including the National Museum of the Royal Navy Portsmouth (n.d.), Verkaik (2009), Jamieson (2009), BBC (2014), East of England Broadband Network (n.d.), Beatty (1807), and Nelson (2005).

2. To support their claim, they even cite approvingly an unpublished paper at the time by Shelley Tremain (Shakespeare and Watson 2001, 18), who—using arguments inspired by Michel Foucault—argues that impairment itself is socially constructed. I should point out that, more recently, although Shakespeare has continued to argue that impairments (or the biological) and disability (or the social) are intertwined (Shakespeare 2014, 22), he has been critical of Tremain's and other scholars' more post-structuralist or post-modernist approach (23, 47–71). I will return to a discussion of Tremain's work shortly.

3. Garland-Thomson cites Butler (1993).

4. This argument was suggested to me by Tremain, although she makes a slightly different point, namely, that Garland-Thomson's concept of "misfits" never really overcomes the impairment/disability distinction (Tremain 2015, 37).

5. We also do not have enough information to know whether she could get up the stairs on her own in a different way from the way nondisabled people get up stairs. In the article by Hockenberry (2004) just mentioned, he says that, when he lived in the Middle East, he "had climbed many stairways and hauled myself and the chair across many filthy floors on my way to interviews, apartments and news conferences. I had also lost my fear of humiliation from living and working there" (146–47). He also describes keeping a promise to a physical therapist during his original rehabilitation that he would be able, as he says, "physically to accomplish everything I had theorized about the subway in Chicago." He decided to keep the promise by using the inaccessible subway station closest to his home in New York City. So he went to the station and lowered himself and his wheelchair down (and then pulled himself and his wheelchair up) flights of stairs to use the subway (147–53). Hockenberry could use stairs, then, just not in the same way that nondisabled people did. Thus, another ableist social expectation that may be blocking the wheelchair user from getting up the stairs is the expectation that she should do things *in the same way* that nondisabled people do, that is, that she should *walk* up the stairs.

Think also of the stevedore or dockworker in the short film by Portuguese director Pedro Amorin called *Midfield* (see the introduction). When, on Sunday, he goes to play soccer with his friends, he takes off his leg prostheses, forgoes arm devices, and plays midfield. His ability to play soccer with his nondisabled friends is possible in part because his friends do not expect him to play soccer *in the same way* that they do. If disabled people were not faced by the ableist expectation that they should do things in the same way that nondisabled people do, disabled people might be able to do a lot more things.

Garland-Thomson's example also requires that we presuppose the current design of wheelchairs. A hovercraft chair of the sort imagined for the character Professor Charles Xavier in Marvel's X-Men franchise can (apparently) navigate stairs. I am not suggesting that Garland-Thomson's imaginary wheelchair user should have to pull herself up and lower herself down flights of stairs—quite the contrary, as we will see (chapter 7). I am just reinforcing my claim that what she can and cannot do cannot be determined outside of social contexts and expectations, including the ableist assumption that disabled people should do things the same way that nondisabled people do, as well as the current socially determined design of wheelchairs. We will return to this point in chapter 7.

6. I am reminded of an episode of a nature show I saw years ago that I have unfortunately been unable to find again. In the episode, the film crew had been following the fate of a female African lion who had given birth to a couple of cubs. Over time, the film crew came to realize that one of the cubs was likely blind. But the cub's blindness did not matter, as the mother cared and later hunted for her two offspring. After the film crew had been following the lions (presumably on and off) for about a year, however, the mother lion began to teach the cubs to hunt and increasingly to require the cubs to catch their own food. As the mother changed her social expectations for the cubs, the one cub, which could not hunt effectively, was beginning not to get enough food. The film crew feared that, as the mother lion expected the cubs to catch more and more of their own food, the cub they suspected was blind would eventually starve to death. At the end of the episode, the crew was debating whether to take the cub away so that he could continue to be fed—this time by humans, of course. I do not know what the crew decided to do or the fate of the cub, but notice that the cub did not misfit at all until, after about a year, the mother lion's social expectations changed.

7. I am grateful to Tiwi D. Marira for suggesting that the misfitting of people of color is just as material as the wheelchair user's misfitting (though I take full responsibility for my explanation for *why* that is the case) as well as for the airport example.

8. Scheer and Groce (1988) discuss the example of a man from one of the indigenous hunter-gatherer groups of San people in Southern Africa (Scheer and Gross refer to him as a "Bushman") who had been regarded as an outstanding hunter but lost his leg to a snake bite. Although he was not the hunter he used to be, he continued to participate in hunts with the help of a walking stick and to be regarded with respect by members of the society (30).

9. In their review of the anthropological literature about disability, Faye Ginsburg and Rayna Rapp (2013) confirm that studies suggest that the general term *disability* does not exist as a category in many cultures (58).

10. In the *Encyclopaedia Logic*, for instance, Hegel distinguishes between items that are real and items that are *actual*. An item is real if it is there or exists, but it is *actual* only if it lives up to the concept of the thing that it is supposed to be. That concept defines not only what the thing is, but also what it should be. Not everything is what it should be, however. As Hegel (1991) says, "Who is not smart enough to be able to see around him quite a lot that is not in fact how it ought to be" (§6, Remark). Hegel's concept of actuality is also closely connected to his concept of truth. He defines *truth* as the agreement between the content of something that is there and its concept. He used the example of a friend. "We speak, for instance," he said, "of a 'true' friend, and by that we understand one whose way of acting conforms with the concept of friendship" (§24, Addition #2). A true friend is someone whose behavior lives up to the concept of friendship, which captures how a friend ought to behave. An untrue friend is thus a bad friend. "To say of something that it is 'untrue' is as much as to say that it is bad, that it involves an inner inadequacy" (§24, Addition #2).

11. I am not suggesting that societies' prescriptive accounts of social roles—their views of what makes someone a good mother, teacher, and so on—can never be criticized. I am

only suggesting that there is a close connection between such concepts' descriptive and prescriptive statuses. I note that Barnartt also uses the example of being a teacher.

12. The view that our modern, scientific constructs of impairments have a legitimate factual basis has been defended more recently by Dimitris Anastasiou and James M. Kauffman (2013). For them, impairments are subject-independent facts, though the experiences of these conditions are socially shaped (443–44). See also their 2011 article in which they defend a "critical scientific realist approach" to disability (Anastasiou and Kauffman 2011, 373), according to which disabilities are best conceived of as "real 'socialized biological' conditions" (373). We will examine claims about biology in chapter 5.

13. For an excellent discussion of the current debate about the genetic underpinnings of schizophrenia, for instance, see Prinz (2014), 26–27.

14. Someone might object to Menkiti's reliance on the concept of "fact" here. Kwasi Wiredu (2003a) has argued that the concept of "fact" is not universal to all cultures, though all cultures, he suggests, will have some concept of what it is for something to "be so" (240–41). But that's all Menkiti needs for his argument. He is claiming that the question of a person's identity depends on what people in a society will regard "as so." His argument does not rest on any technical or specialized notion of a "fact."

15. I use the example of spina bifida because the remains of a thirteen- to fifteen-year-old boy with what we would call spina bifida were found in a grave at the Windover Archeological Site dated from 7,000 to 8,000 years ago in Brevard County, Florida. For a brief discussion of the find, see Richardson (1997).

CHAPTER 5. THE SOCIALLY CONSTRUCTED BODY IN BIOLOGY

1. See, for instance, Foucault's (1988) *Folie et Déraison: Histoire de la Folie à l'âge Classique* (*Madness and Unreason: History of Madness in the Classical Age*), an abridged version of which was published in English as *Madness and Civilization: A History of Insanity in the Age of Reason*. A full translation of the book was recently published in English as *History of Madness* (Foucault 2006).

2. Indeed, Tremain's work helped to inspire my view.

3. I am reminded of a scene from the Cannes Film Festival Palme d'Or winner *I, Daniel Blake*, directed by Ken Loach, which is about an older man, Daniel, trying to navigate the British social services system. In the first scene of the film, as we see the opening credits role, we hear a voice-over of Daniel's interview with a social services worker, Amanda, to determine his eligibility for a government support allowance. "Can you walk more than 50 meters unassisted by any other person?" she begins. Daniel, whose doctor found that the stress and physicality of Daniel's job were too much for his weakening heart and told Daniel to stop working, replies, "Yes." "Can you raise either arm, as if to put something in your top pocket?" Amanda continues. "I filled this in already on your 52-page form," Daniel replies. "Yeah, I can see that you have, but unfortunately I can't make out what you had said there," she answers. "Yes," Daniel says sighing, clearly becoming frustrated. "Can you raise either arm to the top of your head as if you are puttin' on a hat?" Amanda asks. "I've told you, there's not in wrong with me arms and legs," Daniel says. "Could you just answer the question, please?" Amanda says. "Well you've got my medical records. Can we

just talk about me heart?" Daniel asks, raising the pitch of his voice. "Do you think you could just answer these questions?" Amanda asks, matter-of-factly, before pausing and then saying, "so was that a yes that you could put a hat on your head?" "Yes," Daniel says. "Ok, that's great," Amanda comments. "Can you press a button such as a telephone key pad?" she asks. "There's not'in wrong with my fingers either. We're getting' farther and farther away from me heart," Daniel says. "If we could just keep to these questions, thank you," Amanda replies. "Do you have any significant difficulty conveying a simple message to strangers?" she asks. "Yes," Daniel says emphatically, "yes it's me fuckin' heart I'm trying to tell you but you're not listening." Amanda warns him that continuing in this way is not going to be helpful for his assessment. "If you could just answer the question please," she says. "Yes," Daniel replies, now sounding defeated. "Okay," she says, and we hear some papers rustling. "Do you ever experience any loss of control leading to extensive evacuation of the bowel?" she asks. "No," he replies quickly, "but I cannot guarantee there won't be a first if we don't get to the point." "Can you complete the simple task of settin' an alarm clock?" Amanda goes on, ignoring Daniel's commentary. "Jesus," Daniel says under his breath, before replying, "Yes" (Loach 2016, 0:52–2:47).

Daniel's problem is that the questionnaire, which is asking specific questions about discrete bodily movements and bowel function, is *not* constructing him as impaired and so as eligible for government income assistance, even though he needs financial support. The scene thus illustrates Tremain's suggestion that such questionnaires do not discover (or fail to discover, in Daniel's case) preexisting impairment, but construct and define what impairment is while they are defining individual respondents as (or as not) impaired. (I would not say that Daniel is really impaired and that the survey missed that fact. On my view, there is no purely objective, pre-social impairment or fact of impairment—it is always socially defined. If we say that Daniel has impairment, then that, too, is a social decision.)

The film is fiction (and this scene is obviously written to be tragically humorous), but *The Guardian* (2016) newspaper created a short documentary film titled *Meet the Real Daniel Blakes*, profiling people in Daniel's situation. Melvin Newton, for instance, who was out of work due to problems with (what we would call) high blood pressure, was, like Daniel in the film, having financial problems and fighting with the British social services system for support. What is clear in both the film and in the real-life cases profiled by *The Guardian* is that the institutions of British society should make different decisions from the ones they currently make.

4. For further discussions of nonbiological conceptions of illness and Sogolo's views, see Maybee (2017) and Maybee (2018).

5. As I have suggested elsewhere (Maybee 2018), we can capture the distinction Oyěwùmí wants to draw between the Yoruba and English terms by reformulating her observations as *that* clauses of the sort that Hanson used to express how facts are theory-laden or presuppose theoretical commitments about what the world is like (see chapter 4). Because the Yoruba terms and English terms are surrounded by different *that* clauses, or by different theoretical commitments or beliefs about what the world is like, they do not mean the same thing. In particular, unlike the English terms, the Yoruba terms do not refer to a biological or sexual essence that necessarily and always determines someone's identity.

Oyěwùmí's (1997) discussion suggests that *obinrin* implies the following, surrounding *that* clauses or theoretical commitments:

- that it is a human being;
- that it is an adult;
- that it bears babies.

Okùnrin has the following surrounding *that* clauses or theoretical commitments:

- that it is a human being;
- that it is an adult;
- that it does not bear babies. (33–35)

These terms apply only to adult human beings, and never to children. Each person therefore starts out life belonging to neither of these categories, but later, typically, comes to be characterized by one or the other of them. The English terms *female* and *male*, by contrast, are associated with different sets of *that* clauses or theoretical commitments. The term *female*, for instance, includes the following theoretical commitments.

- that it is an essence of the individual (and so applies to someone when she is a child as well as when she is an adult);
- that it is a (biological) sex (which involves more than just a role in reproduction); and
- that it is one of two dimorphic categories, so that a person is necessarily and inherently either one or the other. (35–36).

(For the Yoruba, by contrast, being an *obinrin* nor *okùnrin* is not a fixed identity that someone has since birth, since all children start out as neither *obinrin* nor *okùnrin*.) The Western term *female* is taken to be an essential identity that an individual has all her life, an identity that is therefore not tied only to her role in reproduction, since she has no such role as a child, and is one of only two possible essential categories by which someone must be defined.

We can also see that the terms *obinrin* and *okùnrin* do not map on to the English terms *female* and *male*, Oyěwùmí (1997) continues, by examining the traditional Yoruba social roles of *oko* and *aya*, which have been incorrectly translated as *husband* and *wife*, respectively. Oyěwùmí suggests that *oko* and *aya* are best understood as "owner/insider" and "nonowner/outsider" in relation to a traditional living compound and lineage (44). The *oko* (insiders) were those who were born into the living compound and lineage, while the *aya* (outsiders) were those who were born outside of the living compound and lineage. Because traditional Yoruba society tended to be patrilocal in terms of marriage patterns (44)—though not always (48)—the *aya* (outsiders) in a community were typically *obinrin* (the ones who have babies). But, Oyěwùmí says, the *oko* (insiders) were both *obinrin* (the ones who have babies) and *okùnrin* (the ones who do not have babies). Moreover, *oko* (insiders) who were *obinrin* (the ones who have babies) had all the same rights that equally senior *oko* who were *okùnrin* (the ones who do not have babies) had. *Oko* (insiders) who were *obinrin* (the ones who have babies) even had the right to inherit sexual access to *obinrin* (ones who have babies) whose conjugal partners had died (45–46). And, although the *aya* were typically *obinrin* (ones who have babies), the term *aya* was also used to describe worshippers in the house of a god/goddess—who were all outsiders in relation to the god's/

goddess's house—and in this context referred both to *obinrin* (the ones who have babies) and *okùnrin* (the ones who do not have babies) (47). Like the terms *obinrin* and *okùnrin*, then, the terms *oko* (insider) and *aya* (outsider) do not presuppose that people have biological or sexual essences that would permanently make them either "male" or "female" and hence either a "husband" or a "wife."

6. Hanson suggests that our scientific languages might lead us to see the world in a certain way, in the same way that putting the duck-rabbit drawing (the drawing of a rabbit that also looks like a duck, or vice versa) in the context of other drawings of rabbits will lead us to see the image as a rabbit, while putting the drawing within the context of other drawings of ducks will lead us to see it as a duck. See Hanson (1969, 183), as well as samples of the drawings (96–97).

7. Wiredu (2003a) argues that the Akan have two words for *truth*: *nokware* and *te saa*. However, *nokware*, he argues—which literally means "being of one mouth" (239)—is a moral conception of truth, and is best translated as "truthfulness." *Te saa*, in contrast, belongs to what Wiredu calls a cognitive conception of truth, as do both the English words *true* and *fact* (239–40). The Akan therefore have only one word for a cognitive conception of truth, namely, *te saa*, or "is so."

8. Hanson (1969) makes a similar point. He imagines his opponent offering an objection in which the opponent insists that what makes a statement true is the fact. "Initially," Hanson replies, "nothing makes a statement true. It *is* true or it *isn't* true. It states what is the case or it doesn't do this; and that is the whole story" (195).

CHAPTER 6. BEYOND INDIVIDUAL ACCOMMODATION

1. As disability studies scholars Colin Barnes and Geof Mercer note, disability activists Paul Miller, Sophia Parker, and Sarah Gillinson, for instance, suggested that changes in the nature of work today are precisely what disabled people need for greater access to the labor market, specifically "better rewards and more facility for part-time working, more provision for working from home and greater flexibility in when required hours are worked, for example" (Barnes and Mercer 2005, 539; Miller, Parker, and Gillinson 2004, 44).

2. Baumberg Geiger used Baumberg as his surname for the purposes of publication until 2016, when his surname for the purposes of publication changed to Geiger.

3. Irvine's interview-based study with thirty-eight individuals who defined themselves as having had mental health conditions and who had been employed over the previous twelve months reinforces Baumberg's argument. Irvine (2011) found that increased job control and flexibility allowed people to remain working or minimized sick leave (760–61). Irvine uses her study to suggest that, when policy-makers devise policy, they should "consider not only health circumstances but also structural influences on conceptualizations of being 'fit for work'" (762).

4. These strategies included (1) anti-discrimination legislation, (2) legal and financial measures (grants, funds) that require and help employers to reduce barriers to access or provide accommodations for disabled employees, (3) job creation or financial incentives, such as wage subsidies, for employers to employ disabled or chronically ill people, and (4) return-to-work planning for people who have taken sick leave (Clayton et al. 2012, 435).

5. These strategies included (1) individualized case management for vocational and job-search assistance, (2) reductions in welfare or disability benefits aimed at encouraging people to seek employment, (3) education, training, or job sampling to make individuals more employable, and (4) medical rehabilitation or health management advice to reduce employment limitations (Clayton et al. 2012, 435).

6. There was little evidence to support the claim that reductions in welfare or disability benefits helped people who were not already planning to return to work to return to work (Clayton et al. 2011, 7). In the case of medical rehabilitation and health management advice programs, users found that the programs helped them "to move towards, if not actually into, work" (Clayton et al. 2011, 7).

7. Because the ADA Amendments Act (ADAAA) of 2008 clarified and expanded the definition of disability, legal scholars such as Frank J. Cavaliere, Toni P. Mulvaney, and Marleen R. Swerdlow (2012) have expressed hope that courts will move away from their previous emphasis on whether individuals suing employers qualify as disabled under the law. However, it is still unclear, they suggest, whether the changes to the law will make it easier for plaintiffs to win cases. As Cavaliere and his colleagues write, "The ADAAA will make it easier for plaintiffs to establish that they are disabled, but that alone will not be enough to prevail in a case based on the ADA" (55–56). They predict that the courts will shift attention, not to forcing employers to prove that skills or tasks that are excluding plaintiffs are necessary for the job, as Asch suggests, but to forcing plaintiffs to prove that they were qualified for the job and that the employer discriminated against them—a high legal bar to meet (56–57).

8. For a brief history of the independent living movement, see, for instance Joseph Shapiro's (1993) classic book, *No Pity: People with Disabilities Forging a New Civil Rights Movement*, especially chapter 2.

9. Feminist philosopher Iris Young (1981) analyzes the importance of the "gender division of labor" under capitalism. Sociologist Nona Y. Glazer (1993) describes the shift in the health services and retail industries from paid labor to unpaid women's labor in her book *Women's Paid and Unpaid Labor: The Work Transfer in Health Care and Retailing*. Sociologists Toni M. Calasanti and Carol A. Bailey (1991) offer a structural analysis of gender inequality in the division of household labor in the United States, arguing that "gender inequality stems from the intersection of capitalism and patriarchy" (35).

More recently, sociologist Makiko Fuwa (2004) conducted a study comparing macro-level and micro-level/individual factors in twenty-two industrialized countries affecting the unequal division of household labor between men and women. She concluded that "changes in individual-level factors may not be enough to achieve an equal division of housework, without the reduction of macro-level gender inequality in economic and political power," although she also found that both structural and cultural factors affected micro-level gender relationships (765). For a classic, feminist criticism of the gender injustice of the distinction between paid work and unpaid care and domestic work in the home, see Susan Moller Okin's (1989) *Justice, Gender, and the Family* (75, chapter 7).

10. Sociologist Ann Shola Orloff (1991; 1993) discusses the history of arguments for "Mothers' Pensions" in the United States, for instance (1991, 256–59; 1993, 322). Feminist debates about expanding citizenship to include care labor can be found not only in Fraser's (1994, reprinted in 1997, chapter 2) work, quoted above, but also in the work of

philosopher Eva Kittay (1999, see, e.g., 1, 106-9, 182–88), and in work by feminist legal scholars Vicki Schultz (2000) and Judy Fudge (e.g., 2011). For a discussion of the issue in the popular press, see independent scholar Deborah Stone's (2000) article in *The Nation*.

11. A 2016 report by the nonprofit, nonpartisan civic organization the Citizens Budget Commission, whose mission is "to achieve constructive change in the finances and services of New York City and New York State government" ("About Us" n.d.), examined the financing of New York City's Access-a-Ride and complained that a 2001 settlement requiring travel times on paratransit systems to be comparable to the travel times on an area's equivalent public transportation system decreased Access-a-Ride's financial efficiency because the Metropolitan Transportation Authority (MTA), which runs the system, had to purchase more vehicles and pay contractors more money "to complete the same number of trips in a more timely fashion." This complaint implies that disproportionately wasting disabled people's time in comparison to the time it would take non-disabled people to make the same trip—that is, making disabled people do more work—was preferable to spending additional money on the system.

Later on, the report suggests that one way in which the MTA was able to reduce the number of trips and save money was by increasing the percentage of applicants who were required to be assessed in person to determine if they were eligible for services from approximately 50 percent of the total number of applicants to 100 percent of the total. As the report explains, "Beginning in 2007, all applicants were required to perform an in-person assessment with a certified professional at the eligibility determination unit, providing more scrutiny to the eligibility process and an increase in denials" (Dague 2016). The report thus suggests that forcing disabled people to do more work dealing with the MTA's bureaucracy was a good way to save money. Keep in mind that no one has to do comparable work "applying" for eligibility to use any of the other buses or subways. One also wonders, of course, whether the increase in denials excluded people who cannot access or have difficulty accessing New York City's other public transportation system. Requiring people to travel to an "eligibility determination unit" for assessment would be a barrier for precisely the people who cannot access the other busses or subways and so need to use— but have not yet qualified for—Access-a-Ride services and cannot afford an alternative form of transportation, such as a taxi—assuming, of course, that they can access the taxi.

12. I should note that, since the first draft of this chapter was written, New Jersey Transit's paratransit system, Access Link, shortened the pick-up window to thirty minutes—a move suggesting that the original forty-minute pick-up window was likely a sore spot for users.

CHAPTER 7. DIVERSIFYING ACCESS, REMAKING WORLDS

1. For additional discussion of the notion of disability spread, see, for instance, Wright (1960, 118–19); Wright (1964); Wright (1983, 34–35); Fine and Asch (1988, 13); Olkin (1999, 42); Dunn and Elliott (2005, 185); and Dunn (2014, 51). For additional discussion of disability as a master status, see, for instance, Jaeger and Bowman (2005, 12) and Barnartt (2001). Scholars of race have noted a similar pattern for the category of blackness. The philosophers Lewis R. Gordon and George Yancy, for instance, have suggested that, when individual white people encounter individual black people, the category of blackness comes to overdetermine the black people in the minds of the white people, such that the

white person assumes that he or she knows everything there is to know about the black person. In the minds of the white person, the social category of being black thus spreads, as it were, over the whole black person's personality (Gordon 1997, 74; Yancy 2008, 26).

2. Personal email, May 2018. In a different context, Erik Parens and Adrienne Asch (1999) argue that prospective parents may engage in a similar part/whole fallacy when deciding to abort their fetuses if prenatal screening reveals that the fetus may have a genetic impairment—a decision that echoes disabled people's "daily experience [of] being seeing past because of some single trait they bear" (p. S2).

3. For a classic, feminist critique of "somatophobia," a fear (or rejection) of the body, see chapter 5 of the philosopher Elizabeth V. Spelman's (1988) book *Inessential Woman: Problems of Exclusion in Feminist Thought.*

4. There is an excellent, comprehensive review of the literature on disability and sexual expression by the sociologist Margaret Campbell (2017). It's important to note also that, as disability studies scholar Eunjung Kim (2011) has suggested, some disabled people may define themselves as asexual.

5. A study by Wołowicz-Ruszkowska of twenty-three adult children raised by mothers with moderate to severe intellectual disability in Poland came to the same conclusions. As Wołowicz-Ruszkowska summarizes the results, study participants' experiences "varied, depending in part on the involvement of extended family. It was the stigma of maternal intellectual disability, rather than their mothers' functional limitations, that posed the greatest challenge" (Wołowicz-Ruszkowska and McConnell 2017, 482).

6. Personal conversation, 2009.

7. See also, for instance, Hallenbeck (1984). Psychologists Barbara Krahé and Colette Altwasser (2006) explain that, in their study on attitudes toward disability, they decided not to blindfold the nondisabled student participants or ask the students to use wheelchairs and pretend not to be able to move their lower extremities because doing so could have "detrimental effects" on the students and so would be "ethically questionable" (67).

8. The thirteen categories are autism, deaf-blindness, deafness, hearing impairments, emotional disturbance, mental retardation, orthopedic impairment, specific learning disabilities (e.g., dyslexia), speech or language impairment, traumatic brain injury, visual impairment/blindness, and two more general categories: multiple disabilities and, finally, "other health impairment," which, according to Valle and Conner (2011), refers to students who have "limited strength, vitality or alertness" (65–67).

9. Ironically, Reid and Valle (2005) suggest, special education has tended to be dominated by behavioral approaches to instruction that assume that "disabled students *require* teacher-directed, fragmented, skills-based instruction"—precisely the sorts of instruction that construct disabled students as passive, dependent, and less-capable learners (155).

Bibliography

Abberley, Paul. 1987. "The Concept of Oppression and the Development of a Social Theory of Disability." *Disability, Handicap & Society* 2 (1): 5–19.

"About Us." n.d. *Citizens Budget Commission of New York*. Accessed May 17, 2018. https://cbcny.org/about-us.

Aguilera, Raymond J. 2000. "Disability and Delight: Staring Back at the Devotee Community." *Sexuality & Disability* 18 (4): 255–61.

Ahram, Roey, Edward Fergus, and Pedro Noguera. 2011. "Addressing Racial/Ethnic Disproportionality in Special Education: Case Studies of Suburban School Districts." *Teachers College Record* 113 (10): 2233–66.

Alexander, Jake. 2013. *The Commute*. New York, NY: NyNjGoodwill. www.youtube.com/watch?v=ItDjyJDSDsU.

Allen, Thomas F., Rannveig Traustadottir, and Lisa Spina. 2005. "Sixty Years in the Institution." In *Deinstitutionalization and People with Intellectual Disabilities: In and Out of Institutions*, edited by Kelley Johnson and Rannveig Traustadottir, 33–49. London; Philadelphia: Jessica Kingsley Publishers.

Altamirano, Angy. 2016. "Thousands of Seniors, Disabled Left Stranded by MTA's 'Stress-a-Ride' Program: Comptroller." *Metro US*, May 18, 2016. www.metro.us/new-york/thousands-stranded-botched-service-for-disabled-and-elderly-among-mta-s-access-a-ride-failures-comptroller/zsJpeq—-ieBlbuBYClQwE.

American Experience/PBS. n.d. "Fannie Lou Hamer." *PBS*. Accessed March 19, 2018. www.pbs.org/wgbh/americanexperience/features/freedomsummer-hamer.

Anastasiou, Dimitris, and James M. Kauffman. 2011. "A Social Constructionist Approach to Disability: Implications for Special Education." *Exceptional Children* 77 (3): 367–84.

———. 2013. "The Social Model of Disability: Dichotomy between Impairment and Disability." *Journal of Medicine & Philosophy* 38 (4): 441–59.

Anyadike-Danes, Michael, and Duncan McVicar. 2008. "Has the Boom in Incapacity Benefit Claimant Numbers Passed Its Peak?" *Fiscal Studies* 29 (4): 415–34.

Aptheker, Herbert. 1974. "Sterilization, Experimentation and Imperialism." *Political Affairs* 53 (1): 37–48.

Apuzzo, Matt. 2016. "South Dakota Wrongly Puts Thousands in Nursing Homes, Government Says." *New York Times*, May 2, 2016. www.nytimes.com/2016/05/03/us/south-dakota-disabilities-nursing-homes.html.

Asch, Adrienne. 2001. "Critical Race Theory, Feminism, and Disability: Reflections on Social Justice and Personal Identity." *Ohio State Law Journal* 62 (1): 391–423.

———. 2004. "Critical Race Theory, Feminism, and Disability: Reflections on Social Justice and Personal Identity." In *Gendering Disability*, edited by Bonnie G. Smith and Beth Hutchinson, 9–44. New Brunswick, NJ: Rutgers University Press.

Barnartt, Sharon N. 2001. "Using Role Theory to Describe Disability." In *Exploring Theories and Expanding Methodologies: Where We Are and Where We Need to Go*, edited by Barbara Mandell Altman and Sharon N. Barnartt, 2:53–75. Research in Social Science and Disability 2. Bingly, UK: Emerald Group Publishing Limited.

———. 2010. "Disability as a Fluid State: Introduction." In *Disability as a Fluid State*, edited by Sharon N. Barnartt, 1–22. Bingley, UK: Emerald Group Publishing.

Barnes, Colin, and Geof Mercer. 2005. "Disability, Work, and Welfare Challenging the Social Exclusion of Disabled People." *Work, Employment & Society* 19 (3): 527–45.

Barnes, Elizabeth. 2016. *The Minority Body: A Theory of Disability*. Oxford, UK: Oxford University Press.

Barry, Dan. 2014. "The 'Boys' in the Bunkhouse." *New York Times*, March 8, 2014. www.nytimes.com/interactive/2014/03/09/us/the-boys-in-the-bunkhouse.html.

Batavia, Andrew I., and Kay Schriner. 2001. "The Americans with Disabilities Act as Engine of Social Change: Models of Disability and the Potential of a Civil Rights Approach." *Policy Studies Journal* 29 (4): 690.

Bates-Harris, Cheryl. 2012. "Segregated and Exploited: The Failure of the Disability Service System to Provide Quality Work." *Journal of Vocational Rehabilitation* 36 (1): 39–64.

Baumberg, Ben. 2014. "Fit-for-Work—or Work Fit for Disabled People? The Role of Changing Job Demands and Control in Incapacity Claims." *Journal of Social Policy* 43 (2): 289–310.

BBC. 2014. "History—Admiral Horatio Lord Nelson." *BBC*, 2014. www.bbc.co.uk/history/historic_figures/nelson_admiral_horatio_lord.shtml.

Beatty, William (Sir). 1807. *Authentic Narrative of the Death of Lord Nelson*. London, UK: T. Cadell & W. Davies.

Beck, Ulrich. 2000. *The Brave New World of Work*. Cambridge; Malden, MA: Polity Press.

Bickenbach, Jerome E., Somnath Chatterji, E. M. Badley, and T.B Üstün. 1999. "Models of Disablement, Universalism and the International Classification of Impairments, Disabilities and Handicaps." *Social Science & Medicine* 48 (9): 1173–87.

Black, Edwin. 2003a. "Eugenics and the Nazis—the California Connection." *San Francisco Chronicle*, November 9, 2003. www.sfgate.com/opinion/article/Eugenics-and-the-Nazis-the-California-2549771.php.

———. 2003b. *War against the Weak: Eugenics and America's Campaign to Create a Master Race*. New York: Four Walls Eight Windows.

Bogdan, Robert, and Steven J. Taylor. 1989. "Relationships with Severely Disabled People: The Social Construction of Humanness." *Social Problems* 36 (2): 135–48.

Booth, Tim, and Wendy Booth. 2000. "Against the Odds: Growing Up with Parents Who Have Learning Difficulties." *Mental Retardation* 38 (1): 1–14.

Boundy, Kathyrn. 2008. "'Are You Sure, Sweetheart, That You Want to Be Well?': An Exploration of The Neurodiversity Movement." *Radical Psychology: A Journal of Psychology, Politics & Radicalism* 7 (2): 2.

Braddock, David L., Richard Hemp, Mary C. Rizzolo, Laura Haffer, Emily Shae Tanis, and Jiang Wu. 2011. *The State of the States in Developmental Disabilities 2011.* Boulder, CO: Department of Psychiatry and Coleman Institute for Cognitive Disabilities, University of Colorado.

Braddock, David L., and Susan L. Parish. 2001. "An Institutional History of Disability." In *Handbook of Disability Studies*, edited by Gary L. Albrecht, Katherine Delores Seelman, and Michael Bury. Thousand Oaks, CA: SAGE.

Brown, DeNeen L. 2017. "Civil Rights Crusader Fannie Lou Hamer Defied Men—and Presidents—Who Tried to Silence Her." *Washington Post*, October 6, 2017, sec. Retropolis. www.washingtonpost.com/news/retropolis/wp/2017/10/06/civil-rights-crusader -fannie-lou-hamer-defied-men-and-presidents-who-tried-to-silence-her.

Bruno, Richard L. 1997. "Devotees, Pretenders and Wannabes: Two Cases of Factitious Disability Disorder." *Sexuality & Disability* 15 (4): 243–60.

Buck v. Bell. 1927, 274 U.S. 200. U.S. Supreme Court.

Bumiller, Kristin. 2008. "Quirky Citizens: Autism, Gender, and Reimagining Disability." *Signs: Journal of Women in Culture & Society* 33 (4): 967–91.

Butler, Judith. 1993. *Bodies That Matter: On the Discursive Limits of "Sex."* New York: Routledge.

Calasanti, Toni M., and Carol A. Bailey. 1991. "Gender Inequality and the Division of Household Labor in the United States and Sweden: A Socialist-Feminist Approach." *Social Problems* 38 (1): 34–53.

Campbell, Margaret. 2017. "Disabilities and Sexual Expression: A Review of the Literature." *Sociology Compass* 11 (9): e12508.

Cavaliere, Frank J., Toni P. Mulvaney, and Marleen R. Swerdlow. 2012. "Congress Proposes, the Supreme Court Disposes: Is There Room for Courts to Subvert the Will of Congress after the ADAA Act Broadens the Definition of Disability?" *Southern Law Journal* 22 (1): 37–60.

Chamberlin, Judi. 1995. "Rehabilitating Ourselves: The Psychiatric Survivor Movement." *International Journal of Mental Health* 24 (1): 39–46.

Charlton, James I. 1998. *Nothing about Us without Us: Disability Oppression and Empowerment.* Berkeley: University of California Press.

Charmaz, Kathy. 2003. "Experiencing Chronic Illness." In *The Handbook of Social Studies in Health and Medicine*, edited by Gary L. Albrecht, Ray Fitzpatrick, and Susan C. Scrimshaw, 277–92. London: Sage.

Cimera, Robert Evert. 2011. "Does Being in Sheltered Workshops Improve the Employment Outcomes of Supported Employees with Intellectual Disabilities?" *Journal of Vocational Rehabilitation* 35 (1): 21–27.

Cimera, Robert Evert, Paul Wehman, Michael West, and Sloane Burgess. 2012. "Do Sheltered Workshops Enhance Employment Outcomes for Adults with Autism Spectrum Disorder?" *Autism* 16 (1): 87–94.

Clare, Eli. 2001. "Stolen Bodies, Reclaimed Bodies: Disability and Queerness." *Public Culture* 13 (3): 359.

Clayton, Stephen, Ben Barr, Lotta Nylen, Bo Burström, Karsten Thielen, Finn Diderichsen, Espen Dahl, and Margaret Whitehead. 2012. "Effectiveness of Return-to-Work Interventions for Disabled People: A Systematic Review of Government Initiatives Focused on Changing the Behaviour of Employers." *European Journal of Public Health* 22 (3): 434–39.

Clayton, Stephen, Clare Bambra, Rachael Gosling, Sue Povall, Kate Misso, and Margaret Whitehead. 2011. "Assembling the Evidence Jigsaw: Insights from a Systematic Review of UK Studies of Individual-Focused Return to Work Initiatives for Disabled and Long-Term Ill People." *BMC Public Health* 11 (March): 170.

Connor, David J. 2006. "Michael's Story: 'I Get into So Much Trouble Just by Walking': Narrative Knowing and Life at the Intersections of Learning Disability, Race, and Class." *Equity & Excellence in Education* 39 (2): 154–65.

Cott, Emma, and Kaitlyn Mullin. 2017. "Few Entrances, and Sometimes, No Exit." *The Daily 360, New York Times Video.* www.nytimes.com/video/opinion/100000004791816/ride-the-subway-in-a-wheelchair.html.

Dague, Jamison. 2016. "Access-a-Ride: Ways to Do the Right Thing More Efficiently." *Citizens Budget Commission of New York.* September 20, 2016. https://cbcny.org/research/access-ride.

Davis, Lennard J. 1995. *Enforcing Normalcy: Disability, Deafness, and the Body.* London; New York: Verso.

———. 2006. "Introduction." In *The Disability Studies Reader*, 2nd ed., edited by Lennard J. Davis, xv–xviii. New York: Routledge.

Dembo, Tamara, Gloria L. Leviton, and Beatrice A. Wright. 1975. "Adjustment to Misfortune: A Problem of Social-Psychological Rehabilitation." *Rehabilitation Psychology* 22 (1): 1–100.

Desjardins, Michel. 2012. "The Sexualized Body of the Child: Parents and the Politics of 'Voluntary' Sterilization of People Labeled Intellectually Disabled." In *Sex and Disability*, edited by Robert McRuer and Anna Mollow, 69–85. Durham NC: Duke University Press Books.

Devlieger, Patrick J. 2005. "Generating a Cultural Model of Disability." Paper presented at the 19th Congress of the European Federation of Association of Teachers of the Deaf (FEAPDA). www.researchgate.net/publication/237762101_Generating_a_cultural_model_of_disability;https://is.muni.cz/el/1441/jaro2015/SP_0002/um/50945627/51056873/culturalmodelofdisability.pdf.

Diament, Michelle. 2016. "Segregated Employment, Day Programs May Violate ADA." *Disability Scoop*, November 3, 2016. www.disabilityscoop.com/2016/11/03/segregated-may-violate-ada/22974.

———. 2018. "Justice Department Scraps ADA Guidance." *Disability Scoop*, January 4, 2018. www.disabilityscoop.com/2018/01/04/justice-scraps-ada-guidance/24546.

Doucette, Luticha. 2017. "If You're in a Wheelchair, Segregation Lives." *New York Times*, May 17, 2017, sec. Opinion. www.nytimes.com/2017/05/17/opinion/if-youre-in-a-wheelchair-segregation-lives.html.

Draine, Jeffrey, Mark S. Salzer, Dennis P. Culhane, and Trevor R. Hadley. 2002. "Role of Social Disadvantage in Crime, Joblessness, and Homelessness Among Persons with Serious Mental Illness." *Psychiatric Services* 53 (5): 565–73.

Drainoni, Mari-Lynn, Elizabeth Lee-Hood, Carol Tobias, Sara S. Bachman, Jennifer Andrew, and Lisa Maisels. 2006. "Cross-Disability Experiences of Barriers to Health-Care Access: Consumer Perspectives." *Journal of Disability Policy Studies* 17 (2): 101–15.

Duggan, Paul. 2017. "Deaf, Mute and Accused of Murder, an Undocumented Immigrant Has Been in Legal Limbo for 12 Years." *Washington Post*, March 13, 2017. www.washingtonpost.com/local/social-issues/deaf-mute-and-accused-of-murder-an-un documented-immigrant-has-been-in-legal-limbo-for-12-years/2017/03/13/6f53c29c -fe8d-11e6-99b4-9e613afeb09f_story.html.

Dunn, Dana S. 2014. *The Social Psychology of Disability*. Academy of Rehabilitation Psychology Series. Oxford; New York: Oxford University Press.

Dunn, Dana S., and Timothy R. Elliott. 2005. "Revisiting a Constructive Classic: Wright's Physical Disability: A Psychosocial Approach." *Rehabilitation Psychology* 50 (2): 183–89.

Durbach, Nadja. 2010. *Spectacle of Deformity: Freak Shows and Modern British Culture*. Berkeley: University of California Press.

East of England Broadband Network. n.d. "Horatio Nelson—Timeline." *History's Heroes*. Accessed December 26, 2016. http://historysheroes.e2bn.org/hero/timeline/5.

Ebert, Teresa L. 1996. *Ludic Feminism and After: Postmodernism, Desire, and Labor in Late Capitalism*. Ann Arbor: University of Michigan Press.

Ellis, Katie. 2015. *Disability and Popular Culture: Focusing Passion, Creating Community and Expressing Defiance*. Farnham, UK: Routledge.

Erevelles, Nirmala, and Andrea Minear. 2010. "Unspeakable Offenses: Untangling Race and Disability in Discourses of Intersectionality." *Journal of Literary & Cultural Disability Studies* 4 (2): 127–45.

Erickson, W., C. Lee, and S. von Schrader. 2017. "Disability Statistics from the American Community Survey (ACS)." Ithaca, NY: Cornell University Yang Tan Institute (YTI). www.disabilitystatistics.org.

Etkina, Eugenia. 2015. "Millikan Award Lecture: Students of Physics—Listeners, Observers, or Collaborative Participants in Physics Scientific Practices?" *American Journal of Physics* 83 (8): 669–79.

Etkina, Eugenia, Bor Gregorcic, and Stamatis Vokos. 2017. "Organizing Physics Teacher Professional Education around Productive Habit Development: A Way to Meet Reform Challenges." *Physical Review Physics Education Research* 13 (1).

Ferguson II, Stephen C. 2017. "Exploring the Matter of Race: A Materialist Philosophical Inquiry." In *The Oxford Handbook of Philosophy and Race*, edited by Naomi Zack, 261–70. New York: Oxford University Press.

Fine, Michelle, and Adrienne Asch. 1988. "Disability Beyond Stigma: Social Interaction, Discrimination, and Activism." *Journal of Social Issues* 44 (1): 3–21. https://doi.org/Article.

Finger, Anne. 1992. "Forbidden Fruit: Why Shouldn't Disabled People Have Sex or Become Parents?" *New Internationalist*, July 1, 1992.

Finkelstein, Vic. 2001a. "A Personal Journey into Disability Politics." *The Disability Studies Archive UK, Center for Disability Studies, University of Leeds*. http://disability-studies .leeds.ac.uk/files/library/finkelstein-presentn.pdf.

———. 2001b. "The Social Model of Disability Repossessed (Dec. 1, 2001)." *The Disability Studies Archive UK, Center for Disability Studies, University of Leeds*. http://disability -studies.leeds.ac.uk/files/library/finkelstein-soc-mod-repossessed.pdf.

Fisher, Jack. 1997. "Unforgotten: Twenty-Five Years after Willowbrook." *Castle Hill Productions.* www.youtube.com/watch?v=FcjRIZFQcUY.

Fleischer, Doris Zames, and Frieda Zames. 2001. *The Disability Rights Movement: From Charity to Confrontation.* Philadelphia: Temple University Press.

Fosnot, Catherine Twomey. 2005. *Constructivism: Theory, Perspectives, and Practice.* 2nd ed. New York: Teachers College Press.

Foucault, Michel. 1988. *Madness and Civilization: A History of Insanity in the Age of Reason.* Translated by Richard Howard. New York: Vintage.

———. 2003. *Abnormal: Lectures at the Collège de France, 1974-1975.* Translated by Graham Burchell. New York: Picador.

———. 2006. *History of Madness.* Edited by Jean Khalfa. Translated by Jonathan Murphy. New York: Routledge.

Fraser, Nancy. 1994. "After the Family Wage: Gender Equity and the Welfare State." *Political Theory* 22 (4): 591–618.

———. 1997. *Justice Interruptus: Critical Reflections on the "Postsocialist" Condition.* New York: Routledge.

Fudge, Judy. 2011. "Labour as a 'Fictive Commodity': Radically Reconceptualizing Labour Law." In *The Idea of Labour Law,* edited by Guy Davidov and Brian Langille, 120–35. Oxford: Oxford University Press.

Fuwa, Makiko. 2004. "Macro-Level Gender Inequality and the Division of Household Labor in 22 Countries." *American Sociological Review* 69 (6): 751–67.

Gander, Kashmira. 2016. "The World of People Turned on by Disability." *The Independent,* March 14, 2016. www.independent.co.uk/life-style/love-sex/devotees-the-secret-world -of-people-with-a-fetish-for-disabilities-explored-in-documentary-a6930031.html.

Garland-Thomson, Rosemarie. 1996. *Extraordinary Bodies: Figuring Physical Disability in American Culture and Literature.* New York: Columbia University Press.

Garland-Thomson, Rosemarie. 2011. "Misfits: A Feminist Materialist Disability Concept." *Hypatia* 26 (3): 591–609.

Gill, Carol J., Donald G. Kewman, and Ruth W. Brannon. 2003. "Transforming Psychological Practice and Society: Policies That Reflect the New Paradigm." *American Psychologist* 58 (4): 305–12.

Gill, Michael. 2005. "The Myth of Transition: Contractualizing Disability in the Sheltered Workshop." *Disability & Society* 20 (6): 613–23.

Gill, Michael Carl. 2015. *Already Doing It: Intellectual Disability and Sexual Agency.* Minneapolis: University of Minnesota Press.

Ginsburg, Faye, and Rayna Rapp. 2013. "Disability Worlds." *Annual Review of Anthropology* 42 (1): 53–68.

Glazer, Nona Y. 1993. *Women's Paid and Unpaid Labor: The Work Transfer in Health Care and Retailing.* Women in the Political Economy. Philadelphia: Temple University Press.

Gleeson, B. J. 1997. "Disability Studies: A Historical Materialist View." *Disability & Society* 12 (2): 179–202.

Goode, David. 1994. *A World Without Words: The Social Construction of Children Born Deaf and Blind.* Philadelphia: Temple University Press.

Gordon, Lewis R. 1997. *Her Majesty's Other Children: Sketches of Racism from a Neocolonial Age.* Lanham, MD: Rowman & Littlefield.

Gorz, Andre. 1999. *Reclaiming Work: Beyond the Wage-Based Society.* Cambridge: Polity Press.

Grue, Lars, and Kristin Tafjord Lærum. 2002. "'Doing Motherhood': Some Experiences of Mothers with Physical Disabilities." *Disability and Society* 17 (6): 671–83.

Guldin, Anne. 2000. "Self-Claiming Sexuality: Mobility Impaired People and American Culture." *Sexuality & Disability* 18 (4): 233–38.

Gyekye, Kwame. 2003. "Person and Community in African Thought." In *The African Philosophy Reader: A Text with Readings*, edited by P. H Coetzee and A. P. J Roux, 2nd ed., 297–312. New York: Routledge.

Hahn, Harlan. 1985. "Toward a Politics of Disability: Definitions, Disciplines, and Policies." *The Social Science Journal* 22 (4): 87–105.

———. 1988. "The Politics of Physical Differences: Disability and Discrimination." *Journal of Social Issues* 44 (1): 39–47.

———. 1996. "Antidiscrimination Laws and Social Research on Disability: The Minority Group Perspective." *Behavioral Sciences & the Law* 14 (1): 41–59.

Hallenbeck, Charles E. 1984. "The Trouble with Simulation." *Bulletin of the Association on Handicapped Student Service Programs in Post-Secondary Education (AHSSPPE)* 2 (3): 11–12.

Hammell, Karen Whalley. 2006. *Perspectives on Disability and Rehabilitation: Contesting Assumptions; Challenging Practices*. Edinburgh, UK: Churchill Livinstone/Elsevier.

Hammer, David. 2000. "Student Resources for Learning Introductory Physics." *American Journal of Physics* 68 (S1): S52–59.

Hanson, Norwood Russell. 1969. *Perception and Discovery: An Introduction to Scientific Inquiry*. Edited by Willard C. Humphreys. San Francisco: Freeman, Cooper.

Harris, John. 2000. "Is There a Coherent Social Conception of Disability?" *Journal of Medical Ethics* 26 (2): 95–100.

Harris Interactive. 2010a. "Kessler Foundation/NOD Survey of Americans with Disabilities." New York, NY: Kessler Foundation & National Organization on Disability. www.socalgrantmakers.org/sites/default/files/resources/Suvery%20of%20Americans%20with%20Disabilities.pdf.

———. 2010b. "Kessler Foundation/NOD Survey of Employment of Americans with Disabilities." New York, NY: Kessler Foundation & National Organization on Disability. www.adminitrustllc.com/wp-content/uploads/2013/12/Kessler-NOD-2010-Survey.pdf.

Hattori, Tomoko. 2016. "The Integration of People with Disabilities into the Labor Market." Unpublished. New York, NY.

Hayes, Jeanne, and Elizabeth "Lisa" M. Hannold. 2007. "The Road to Empowerment: A Historical Perspective on the Medicalization of Disability." *Journal of Health & Human Services Administration* 30 (3): 352–77.

Hegel, G. W. F. 1991. *The Encyclopaedia Logic: Part I of the Encyclopaedia of the Philosophical Sciences with the Zustze*. Translated by T. F. Geraets, W. A. Suchting, and H. S. Harris. Indianapolis: Hackett.

Hehir, Thomas. 2002. "Eliminating Ableism in Education." *Harvard Educational Review* 72 (1): 1–32.

Hentoff, Nat. 1985. "The Awful Privacy of Baby Doe: Should Infants Born with Treatable or Manageable Handicaps Be 'Allowed' to Die? One Civil Libertarian Says No." *Atlantic Monthly (02769077)* 255 (1): 54.

Hockenberry, John. 2004. "Public Transit." In *Voices from the Edge: Narratives about the Americans with Disabilities Act*, edited by Ruth O'Brien, 137–53. Oxford: Oxford University Press.

Holland, Paula, Bo Burström, Margaret Whitehead, Finn Diderichsen, Espen Dahl, Ben Barr, Lotta Nylén, et al. 2011. "How Do Macro-Level Contexts and Policies Affect the Employment Chances of Chronically Ill and Disabled People? Part I: The Impact of Recession and Deindustrialization." *International Journal of Health Services* 41 (3): 395–413.

Holland, Paula, Lotta Nylén, Karsten Thielen, Kjetil A. van der Wel, Wen-Hao Chen, Ben Barr, Bo Burström, et al. 2011. "How Do Macro-Level Contexts and Policies Affect the Employment Chances of Chronically Ill and Disabled People? Part II: The Impact of Active and Passive Labor Market Policies." *International Journal of Health Services* 41 (3): 415–30.

Hord, Fred L, and Jonathan Scott Lee. 1995. *I Am Because We Are: Readings in Black Philosophy*. Amherst: University of Massachusetts Press.

Hughes, Bill. 2007. "Being Disabled: Towards a Critical Social Ontology for Disability Studies." *Disability & Society* 22 (7): 673–84.

Hughes, Bill, and Kevin Paterson. 1997. "The Social Model of Disability and the Disappearing Body: Towards a Sociology of Impairment." *Disability & Society* 12 (3): 325–40.

Ingstad, Benedicte. 2007. "Seeing Disability and Human Rights in the Local Context: Botswana Revisted." In *Disability in Local and Global Worlds*, edited by Benedicte Ingstad and Susan Reynolds Whyte, 237–58. Berkeley: University of California Press.

Ingstad, Benedicte, and Susan Reynolds Whyte. 1995. *Disability and Culture*. Berkeley: University of California Press.

Irvine, Annie. 2011. "Fit for Work? The Influence of Sick Pay and Job Flexibility on Sickness Absence and Implications for Presenteeism." *Social Policy & Administration* 45 (7): 752–69.

Jaeger, Paul T., and Cynthia Ann Bowman. 2005. *Understanding Disability: Inclusion, Access, Diversity, and Civil Rights*. Westport: Praeger.

Jamieson, Alastair. 2009. "Lord Nelson Returned to Work Half an Hour after Losing Arm." *The Telegraph*, October 28, 2009. www.telegraph.co.uk/news/uknews/6451152/Lord-Nelson-returned-to-work-half-an-hour-after-losing-arm.html.

Johnson, Guy, and Chris Chamberlain. 2011. "Are the Homeless Mentally Ill?" *Australian Journal of Social Issues (Australian Council of Social Service)* 46 (1): 29–48.

Johnson, Kelley, and Rannveig Traustadottir, eds. 2005. *Deinstitutionalization and People with Intellectual Disabilities*. London: Jessica Kingsley Publishers. www.jkp.com/uk/deinstitutionalization-and-people-with-intellectual-disabilities.html.

Johnson, Samuel, and Obadiah Johnson. 2010. *The History of the Yorubas: From the Earliest Times to the Beginning of the British Protectorate*. Cambridge: Cambridge University Press.

Jones, Melanie K. 2008. "Disability and the Labour Market: A Review of the Empirical Evidence." *Journal of Economic Policy Studies* 35 (5): 405–24.

"Joseph Merrick." 2018. *Wikipedia*. https://en.wikipedia.org/w/index.php?title=Joseph_Merrick&oldid=832770600.

Kafer, Alison. 2012. "Desire and Disgust: My Ambivalent Adventures in Devoteeism." In *Sex and Disability*, edited by Robert McRuer and Anna Mollow, 331–54. Durham, NC: Duke University Press.

Kempton, Winifred, and Emily Kahn. 1991. "Sexuality and People with Intellectual Disabilities: A Historical Perspective." *Sexuality and Disability* 9 (2): 93–111.

Kim, Eunjung. 2011. "Asexuality in Disability Narratives." *Sexualities* 14 (4): 479–93.

Kittay, Eva. 2002. "Love's Labor Revisited." *Hypatia* 17 (3): 237–50.

Kittay, Eva Feder. 1999. *Love's Labor: Essays on Women, Equality, and Dependency*. Thinking Gender. New York: Routledge.

Kline, Wendy. 2005. *Building a Better Race: Gender, Sexuality, and Eugenics from the Turn of the Century to the Baby Boom*. Berkeley, CA: University of California Press.

———. 2013. "Sterilization." Eugenicsarchive.ca. http://eugenicsarchive.ca/discover/ency clopedia/5233e4e35c2ec500000000e0.

Kluchin, Rebecca M. 2011. *Fit to Be Tied: Sterilization and Reproductive Rights in America, 1950–1980*. New Brunswick, NJ: Rutgers University Press.

Krahé, Barbara, and Colette Altwasser. 2006. "Changing Negative Attitudes towards Persons with Physical Disabilities: An Experimental Intervention." *Journal of Community & Applied Social Psychology* 16 (1): 59–69.

Kuhl, Stefan. 2002. *The Nazi Connection: Eugenics, American Racism, and German National Socialism*. New edition. Oxford; New York: Oxford University Press.

Ladieu, Gloria, Dan L. Adler, and Tamara Dembo. 1948. "Studies in Adjustment to Visible Injuries: Social Acceptance of the Injured." *Journal of Social Issues* 4 (4): 55–61.

LaNear, John, and Elise Frattura. 2007. "Getting the Stories Straight: Allowing Different Voices to Tell an 'Effective History' of Special Education Law in the United States." *Education & the Law* 19 (2): 87–109.

Leach, Anna. 2015. "Exporting Trauma: Can the Talking Cure Do More Harm Than Good?" *The Guardian*, February 5, 2015, sec. Global Development Professionals Network. www.theguardian.com/global-development-professionals-network/2015/feb/05/mental-health-aid-western-talking-cure-harm-good-humanitarian-anthropologist.

Lee, Theresa Man Ling. 2006. "Multicultural Citizenship: The Case of the Disabled." In *Critical Disability Theory: Essays in Philosophy, Politics, Policy, and Law*, edited by Dianne Pothier and Richard Devlin, 87–105. Vancouver, BC: University of British Columbia Press.

Lehrer, Riva. 2012. "Golem Girl Gets Lucky." In *Sex and Disability*, edited by Robert McRuer and Anna Mollow, 231–55. Durham, NC: Duke University Press.

Liddiard, Kirsty. 2017. *The Intimate Lives of Disabled People*. New York: Routledge.

Liesener, James J., and Judson Mills. 1999. "An Experimental Study of Disability Spread: Talking to an Adult in a Wheelchair Like a Child." *Journal of Applied Social Psychology* 29 (10): 2083–92.

Loach, Ken. 2016. *I, Daniel Blake*. DVD. London: Entertainment One UK.

Longmore, Paul K. 2003. *Why I Burned My Book and Other Essays on Disability*. American Subjects. Philadelphia: Temple University Press.

———. 2005. "Policy, Prejudice, and Reality: Two Case Studies of Physician-Assisted Suicide." *Journal of Disability Policy Studies* 16 (1): 38–45.

Magruder, Frank Abbott. 1921. *American Government in 1921: A Consideration of the Problems of Democracy*. Boston, MA: Allyn and Bacon.

———. 1950. *American Government: A Textbook on the Problems of Democracy*. Boston, MA: Allyn and Bacon.

Magruder, Frank Abbott, and William A. McClenaghan. 2004. *Magruder's American Government*. Needham, MA: Pearson/Prentice Hall.

Marks, Deborah. 1999. "Dimensions of Oppression: Theorising the Embodied Subject." *Disability & Society* 14 (5): 611–26.

Marx, Karl. 1909. *Capital: A Critique of Political Economy*. Edited by Frederick Engels. Translated by Ernest Untermann. Vol. III: The Process of Capitalist Production as a Whole. Chicago: Charles H. Kerr & Company. http://oll.libertyfund.org/titles/marx -capital-a-critique-of-political-economy-volume-iii-the-process-of-capitalist-production -as-a-whole.

Maybee, Julie E. 2002. "Politicizing the Personal and Other Tales from the Front Lines." In *Theorizing Backlash: Philosophical Reflections on the Resistance to Feminism*, edited by Anita M. Superson and Ann E. Cudd, 133–52. Lanham, MD: Rowman & Littlefield.

———. 2017. "Em'body'ment and Disability: On Taking the (Biological) 'Body' out of Em'body'ment." *Journal of Social Philosophy* 48 (3): 297–320.

———. 2018. "African Philosophy, Disability, and the Social Conception of the Self." In *Debating African Philosophy: Perspectives on Identity, Decolonial Ethics and Comparative Philosophy*, edited by George Hull, 289–304. London; New York: Routledge.

———. Forthcoming. "Homelessness, Disability and Oppression." In *The Ethics of Homelessness: Philosophical Perspectives* (revised edition), edited by G. John M. Abbarno. Netherlands: Brill Publishing.

McElvaney, Claire. 2011. "Client Evaluations and Summaries: How Person-Centered Planning Is Tainted by a Diagnosis." *Intellectual & Developmental Disabilities* 49 (3): 203–5.

McKeever, Patricia, and Karen-Lee Miller. 2004. "Mothering Children Who Have Disabilities: A Bourdieusian Interpretation of Maternal Practices." *Social Science & Medicine* 59 (6): 1177–91.

McWhorter, Ladelle. 2006. "In Perpetual Disintegration." Keynote Address delivered to the Foucault Society Conference on the Body: Ethos and Ethics. New School for Social Research, New York, NY.

———. 2009. *Racism and Sexual Oppression in Anglo-America: A Genealogy*. Bloomington: Indiana University Press.

Menkiti, Ifeanyi A. 1984. "Person and Community in African Traditional Thought." In *African Philosophy: An Introduction*, edited by Richard A. Wright, 171–81. Lanham, MD: University Press of America.

Metzler, Irina. 2006. *Disability in Medieval Europe: Thinking about Physical Impairment in the High Middle Ages, c.1100–c.1400*. London: Routledge.

———. 2015. *A Social History of Disability in the Middle Ages: Cultural Considerations of Physical Impairment*. New York: Routledge.

Miles, M. 2000. "Disability on a Different Model: Glimpses of an Asian Heritage." *Disability & Society* 15 (4): 603–18.

Miller, Paul, Sophia Parker, and Sarah Gillinson. 2004. *Disablism: How to Tackle the Last Prejudice*. London: Demos. http://lx.iriss.org.uk/sites/default/files/resources/Disablism.pdf.

Morris, Jenny. 2001. "Impairment and Disability: Constructing an Ethics of Care That Promotes Human Rights." *Hypatia* 16 (4): 1–16.

Nario-Redmond, Michelle R. 2010. "Cultural Stereotypes of Disabled and Non-Disabled Men and Women: Consensus for Global Category Representations and Diagnostic Domains." *British Journal of Social Psychology* 49 (3): 471–88.

National Council on Disability. 2017. "National Disability Policy: A Progress Report." Washington, DC: National Council on Disability. https://ncd.gov/progressreport/2017/ national-disability-policy-progress-report-october-2017.

———. 2018. "The Segregation of Students with Disabilities." IDEA Series. Washington, DC: National Council on Disability. https://ncd.gov/sites/default/files/NCD_Segrega tion-SWD_508.pdf.

National Museum of the Royal Navy. 2004. "Biography: Horatio Nelson: Admiral Horatio Nelson, Hero of Trafalgar." *Royal Naval Museum*, 2004. www.royalnavalmuseum.org/ info_sheets_horatio_nelson.htm.

National Museum of the Royal Navy Portsmouth. n.d. "Nelson Gallery—Frequently Asked Questions." *National Museum of the Royal Navy Portsmouth*. Accessed December 26, 2016. www.nmrn-portsmouth.org.uk/nelson-gallery-frequently-asked-questions.

Nelson, Horatio. 2005. *Nelson: The New Letters*. Edited by Colin White. Woodbridge, VA: Boydell & Brewer in association with The National Maritime Museum and The Royal Navy Museum.

Nguyen, Java. 2014. "Let's (Not) Talk about Sex." *THIS*, February 3, 2014. https://this .org/2014/02/03/lets-not-talk-about-sex.

Nicolaisen, Ida. 2008 "Persons and Nonpersons: Disability and Personhood among the Punan Bah of Central Borneo." In *Disability and Culture*, edited by Benedicte Ingstad and Susan Reynolds Whyte, 38–55. Berkeley: University of California Press.

Nietzsche, Friedrich Wilhelm. 1976. *The Portable Nietzsche: Selected and Translated, with an Introduction, Prefaces, and Notes, by Walter Kaufmann*. Translated by Walter Kaufmann. Harmondsworth, UK: Penguin Books.

Nishio, Akihiro, Ryo Horita, Tadahiro Sado, Seiko Mizutani, Takahiro Watanabe, Ryosuke Uehara, and Mayumi Yamamoto. 2017. "Causes of Homelessness Prevalence: Relationship between Homelessness and Disability." *Psychiatry and Clinical Neurosciences* 71 (3): 180–88.

Okin, Susan Moller. 1989. *Justice, Gender, and the Family*. New York: Basic Books.

Oliver, Mike. 1996. "Defining Impairment and Disability: Issues at Stake." *Centre for Disability Studies*. http://disability-studies.leeds.ac.uk/files/library/Oliver-ex-div-ch3.pdf.

Olkin, Rhoda. 1999. *What Psychotherapists Should Know about Disability*. New York: Guilford Press.

Olkin, Rhoda, and Constance Pledger. 2003. "Can Disability Studies and Psychology Join Hands?" *American Psychologist* 58 (4): 296.

Olmstead v. L. C. [Syllabus]. 1999, 527 U.S. 581. U.S. Supreme Court.

Orloff, Ann Shola. 1991. "Gender in Early U.S. Social Policy." *Journal of Policy History* 3 (3): 249–81.

———. 1993. "Gender and the Social Rights of Citizenship: The Comparative Analysis of State Policies and Gender Relations." *American Sociological Review* 58 (3): 303–28.

Ormrod, Jeanne Ellis, Eric M. Anderman, and Lynley Anderman. 2017. *Educational Psychology: Developing Learners*. 9th edition. Hoboken, NJ: Pearson Education.

O'Toole, Corbett. 2002. "Sex, Disability and Motherhood: Access to Sexuality for Disabled Mothers." *Disability Studies Quarterly* 22 (4): 81–101.

Oyěwùmí, Oyèrónké. 1997. *The Invention of Women: Making an African Sense of Western Gender Discourses*. Minneapolis: University of Minnesota Press.

Padden, Carol, and Tom Humphries. 2005. *Inside Deaf Culture*. Cambridge, MA: Harvard University Press.

Parens, Erik, and Adrienne Asch. 1999. "Special Supplement: The Disability Rights Critique of Prenatal Genetic Testing Reflections and Recommendations." *The Hastings Center Report* 29 (5): S1–22.

Parker, Pat. 2000. "For the White Person Who Wants to Know How to Be My Friend." *Callaloo* 23 (1): 73.

Parrey, Donna, Eric Davis, Lorrie Lykins, Paula Johnson, and Erin Riehle. 2014. "Employing People with Intellectual and Developmental Disabilities: A Report by the Institute for Corporate Productivity (I4cp)." Seattle, WA: Institute for Corporate Productivity (i4cp). www.ohioemploymentfirst.org/up_doc/Employing_People_With_Intellectual_and_Developmental_Disabilities.pdf.

p'Bitek, Okot. 1998. "The Sociality of Self." In *African Philosophy: An Anthology*, edited by Emmanuel Chukwudi Eze, 73–74. Malden, MA: Blackwell.

Pelling, Margaret. 2014. *The Common Lot: Sickness, Medical Occupations and the Urban Poor in Early Modern England*. New York: Routledge.

Perry, David M. 2016. "Disabled People Need Not Apply." *Al Jazeera America*, February 5, 2016. http://america.aljazeera.com/opinions/2016/2/disabled-people-need-not-apply.html.

Phillips, Marilynn J. 1990. "Damaged Goods: Oral Narratives of the Experience of Disability in American Culture." *Social Science & Medicine* 30 (8): 849–57.

Pledger, Constance. 2003. "Discourse on Disability and Rehabilitation Issues: Opportunities for Psychology." *American Psychologist* 58 (4): 279.

Plummer, Ken. 2001. "The Square of Intimate Citizenship: Some Preliminary Proposals." *Citizenship Studies* 5 (3): 237–53.

PricewaterhouseCoopers LLP. 2015. "Economic and Social Contributions of the US Personal Care Products Industry, 2013." Washington, DC: Personal Care Products Council. www.personalcarecouncil.org/sites/default/files/PCPC%20Economic%20and%20Social%20Contributions%20in%202013_FINAL_20150925.pdf.

Prilleltensky, Ora. 2003. "A Ramp to Motherhood: The Experiences of Mothers with Physical Disabilities." *Sexuality and Disability* 21 (1): 21–47.

Prinz, Jesse J. 2014. *Beyond Human Nature: How Culture and Experience Shape the Human Mind*. New York: W. W. Norton.

"Public Health." 1896. *Journal of the American Medical Association* 24 (23): 1138–40.

Reid, D. Kim, and Jan Weatherly Valle. 2005. "A Constructivist Perspective from the Emerging Field of Disability Studies." In *Constructivism: Theory, Perspectives, and Practice*, edited by Catherine Twomey Fosnot, 2nd ed., 150–71. New York: Teachers College Press.

Rhodan, Maya. 2017. "Protesters Dragged Out of Hearing on GOP Health Care Repeal Bill." *Time*, September 25, 2017. http://time.com/4956397/graham-cassidy-republican-health-care-protests.

Richardson, Joseph L. 1997. "The Windover Archeological Research Project." *North Brevard Business Directory*. www.nbbd.com/godo/history/windover.

Rivera, Geraldo. 1972. *The Last Disgrace*. New York: WABC-TV. http://geraldo.com/page/willowbrook.

Roberts, Dorothy. 1998. *Killing the Black Body: Race, Reproduction, and the Meaning of Liberty*. New York: Vintage.

Russell, Martha, and Ravi Malhotra. 2002. "Capitalism and Disability." *The Socialist Register* 14: 211–28.

Samuel, Raphael. 1981. "The Elephant Man as a Fable of Class." *New Society* 19 (2): 315–17.

Samuels, Ellen Jean. 2003. "My Body, My Closet: Invisible Disability and the Limits of Coming-Out Discourse." *GLQ: A Journal of Lesbian and Gay Studies* 9 (1): 233–55.

Scheer, Jessica, and Nora Groce. 1988. "Impairment as a Human Constant: Cross-Cultural and Historical Perspectives on Variation." *Journal of Social Issues* 44 (1): 23–37.

Scheper-Hughes, Nancy, and Margaret M. Lock. 1987. "The Mindful Body: A Prolegomenon to Future Work in Medical Anthropology." *Medical Anthropology Quarterly* 1 (1): 6–41.

Scheper-Hughes, Nancy, and Mariana Leal Ferreira. 2007. "Dombá's Spirit Kidney: Transplant Medicine and Suyá Indian Cosmology." In *Disability in Local and Global Worlds*, edited by Benedicte Ingstad and Susan Reynolds Whyte, 149–85. Berkeley: University of California Press.

Schultz, Vicki. 2000. "Life's Work." *Columbia Law Review* 100 (7): 1881–1964.

Schweik, Susan M. 2010. *The Ugly Laws: Disability in Public*. New York: New York University Press.

Scotch, Richard K., and Kay Schriner. 1997. "Disability as Human Variation: Implications for Policy." *Annals of the American Academy of Political and Social Science* 549 (January): 148–59.

Semega, Jessica L., Kayla R. Fontenot, and Melissa A. Kollar. 2017. "Income and Poverty in the United States: 2016." P60-259. Washington, DC: U.S. Census Bureau. www.census.gov/library/publications/2017/demo/p60-259.html.

Shakespeare, Tom. 1994. "Cultural Representation of Disabled People: Dustbins for Disavowal?" *Disability & Society* 9 (3): 283–99.

———. 2014. *Disability Rights and Wrongs Revisited*, 2nd ed. London; New York: Routledge.

Shakespeare, Tom, and Nicholas Watson. 2001. "The Social Model of Disability: An Outdated Ideology?" *Research in Social Science and Disability* 2: 9–28.

Shapiro, Joseph P. 1993. *No Pity: People with Disabilities Forging a New Civil Rights Movement*. New York: Times Books.

Sheldon, Alison. 1999. "Personal and Perplexing: Feminist Disability Politics Evaluated." *Disability & Society* 14 (5): 643–57.

Shildrick, Margrit, and Janet Price. 1996. "Breaking the Boundaries of the Broken Body." *Body & Society* 2 (4): 93–113.

Shuttleworth, Russell. 2002. "Defusing the Adverse Context of Disability and Desirability as a Practice of the Self for Men with Cerebral Palsy." In *Disability/Postmodernity: Embodying Disability Theory*, edited by Mairian Corker and Tom Shakespeare, 112–26. London; New York: Continuum.

———. 2012. "Bridging Theory and Experience: A Critical-Interpretive Ethnography of Sexuality and Disability." In *Sex and Disability*, edited by Robert McRuer and Anna Mollow, 54–68. Durham, NC: Duke University Press Books.

Siebers, Tobin. 2008. *Disability Theory*. Ann Arbor: University of Michigan Press.

———. 2012. "A Sexual Culture for Disabled People." In *Sex and Disability*, edited by Robert McRuer and Anna Mollow, 37–53. Durham, NC: Duke University Press Books.

Silvers, Anita. 1998. "Formal Justice." In *Disability, Difference, Discrimination: Perspectives on Justice in Bioethics and Public Policy*, edited by Anita Silvers, David T. Wasserman, and Mary Briody Mahowald, 13–146. Lanham, MD: Rowman & Littlefield.

Sinason, Valerie. 1992. *Mental Handicap and the Human Condition: New Approaches from the Tavistock*. London: Free Association Books.

Smith, S.E. n.d. "Your Body Is Not a Sex Object: Devotees and Disability." Scarleteen. Accessed May 10, 2018. www.scarleteen.com/your_body_is_not_a_sex_object_devotees_and_disability.

Sogolo, Godwin S. 2003. "The Concept of Cause in African Thought." In *The African Philosophy Reader*, edited by P. H. Coetzee and A. P. J. Roux, 2nd ed., 192–99. New York: Routledge.

Sommer, Will. 2017. "Police Remove Protesters Opposed to ObamaCare Repeal from McConnell's Office." *The Hill*, June 22, 2017. https://thehill.com/policy/healthcare/ 338985-police-force-protesters-staging-die-in-over-obamacare-repeal-from.

Spelman, Elizabeth V. 1988. *Inessential Woman: Problems of Exclusion in Feminist Thought*. Boston: Beacon Press.

Standing, Guy. 2016. *The Precariat: The New Dangerous Class*. Reprint edition. London; New York: Bloomsbury Academic.

Stone, Anna, and Toby Wright. 2013. "When Your Face Doesn't Fit: Employment Discrimination against People with Facial Disfigurements." *Journal of Applied Social Psychology* 43 (3): 515–26.

Stone, Deborah. 2000. "Why We Need a Care Movement." *The Nation*, March 13, 2000.

Stout, David. 1997. "Clinton Calls for Sculpture of Roosevelt in Wheelchair." *New York Times*, April 24, 1997, sec. U.S. www.nytimes.com/1997/04/24/us/clinton-calls-for -sculpture-of-roosevelt-in-wheelchair.html.

Stubblefield, Anna. 2007. "'Beyond the Pale': Tainted Whiteness, Cognitive Disability, and Eugenic Sterilization." *Hypatia: A Journal of Feminist Philosophy* 22 (2): 162–81.

———. 2009, January. "Race, Disability, and the Social Contract." Race, Racism, and Liberalism in the Twenty-First Century: Spindel Conference, September 25–27, 2008. *Southern Journal of Philosophy* 47 (January): 104–11.

Sutherland, Allan T. 1984. *Disabled We Stand*. Bloomington: Indiana University Press.

———. 1989. "Disability Arts, Disability Politics." *University of Leeds, Center for Disability Studies*. https://disability-studies.leeds.ac.uk/wp-content/uploads/sites/40/library/ Sutherland-Disability-Arts-Disability-Politics.pdf.

Taylor, James E., and Jessica Averitt Taylor. 2013. "Person-Centered Planning: Evidence-Based Practice, Challenges, and Potential for the 21st Century." *Journal of Social Work in Disability & Rehabilitation* 12 (3): 213–35.

Teffo, Lebisa J., and Abraham P. J. Roux. 2003. "Themes in African Metaphysics." In *The African Philosophy Reader*, edited by P. H. Coetzee and A. P. J. Roux, 2nd ed., 161–74. New York: Routledge.

The Guardian. 2016. *Meet the Real Daniel Blakes*. www.youtube.com/watch?v=cKaX5w MyMqQ.

Titchkosky, Tanya. 2002. "Cultural Maps: Which Way to Disability?" In *Disability/ Postmodernity: Embodying Disability Theory*, edited by Mairian Corker and Tom Shakespeare, 101–11. London; New York: Continuum.

Tremain, Shelley. 2001. "On the Government of Disability." *Social Theory & Practice* 27 (4): 617–36.

———. 2015. "This Is What a Historicist and Relativist Feminist Philosophy of Disability Looks Like." *Foucault Studies* (19): 7–42.

———. 2016. "Disabled People Need Not Apply." *Discrimination and Disadvantage* (blog). February 6, 2016. http://philosophycommons.typepad.com/disability_and_dis advanta/2016/02/disabled-people-need-not-apply.html.

Turner, David M. 2012. *Disability in Eighteenth-Century England: Imagining Physical Impairment*. New York: Routledge.

UPIAS. 1976. "Fundamental Principles of Disability." Union of the Physically Impaired Against Segregation. The Disability Archive UK. http://disability-studies.leeds.ac.uk/files/library/UPIAS-fundamental-principles.pdf.

U.S. Department of Labor. 2008. "Fact Sheet 39: The Employment of Workers with Disabilities at Subminimum Wages." July 2008. www.dol.gov/whd/regs/compliance/whdfs39.htm.

———. 2018. "Office of Disability Employment Policy (ODEP)." January 2018. www.dol.gov/odep.

U.S. Government Accountability Office. 2001. "Special Minimum Wage Program: Centers Offer Employment and Support Services to Workers with Disabilities, But Labor Should Improve Oversight." GAO-01-886. Washington DC: U.S. Government Accountability Office. www.gao.gov/products/GAO-01-886.

U.S. Holocaust Memorial Museum. n.d. "Euthanasia Program." *Holocaust Encyclopedia*. Accessed March 19, 2018. https://encyclopedia.ushmm.org/content/en/article/euthanasia-program

Valle, Jan W., and David J. Connor. 2011. *Rethinking Disability: A Disability Studies Approach to Inclusive Practices*. The Practical Guide Series. New York: McGraw-Hill.

Verkaik, Robert. 2009. "When Nelson Lost His Arm (and Returned to Work Half an Hour Later)." *The Independent*, October 27, 2009. www.independent.co.uk/news/uk/this-britain/when-nelson-lost-his-arm-and-returned-to-work-half-an-hour-later-1810511.html.

Wacquant, Loïc J. D. 1995. "Pugs at Work: Bodily Capital and Bodily Labour among Professional Boxers." *Body and Society* 1 (1): 65–93.

Waldschmidt, Anne. 2017. "Disability Goes Cultural: The Cultural Model of Disability as an Analytical Tool." In *Culture—Theory—Disability*, edited by Anne Waldschmidt, Hanjo Berressem, and Moritz Ingwersen, 19–28.

Wanshel, Elyse. 2017. "Protestors with Disabilities Deserve the Credit for Saving Obamacare." *The Huffington Post*, July 28, 2017. www.huffpost.com/entry/activists-disabilities-adapt-healthcare-bill_n_597b5508e4b02a4ebb751e2e.

Wasserman, David. 1993. "Disability, Discrimination, and Fairness." *Report from the Institute for Philosophy and Public Policy* 13 (1/2): 7–12.

———. 1994. "Impairment, Disadvantage, and Equality: A Reply to Anita Silvers." *Journal of Social Philosophy* 25 (3): 181–88.

Waxman, B. F., and A. Finger. 1989. "The Politics of Sex and Disability." *Disability Studies Quarterly* 9 (3): 1–5.

Wehmeyer, Michael L., and Nancy W. Gamer. 2003. "The Impact of Personal Characteristics of People with Intellectual and Developmental Disability on Self-Determination and Autonomous Functioning." *Journal of Applied Research in Intellectual Disabilities* 16 (4): 255–65.

White, Glen W., Jamie Lloyd Simpson, Chiaki Gonda, Craig Ravesloot, and Zach Coble. 2010. "Moving from Independence to Interdependence: A Conceptual Model for Better Understanding Community Participation of Centers for Independent Living Consumers." *Journal of Disability Policy Studies* 20 (4): 233–40.

Whitney, Shiloh Y. 2011. "Dependency Relations: Corporeal Vulnerability and Norms of Personhood in Hobbes and Kittay." *Hypatia* 26 (3): 554–74.

Williams, Simon J. 1999. "Is Anybody There? Critical Realism, Chronic Illness and the Disability Debate." *Sociology of Health & Illness* 21 (6): 797.

Williams, Spencer. 2016. "Are Disability Fetishists Exploiting People with Disabilities?" *Vice*. November 24, 2016. www.vice.com/en_us/article/bn373a/are-disability-fetishists -exploiting-people-with-disabilities.

Wilson, Anne, and Peter Beresford. 2002. "Madness, Distress and Postmodernity: Putting the Record Straight." In *Disability/Postmodernity: Embodying Disability Theory*, edited by Mairian Corker and Tom Shakespeare, 143–58. London; New York: Continuum.

Winkler, Petr, Barbara Barrett, Paul McCrone, Ladislav Csémy, Miroslava Janoušková, and Cyril Höschl. 2016. "Deinstitutionalised Patients, Homelessness and Imprisonment: Systematic Review." *The British Journal of Psychiatry: The Journal of Mental Science* 208 (5): 421–28.

Wiredu, Kwasi. 1992. "Moral Foundations of an African Culture." In *Person and Community: Ghanaian Philosophical Studies, I*, edited by Kwasi Wiredu and Kwame Gyekye. Vol. I. Cultural Heritage and Contemporary Change, Series II. Washington, DC: CRVP (Council for Research in Values Philosophy. www.crvp.org/book/Series02/II-1/chapter_ix.htm.

———. 2003a. "The Concept of Truth in the Akan Language." In *The African Philosophy Reader*, edited by P. H. Coetzee and A. P. J. Roux, 2nd ed., 239–43. New York: Routledge.

———. 2003b. "The Moral Foundations of an African Culture." In *The African Philosophy Reader: A Text with Readings*, edited by P. H. Coetzee and A. P. J Roux, 2nd ed., 287–96. New York: Routledge.

Wołowicz-Ruszkowska, Agnieszka. 2016. "How Polish Women with Disabilities Challenge the Meaning of Motherhood." *Psychology of Women Quarterly* 40 (1): 80–95.

Wołowicz-Ruszkowska, Agnieszka, and David McConnell. 2017. "The Experience of Adult Children of Mothers with Intellectual Disability: A Qualitative Retrospective Study from Poland." *Journal of Applied Research in Intellectual Disabilities* 30 (3): 482–91.

Wright, B. A. 1964. "Spread in Adjustment to Disability." *Bulletin of the Menninger Clinic* 28 (July): 198–208.

Wright, Beatrice Ann Posner. 1960. *Physical Disability—A Psychological Approach*. New York: Harper.

———. 1983. *Physical Disability—A Psychosocial Approach*. 2nd ed. New York: Harper & Row. http://search.ebscohost.com/direct.asp?db=pzh&jid=%22200416324%22&scope=site.

Yancy, George. 2008. *Black Bodies, White Gazes: The Continuing Significance of Race*. Lanham, MD: Rowman & Littlefield Pub.

Young, Iris. 1981. "Beyond the Unhappy Marriage: A Critique of the Dual Systems Theory." In *Women and Revolution: A Discussion of the Unhappy Marriage of Marxism and Feminism*, edited by Lydia Sargent, 43–69. Montreal: Black Rose Books Ltd.

Zdanowicz, Christina. 2018. "7 Years after a Football Accident Paralyzed Him, She Helped Him Walk Down the Aisle." *CNN*, April 27, 2018. www.cnn.com/2018/04/27/health/paralyzed-football-player-walks-with-bride-trnd/index.html.

Zola, Irving K. 1991. "Bringing Our Bodies and Ourselves Back In: Reflections on a Past, Present, and Future 'Medical Sociology.'" *Journal of Health and Social Behavior* 32 (1): 1–16.

———. 1993. "Disability Statistics, What We Count and What It Tells Us: A Personal and Political Analysis." *Journal of Disability Policy Studies* 4 (2): 9–39.

Index

About the Author

Julie E. Maybee is professor and chair of the Department of Philosophy as well as the director of the interdisciplinary disability studies minor at Lehman College, City University of New York (CUNY). She also teaches in the disability studies master's program for CUNY's School of Professional Studies. For many years, her research areas were nineteenth-century continental philosophy, particularly the work of G. W. F. Hegel, African philosophy, and race and philosophy. After her daughter had a brain aneurysm and became what our society would call "disabled" in 2002, Maybee also became interested in the analysis of disability as a social category.

In addition to this book, she is the author of *Picturing Hegel: An Illustrated Guide to Hegel's Encyclopaedia Logic*, as well as articles on disability studies, African philosophy, educational theory, and race. What unites her seemingly eclectic specialties is an overriding interest in the way socially defined differences as well as time and place shape people's identities, knowledge, and experiences. Maybee is also currently working on a book about Hegel's *Phenomenology of Spirit*.